BY ARTHUR JANOV

The Primal Revolution
The Primal Scream
The Anatomy of Mental Illness

THE PRIMAL
REVOLUTION
Toward a Real World

ARTHUR JANOV

Simon and Schuster / New York

FIRST PRINTING
SBN 671-21349-0
LIBRARY OF CONGRESS CATALOG CARD NUMBER: 72-83916
DESIGNED BY IRVING PERKINS
MANUFACTURED IN THE UNITED STATES OF AMERICA

For Vivian

Contents

7

Is Potential · Neurosis as Something Physical · The
Unreal Front · On Phobias and Fear · The Cold Warrior
· On Speech · Ambivalence · On Crying · On Wanting
and Caring · On Marriage · On Death and Mourning ·
You Can't Go Home Again · Violence in the Media ·
The Myths of the Growth Center · The Nature of the
Self · On the Nature of Freedom · On Being Honest

Glossary

Primal Pain—The pain resulting when the child cannot be himself. Primal Pain is the result of parental denial of basic need and natural development.

Feelings—Sensation conceptualized. Primal Pains are the sensations of pain until connected to their early origins, at which point they become Primal feelings.

Tension—The inner pressure resulting from denied or repressed feelings. Tension is the product of a disconnection of thought from its original feeling counterpart.

Defense—The way the body and mind suppress Primal Pains.

Symbolic Behavior—Acting out the past in the present. Treating current situations and people as though they were parent surrogates.

The Struggle—The specific way one behaves symbolically. Struggle includes those behaviors designed to quell Primal Pain and gain love.

Unreal Hope—The unconscious hope for love implicit in the struggle. Unreal hope and the struggle are what the neurotic uses to cover the hopelessness of ever being loved for himself.

Neurosis—The symbolization of Primal Pain. The constellation of defenses to cover Primal feelings.

The Split—The disengagement of feelings from thoughts. To be split is to be disconnected from one's feelings.

Primal Scenes—Key early traumas representative of many other events when the child could not be himself.

Major Primal Scene—The early critical event which sets neurosis on its course. It is the signal occurrence which makes the child predominantly unreal.

Real Self—Our natural selves. Our true feelings and impulses.

Unreal Self—The front which comes into being as a viable entity at the Major Primal Scene. The unreal self is the cover for the real one.

A Primal—Reliving key Primal Scenes and their painful feelings in a totally encompassing way, mind and body.

Insight—The mental nucleus of Primal Pain. It is the meaning of painful events that have been shut away with the Pain.

The Primal Pool—The inner reservoir of Primal Pains. The sum total of all the various kinds of hurts the child has suffered in his early relationships.

The Cure—The systematic emptying out of the Primal Pool. The final dismantling of all defenses, leaving only a real self.

Introduction

For the past several years, since the publication of *The Primal Scream,* I have been lecturing to both lay and professional groups. Their questions indicate that a great deal was left unsaid in that book. This work is an effort to deal with some of those questions. For example, why can't Primal Therapy be integrated into other therapies and used in an eclectic way? Why must it be so exclusive? I have tried to answer that in the first chapter, titled, "Why There Can Be Only One Cure." I do believe that it cannot be integrated with other therapeutic forms, and I hope that the first chapter will explain why.

Other questions, such as, "Are post-Primal patients happy?" indicate to me the confusion about the nature of happiness and depression, for that matter; and so I have discussed this in the chapter on Happiness and Depression. Some have said that I left myself out of *The Primal Scream.* Have I had the therapy, how have I done, etcetera? I have included some of my Primals and what they have meant, not as autobiography but rather because these Primals help elucidate a point—in this case, the nature of mourning. What is surprising is how similar the questions are from both lay and professional audiences. For example, both groups frequently want to know about regression. If you regress back to childhood, will you ever return? How can you guarantee it? First of all, I have a different notion about what regression is, and it is different from the historic conceptions. I hope that the section on Regression clarifies my views.

What I have tried to do is expand on some points just touched upon in my previous publications. The nature of meaning, the difference between tension and feeling, what is homosexuality, are examples. I have included some case histories for those unfamiliar with what Primals are like and have chosen those few that are well-written and offer poignant accounts of the feeling of a Primal. I have included, as well, some short statements written by patients about the kinds of changes that have taken place in them. One can see from their stories how difficult it is to design a research project to predict and measure change in Primal Therapy. The kinds of changes are often totally unexpected and unpredictable. Having one's baby teeth finally descend, or having one's jaw and teeth go back to pre-orthodontia times, is nothing we set out to do in Primal Therapy, but these changes do occur and are reported.

Finally, in the last chapter I have tried to indicate what the world would be like if it were a real and feeling place. It is not a Utopian account; it is what could actually be if we set out to produce real people in this world. This is not as difficult as it may seem. Radical changes in child-rearing practices would give us a good head start. Alterations in the school system would help. Producing these changes in child-rearing practices can have widespread effects; the same kinds of effects (in reverse) that the Behaviorists had on us in the thirties and forties, when they urged that babies not be picked up when they cry, that they be fed on a strict schedule, and so on. They did a lot of damage, but the point is that they had a broad effect on the people, so it is possible to influence masses of human beings. I believe that if we don't have a real world, we will have no world. It is not a matter of being a prophet of doom. It is a matter of observing the signs, of seeing the acceleration of destruction of human beings in environmental terms and in psychological ones as well. We have lost our touch with nature and so have relied on machines for our existence, and we in psychology have seen the proliferation of machines in use in psychotherapy. We have shocked people to make them behave, shocked them when they go crazy, shocked them when they wet the bed, and shocked them when they take a drink. We have relied on the mystical powers of the machine because mental illness has been an arcane mystery that needed some kind of magic to dispel it. But it is not such a mystery, and we need not use magic and machines. We need to help people understand what makes for mental illness, and we need a new view of the treatment for it.

THE PRIMAL REVOLUTION

I think I could turn and live with animals, they are so placid and self-contain'd,
I stand and look at them long and long.
They do not sweat and whine about their condition,
They do not lie awake in the dark and weep for their sins,
They do not make me sick discussing their duty to God,
Not one is dissatisfied, not one is demented with the mania of owning things,
Not one kneels to another, nor to his kind that lived thousands of years ago,
Not one is respectable or unhappy over the whole earth.

WALT WHITMAN

1 Why There Can Be Only One Cure for Mental Illness

Primal Therapy purports to *cure* mental illness (psychophysical illness, to be exact). Moreover, it claims to be the *only* cure. By implication, this renders all other psychologic theories obsolete and invalid. It means that there can be only one valid approach to treating neuroses and psychoses. In this chapter I shall explain why this is so.

The term "cure" is an elusive one in the field of psychology. It is rarely used in the psychiatric literature. Instead, one finds "remission of symptoms," "improved social adjustment," "enhanced ego integration," and so on. One of the reasons the term "cure" is not used is that it is inseparably tied to "cause." Cure implies eradicating cause. Otherwise, one is dealing in symptomatic relief alone. To "cure" a bacterial infection implies that the symptoms of a fever, headache, and sore throat, for example, are the result of an underlying bacillary process, that such specific bacillus exists, and that a certain antibiotic will kill such a bacillus. When such a bacillus is discovered in culture, and when it is shown that the antibiotic can predictably destroy it, we can then speak about cure. Without such knowledge, the best we can do is produce symptomatic relief, and this, I suggest, is the state of psychotherapy today. It is the treatment of symptoms, and the results are couched in terms of symptomatic improvement. Part of the symptomatology of neurosis is irrational or inadequate behavior. Improvement of neurosis, therefore, is thought of in terms of changes in behavior. Psychology is called a "behavioral science," and the accepted definition of its purpose is to study human behavior, not human feelings.

Because we have found mental illness to be so manifold, we have heretofore despaired of finding a single cause or even a few basic causes. Most psychologic theorists believe that its complexity is almost overwhelming. For example, a recent book called *Neurotic Styles* states on the flyleaf:

> An original, clinical study of four kinds of neuroses . . . how their development is influenced by instinctual drives; their possible significance for drive-tension control and regulation, and their relationship to defense mechanisms.

Fourteen pages into the introduction the author states:

> It is clear that the problem of origins and sources of [neurotic] forms or styles of functioning is not simple; much already suggests that they must be products of multiple interacting sources. I will have little to say about the possible origins of the neurotic styles. . . . Careful study of the styles themselves and a clearer, more detailed picture of the forms of cognition, activity, emotional experience, is, I am convinced, an indispensable prerequisite to an understanding of origins.*

Having given up the search for origins, psychologists have been fragmented in their studies, so that one observes cognition, another studies perception, still another examines emotion, failing to see how each is part of an integrated whole. Furthermore, they fail to understand that it is feeling that makes us human and integrates human behavior, irrespective of its form. Overwhelmed by the complexity of neurosis, we have been driven to compartmentalize our studies, to isolate one from the other with the result that we never really deal with the whole man. Conse-

---

* David Shapiro, *Neurotic Styles*, Basic Books, New York, 1965.

quently, these fragmentations generate no cures for neurosis, meaning the pathology of *whole* man, physiologically and psychologically. In the foregoing quote, chosen because it represents the thinking of much of the field, we see that the author takes refuge in *descriptions* of *behavior* (cognition, activity), hoping somehow that refinement of description will lead to deeper understanding. It is a compound error. First, descriptions of the manifestations or symptoms of disease are still merely descriptions and do not speak of origins. Secondly, the descriptions are of behaviors and not inner states, which is what neurosis is, in my opinion. Because neurosis is an inner state, something we always carry around with us, it is persistent, predictable, and impelling. One could describe the common cold in scientific language or in the language of the layman—sore throat, stuffy nose, etcetera—and still not be any closer to a cure. Scientized descriptions, then, help communication, aid in categorization, but are not involved with the modes of the generation of disease. Moreover, description of behavior is ahistoric. It deals with presenting conduct, and, by definition, it cannot be teleologic. Any description, diagnosis, explanation, or method of treatment that is ahistoric and deals with current behavior and symptoms is doomed to failure, because the causes of mental illness lie in one's history; by and large, they are centered in one's early childhood and the early relationships that altered a healthy, innocent, pure infant into a tense neurotic. No cure can exist without accounting for those early experiences, as Freud knew so well. And no cure can exist which cannot in some way alter the internal reaction to those early events; for as I have shown elsewhere in *The Anatomy of Mental Illness*, those early Pains remained locked in our system, hidden below the level of consciousness, relentlessly driving later neurotic behavior.

Descriptions are doubly deceptive because they frequently offer the illusion of clarification while enmeshing us deeper in the morass of the complexities of behavior. If we look only at behavior, the field of study is, indeed, overwhelming because the possibilities of neurotic acting-out are enormous. If we stand away for a moment from the neurotic entanglements and look deeper, we do not find such complexity. We find human need, similar in all of us; it is basic, profound, and simple. And unfulfilled need is the fount from which spring all the varieties of mental aberration. We have not seen this because we have been led astray, almost from the beginning of psychotherapy, by the writings of Freud, who posited an innate neurotic process in all of us. What *is* innate is human need. Lack of satisfaction of that need, or conditional satisfaction of need, provides the grounds for psychologic disease.

We see the Freudian legacy in the preceding book from which I quoted. Tension is a given—either controlled or regulated, never eradicated. The best controller is, perforce, the healthiest; not "normal," you understand, simply the best integrated. When you consider neurosis to be an innate, genetic state, or even congenital, then to speak about cure makes one suspect, a "quack." "Cure" is an opprobrious term in the social sciences because it means that one holds "the Truth"—the final answer. The safest way for the social scientist, then, is to remain isolated from the whole man, and instead study his perceptions, his reaction times, his movements, or study animals and compare their reactions to those of humans.

The belief that neurotic and psychotic processes are innate makes the notion of defenses necessary. To believe in the necessity for defenses is to divert ourselves from studying what lies below them. To posit the need for defenses is to place neurosis in the natural order of things. It produces a circular bind: neurosis is normal, the "best" neurotic the most normal. If we are ever to comprehend what a cure really means, we must rethink the entire base of our theories.

It is because we have not properly understood causes, or because we have believed the causes of mental illness to be so arcane, that we have been forced to develop theories that circumvent the notion of cure. We have failed to understand that experience validates a theory about human neurosis, and that the only person who can find a truth about himself is that person.

In order to talk about curing neurosis we need to have an

exact idea of what it is. Neurosis is just a word which indicates the lack of proper integration of all physiologic systems. There is no part of our biology that has "neurosis" written on it. Psychologists have labeled people "neurotic" when their behavior did not conform to professional conceptions of rational conduct. So, to an Analyst, not being able to postpone pleasure could be a sign of neurosis. To a Primal patient, postponing pleasure could just as well be neurotic.

Neurosis is a state of being, and its chief characteristic is tension. Neurotic tension comes from repressed Pain, whether of physical or psychological origin. Each time an *experience* is unfelt because it cannot be integrated, tension ensues. Tension accumulates with each repression until a certain critical level occurs where the person is more repressed and defended than feeling, more unreal than real, more irrational than rational. We call that state "neurosis." *It is possible to have tension without neurosis; but it is not possible to have neurosis without tension.*

I am suggesting that the substrate for all irrational behavior is Pain, no matter of what origin. Enough surgery early in life may produce later neurosis just as psychological traumas might. One trauma, if severe enough and early enough may produce neurosis.

One severe trauma or many accumulated smaller ones can produce that critical qualitative leap from a tense person to a neurotic one. Usually it takes a slow accretion of one Pain after another for several years to make a person more defended than feeling. The critical shift from tension to neurosis is usually accompanied by both physical symptoms and irrational conduct, such as being unable to sit still and concentrate. Heretofore, psychologists have called those irrational behaviors "neurosis." But neurosis is not just an overt behavior. Each overt behavior is part of an organismic behavior pattern, which includes what the blood vessels, muscles, and nerve cells are doing. To study social behavior alone is but one more fragmentation of the human being.

Internal neurotic behaviors can include asthma and ulcers. External behavior may involve stealing or the use of drugs. Both sets of behaviors are responding to a total psychophysiologic state—the result of a peculiar life history.

Tension levels do drop in Primal Therapy; and we have used the armamentarium of science to measure the phenomenon.* It is of no small consequence that Primal patients feel less tense. These subjective reports are valid data as well.

What about defenses? Are they always necessary? It doesn't matter whether we think they are or are not necessary; they are natural reactions to threats to the integrity of the organism. In that sense, they are "natural" states that occur when life does not permit us to be wholly natural . . . a kind of second-order "naturalness." Defenses are necessary when we are young and fragile and cannot take too much assault. As we mature and become independent, they are no longer needed. We can shed them if we know how.†

The first universal reaction to Pain overload is repression. Repression is something we all have in common. We diverge in terms of how we act out the Pain, depending upon our peculiar life circumstances. These varieties of ways we each act out are the forms of neurosis . . . homosexuality, addiction, transvestism, etcetera. Psychologists have become experts in the categories. . . . and the symbolic paths chosen by neurotics.

The severity of neurosis really depends on the amount of accumulated Pain. It is the level of Pain which determines how generalized one's behavior will be; how much of the present will be not seen and reacted to, and how much of the past will be superimposed on the present. Indiscriminate sex with anyone at any time is one example of this generalization pattern. Eating all the time and feeling hungry every hour is another example.

No behavior is neurotic in and of itself. One can eat due to neurosis or not. We can only define a behavior as neurotic when it is taken in total context. Many inner processes are going on

* Arthur Janov, *The Anatomy of Mental Illness,* G. P. Putnam's, New York, 1972, for exposition of this.

† I reiterate—defenses are neurophysiologic phenomena. This means that when they are diminished, anesthetic levels change and Primal patients are far more susceptible to anesthetic drugs. One Primal patient given the so-called "normal" dose of anesthesia during surgery almost died as a result of the neglect of this fact.

to produce such behavior. We are not just eating. It isn't just a hand moving to the mouth. It is blood sugar levels, brain activation, adrenal output, and so on. Excessive talking is not just a mouth moving and a tongue flapping. It is a *need* that pushes torrents of words out of a neurotic's mouth. And need is a total psychophysiologic state.

All "curing" neurosis involves is bringing down the tension level through Primals to a level where the person is more feeling than defended; where his feelings are accessible to him; and where the initial automatic reflex to situations is not to repress. Once that state occurs, it is a matter of time until enough old Pains are resolved so that neurotic tension is no longer a problem.

Pains have many labels but the inner processes mediating Pain are the same. The automatic response is repression; the result is tension. If the child can feel all of the humiliation and its horrible implications in terms of how his parents really feel about him, then he will not repress and he will not be tense. Instead, he will be in agony. Neither the Pains nor the defenses can be erased by a warm environment (good doesn't erase bad), by apologies, or by anything "external" such as a therapeutic encounter. In order for a person to be cured—that is, to be without unconscious Pains which drive neurosis—he must go through deep-feeling experiences which finally render defenses unnecessary. The causes are early Pains, the results are neurotic defenses, the cure is in eliminating those Pains from our systems. There is no way to be totally oneself until every bit of the blocked or defended self is liberated. There can be no instant "crash-through" to oneself. Dismantling of defenses is accomplished step by step in the same way that those defenses were originally built. We erect our defenses, and only *we* can dismantle them. No warm embrace, no smiling therapist, no shedding of one's clothes will alter the defense system. Therefore, nothing which deals with the here-and-now, the presenting behavior, or with symptoms can be a cure. Neurosis can always be redirected for a time, but there is a history inside our bodies that must be dealt with.

The most basic difference between the classical Freudian

approach and the Primal one is that the Freudians believe that
the unconscious, or the id, is basically destructive and maladap-
tive, and that defenses are needed to hold it back and help us
adapt to outside realities. We think that what is unconscious is
real and healthy, and that defenses against that reality are what
make us unreal and maladapted. The Primal unconscious is
filled with want and need, a desire for tenderness as well as rage
and fear. Liberating those feelings is what makes us healthy. The
Freudians believe that liberating the unconscious, i.e., "losing
control," is basically disintegrative. The Freudian unconscious is
negative; the Primal unconscious is positive. These are diametri-
cally opposed concepts. The Freudian adaptive self, to us, is unreal and neurotic. *It* is what is destructive—destructive of the
inner reality.

All of this does not mean that some things will not help for
a time. Certainly, body approaches in which muscle blocks are
massaged do help release tension in those muscle groups. People
do feel better afterwards. But being helped and being cured are
two distinct conditions. One does not massage need away. If a
child grew tense and his musculature became taut because he
had a lifelong aggravating need for a father who never held him,
never paid attention to him, that need will not go away with an
easing of the musculature. But if massaging the tight muscles
eases the physical defense enough for the person to *feel his need*,
then massage is more than helpful. In other words, massage by
itself is ahistoric. It does not deal with stored history. Massage
which leads to unblocking that history, which leads to Primals,
becomes an entirely different phenomenon.

Meditation provides a good example of an ahistoric mode of
dealing with neurosis in its most obvious form—tension. The
meditator cannot truly experience his body fully and *continuously*
because there are *historic* blocks preventing it. All of the early
Pains he did not feelingly experience act to block all subsequent
feelings. Thus, the only way he can become a feeling person is to
have those blocks removed and feel what he *did not* fully feel
originally. Furthermore, meditation has no reality focus. Primals

focus directly on reality. The altered state of consciousness in Primals is real consciousness, not socially (meaning neurotically) acquired consciousness. With meditation, the focus is on a mantrum, a flower, a vase, which means that the individual is focusing away from what is real—himself. The result is that he widens the split between what is real and unreal, and *increases* the tension in his body.

By far the best example for redirecting neurosis is hypnosis. Hypnosis can make someone into someone else for a time—into a "movie star," for example. Hypnosis can split consciousness so that one is completely unaware and even untroubled by a symptom. Hypnosis can even dispel the desire for alcohol or cigarettes for a time. In self-hypnosis one can render oneself unconscious simply by uttering the right phrase, testimony to the facility by which unconsciousness (and neurosis) can be accomplished. But hypnosis is as temporary as any other treatment or approach for neurosis. Neurosis always triumphs because the Pains underlying it *are* real.

Why, then, is there only one cure? Why can't many theories contribute something and have their equal shares of validity? Because any theory which ignores Primal Pains ignores a basic truth in the patient—it ignores the causes for neurosis. Validity means truth. One cannot ignore it and develop a valid theory. What is valid is the truth *for the patient* and no one else. Primal theory has validity because it *does not* attempt to imply what drives a specific neurosis. Only a person who experiences a Primal can say what does. Primal theory simply says that the only validity is *in* experience. The only psychologic truth is experienced truth. Anything else is open to interpretation and therefore falsification and misinterpretation. Interpretation by a therapist about a patient's thoughts and feelings is ideation about ideation. So long as a therapist himself has blocked consciousness, his interpretation must in some way be derivative of his own Pains, and his views about his patient must remain unobjective.

If we grant that an adult neurotic can act-out a trauma that occurred to him at the age of five, does it not make sense to say that once he feels that trauma, all of the acting-out based on it will become clear to him? Why would he need someone else to make it clear?

What is the essence of conventional insight therapy? Isn't it a process of matching today's behavior or symptoms with what went on in the patient's past? The reason that a person must go to a stranger to find out about himself is that his past is usually buried and forgotten. Symptoms that occur in the present may result from events that took place decades before. The conventional therapist usually explores those past events and attempts to extrapolate from them with the patient the reasons for present behavior. Does it not make more sense for the patient to reexperience that past and make his own extrapolations? Is it not likely to be more accurate? I think so.

The only thing a neurotic must confront is himself. Deep personal experience, consciously connected, cannot be falsified. Ideas about someone else's experience can be. When one does not feel, such as in hypnotic states, then he can be told anything and he may believe it. Indeed, he may even act like the "star" until the hypnotist (or parents, in more subtle ways) tells him to be someone else or think something else. Psychotherapy is very much in the same position of dealing with someone who is in a post-hypnotic state, behaving under post-hypnotic suggestion and trying to figure out what suggestions are driving the behavior. If the person were allowed to be totally conscious of the hypnotic suggestion, then there would be nothing to figure out. The person would know the source of his seemingly irrational behavior. This is no more than the position of Primals. Once the patient *feels* what is unconscious, there is nothing to figure out or infer.

We need to understand that a theory about behavior is still one person's idea, and the fact that we call it a theory doesn't make it any more right than a guess by a bartender about someone's behavior. There are two components of Primal theory that make it truly a science. The first is replicability, the crucial test of any concept in science. Primal Therapy methods are replicable in the hands of any competent Primal Therapist who can produce Primals and cures consistently. In the hands of a neurotic, these methods are useless and even dangerous to the patient. The second component is predictability. Prediction is what counts—predicting behavior and cure. Until one can predict, one guess is as good as another, and any treatment method is as good or bad as another, whether it be advice from a neighbor, or "counseling" by someone who is called an "expert." Prediction is the cornerstone of science, and it is only when we understand the laws of development of neurosis that we can predict. Perhaps, being humans, we like to think of ourselves as more intricate, less predictable than physical phenomena such as electricity. But we are, among other things, electrical and chemical matter, and are subject to physical laws. When I say, "I'm going to cross these two wires and the result will be that the light bulb will light up," and it does so each and every time, then it can be said that an important fact has been discovered. It should be no less true when a statement is made that feeling inner Pains dispels tension and its symptoms, and such occurs time after time in predictable order. If the laws governing the development of neurosis and psychosis are specific, then there can be no leeway, no false modesty or false democratic ideals, all of which would leave room for many approaches to the problem. There can be but one approach.

One might cavil and question about my intolerance of others. But I am not the one who is intolerant; it is the Primal hypothesis. The truth is highly intolerant of untruths. Valid scientific hypotheses drive out the invalid ones. Given two hypotheses, if one is more comprehensive, less symbolic, and can lay bare the fundamental structure of the phenomenon observed, then that hypothesis will be the more powerful. That hypothesis must be testable. And it must be part of a theory that generates other testable hypotheses. This is a central point. A good theory is a simple one. It should explain a broad range of facts with a minimum number of hypotheses. The theory is simple; the phenomenon observed complex. Somehow we have gotten this twisted and have come to believe that a complex theory is a truly profound one. Psychotherapy up until now has been divided into schools, into schisms that resemble phenomena in religion rather than science. Schisms occur in religion because things are not testable. Religion deals with events outside of known or verifiable reality. The fact that schools, dozens of them, exist in psychology is *de facto* indication that mysticism and religious fervor have replaced science in our field. Schisms can occur so easily in our field because thoughts have not been anchored into and derived from the inner reality of our patients. Even though we might all agree that that is the reality we are dealing with, we have somehow lost sight of the fact and have relied instead on our interpretations of the patient's reality. *We* decide what is real for him, what he might be feeling, why he behaves the way he does. The patient, by this curious twist, comes to believe this nonsense and tailors his reality to that of the therapist. He believes in his id, his mass unconscious, his existential void, his need to handle responsibility, and so on. He believes what he is told, instead of what he feels. And the therapist comes to believe what he is saying to the patient.

Let us take several examples to clarify my point: Three homosexuals are now undergoing Primal Therapy. Each has *felt* one of the central factors of his homosexuality. The first had sex with a woman after four months of therapy. Immediately after ejaculation, he went into a deep Primal over the Pain of never having a mother. He had shied away from women most of his life to avoid the great Pain of wanting a woman—his mother. The second homosexual has had Primals over trying to get his father to pay attention to him and not his younger brother, who was really more handsome and talented and got the attention. *Part* of his homosexual drive was trying to attract men, competing with other males for a man's love. The third homosexual has had Primals about his father's rages and how early in life he sensed a jealousy from his father when he kissed and hugged his mother. He learned early to avoid his mother (and later women) to mollify his father. Obviously, there are many more Primals to be experienced by all of them so that the entire dynamic behind their homosexual drives will be laid bare. But what we learn here is that there is no "homosexual" to be studied by specialists, any more than there is a "heterosexual" to be studied by specialists. People become homosexual for idiosyncratic reasons, just as they may become sexually aberrant in other ways. The reason for the homosexuality in a person will be discovered *only* by him. In the same way, we can see how ridiculous it is to discuss the dynamics of the overeater. Obese patients have had Primals about being starved in the crib, and other patients have felt that the only way they were ever satisfied early in life was by a mother who prepared tasty meals. No theory or approach can cure anyone of anything which neglects that history.

Out of the welter of human experience, how can a therapist ever know what produced heroin addiction or homosexuality? The *question* is wrong. A *therapist* can't. How can we measure the valence of a particular early experience in terms of its effect on a later neurotic symptom? *We* can't. But a patient who *feels* that experience will know by the intensity of his feeling how important it was. To feel an early Pain and to be immediately relieved of a headache is eloquent testimony to the relationship of early experience to neurosis. Treating the symptom—overweight, stuttering, alcoholism, learning disorders—must end ultimately in failure. Symptoms can be conditioned or punished out of existence. But Pain, the encoded, physiologic personal history, will never be conditioned out of our systems, any more than any other part of our physiology could be conditioned away. What solves/cures psychogenic stuttering is when the person is allowed to scream out all the words he has been hiding. What *helps* stuttering is speech therapy. What it helps do is create more tension by taking away a critical outlet. A person talks baby-talk usually because there is one last part of him clinging to a childhood he never had. Speech therapy can't give him back his childhood; indeed, it makes the person act even more grown-up in his speech.

Once a person has relived Primal Pains and interpreted their meaning for himself, *he will never need therapy again;* neither will he ever need to have any of his behavior interpreted by anyone. When he goes through a Primal unable to speak because he is reliving a scene that occurred before he learned language, there is no need to theorize about whether early experience, left unresolved, lingers on in our systems.

The implications of what I am saying are many: First, psychotherapy is not a learning situation in which someone learns to cope in new ways. Everything he is ever going to experience is already there inside, lying in wait. He has only to experience it piece by piece. Any therapy that involves a relationship to a therapist (the Freudian "transference," for example) is false. The patient will not get better in learning how to "confront" anyone, even the father-figure-therapist. In Primal Therapy, the patient doesn't confront his therapist but rather the past that is locked up within him. Neurosis is not *between* people; it is an inner state. We carry our neurosis around and it exists even if we are locked in a closet alone.

A patient cannot *learn* to be more aggressive or kind or humble at the counsel of a therapist. Too many early blocks stand in the way for a bit of advice to do anything. A patient may learn to act more aggressive in group therapy but it is an *act*, and a therapist can teach new acts to neurotics all the time. But it is not natural behavior. To have to *learn* a certain way of acting means that it is not natural. It is far better to have faith in what is natural in humans. They will be aggressive if necessary when they are well. Secondly, any group confrontation is only symbolic of an early situation. Being aggressive in group therapy only symbolically solves the early blocks, and, as we know, symbolic solutions are not real ones. A neurotic is afraid of his group peers or Analyst because of early experience. A normal adult has no reason to fear another adult unless the other person is actually dangerous or threatening. One can *act* less afraid in encounter situations, but the fear will always be there to take its various forms outside the conventional therapeutic situation. Thus, the best defense for any of us is to be defense-free. To be armed with our feelings is to be in a position of strength—a position of self. How can we get well if we are in a therapy that posits a need for defenses? To be natural is to be rooted in something very solid.

Theorists need to hypothecate theories that include defenses because they themselves are defended. They are defended (as we all are) so early that defenses seem as natural as having an arm. When one is blocking feelings, he needs defenses, and, if a psychologist, he needs to build them into a theoretical system. The kind of theory one chooses depends on the nature of what is being defended. To grow up in an "old world" home where children are pawns, defenseless and powerless against the authoritarian father, possibly will lead to the creation of a theory about the "need for power." Generally, theories are built to figure out what lies below defenses. If we can get below the idea of defenses, we can do away with the need for those theories. To be open to oneself allows one to know everything important about one's behavior. No theory about human behavior can help any more than that. If everyone were open to himself, there surely would be no psychologic theory business.

It is when we superimpose our ideation (theory) on experience that we go astray. We learn to trust the theory and not our own experience. Neurotics, cut off from their experience, are the most vulnerable to this, and yet are most in need of experience. They will talk "castration anxiety," "penis envy," "ego strength," "identity crisis," "bad karma," if that is the therapist's bent; all they should be talking about is what they felt. In a dual feedback, the patient learns to talk the therapist's lingo and the therapist verifies his theory by his patient's reports. His concepts become "validated." Yet, it doesn't make sense to be innately jealous or envious of a penis. It doesn't make sense to have a genetic code that dictates that at a certain age a boy will turn to his mother and hate his father. It doesn't make sense to think that there are anal and oral stages of development. We develop as organic, whole beings. It is when we superimpose theoretical concepts on personal experience that life and people become mystical and inexplicable, just as when parents superimpose their "ideas" on a child's feelings that he becomes a mystery to himself.

Even when a theory seems to make sense, it cannot make exact sense unless it grows out of personal experience. I am thinking of

Otto Rank's theory about birth trauma. Rank believed that all birth was traumatic, and that neurotic anxiety was a repetition of the prototypic anxiety surrounding birth. His ideas had to remain in the realm of theory, because he had no way to observe the effects of birth on later behavior. Nor could he really know only by observation that the newborn was actually undergoing a trauma. We have videotaped dozens of birth Primals, hands and legs in fetal position, eyes rolled back in the head, grunts and groans but no words, and these videotapes leave no doubt in the minds of observers as to what is occurring. More importantly, the person going through the Primal has no doubt as to what he has experienced. What we see on these videotapes and films is an unconscious and involuntary neurologic sequence being run off for one or two hours—coming down the canal, convulsing every few seconds, being strangled by the cord, being hurt in a breech entry, and so on. The theory I had at the time I first witnessed such events did not allow me to understand what was really going on. Even after the patient told me what he thought it was, I discounted it. After two dozen of them had taken place, I became a believer—a believer in the truth of a patient's experience and not in my theory. We know now *from our observations* that not all birth is traumatic; it is traumatic birth which is traumatic. This trauma is laid down in the nervous system, producing enormous lifelong tension. Patients with years of personal analysis behind them are amazed when they undergo such an experience. Though they have been introspecting for years in their own therapies, they are astounded to find such a powerhouse inside them—just minutes away from experience, yet never having any idea that it is there. Nor would there be any way to *infer* that such a dramatic event lies inside them.

What is the state of psychotherapy today? It is very much like the state of the stock exchange. It can spin elaborate rationales to explain change that has already occurred, but it cannot produce that change systematically. Both psychotherapy and the stock exchange deal in symptoms—in indices. When the bank reserve ratio is low, and the manufacturing inventory index is high, we *post hoc* decide that that is the reason for a lower stock level. In the same way, when a person taking a psychological test writes that he can't sleep nights, that he has to keep on the move, and that he often has nightmares, we decide that he is anxious. We take what he says on the test, put it together, label it, and believe that we are making a serious scientific statement. Or, worse, when a person tells his therapist that he has been off drugs for two years, we say that he is a therapeutic success. He may be a social success, that is, he may conform to society's ideas of good behavior, but he may by no means be considered well or a success. If his tension level is high, he is still an addict even if he never shoots up again. It is the biologic state that tells the truth, not only what a neurotic says or how he conforms. Our biology is our truth; it contains our real history. No lie of the mind can change it, just as no "correct" behavior can alter it. *If psychotherapy cannot change that biology, it fails.* Neurotic parents have usually tried to alter the *behavio*r of their children toward some established idea, and have produced neurosis. A "good" therapist who circumvents Primal Pains becomes just another parent trying to change the *behavior* of his patient—leaving the neurosis intact.

How can we be sure we have a "cure"? How does one measure cure? Since cure involves making a person into himself, the question might well be phrased, "How can you prove you are you?" No one should have to prove it, least of all Primal patients, who are not concerned with any *idea* such as "cure" but are only concerned with feeling the life they lead. If we take a mentalistic or psychologic approach, then if a person says he feels fine, that his mind is clear and that he has "new" values and "proper" goals, we would consider that significant evidence of therapeutic effectiveness. Indeed, this is what any number of "finished" analysands do report about their psychoanalysis. But what if at the same time we take elaborate measurements of that person's physiologic functioning and find that his tension level has been raised instead of lowered? What could we say then? One conclusion might be that the person has only *convinced* himself that he is doing better—that he has adopted mental attitudes which make him feel more comfortable even though his body contradicts him.

A coronary at the age of fifty-seven is eloquent testimony that he never got it all together.

Thus, mentalistic statements about improvement must be taken as just one factor in a "cure." What we are after are psychobiologic truths, with an emphasis on the biologic. We want to document the integration of the physiologic systems. To that end, we are engaged in research at the present time, measuring, among other things, deep body temperature, brain waves, and blood pressure. We are getting one- to three-degree drops in the core body temperature, which alone is a highly significant finding, and which does not occur with any other treatment method. Indeed, such a phenomenon is unknown in the annals of medicine, except in cases of severe physical illness. I believe that core body temperature must be related to tension and drops when tension drops. A full report of our research will be published upon completion of the project. The point, of course, is that people can often delude themselves into false states of contentment—witness Christian Science, for example. So that what people *say* about themselves and their adjustment cannot be taken at face value.

In no other field of medicine outside of psychiatry is there the delusion that understanding a disease makes it go away. For some reason, the insight therapies have operated on the belief that it is beneficial to understand one's problems, and that the greater the understanding the more well the person. In my opinion, it is analogous to a physician informing his patient about what is happening to his sinuses during a cold and then expecting the cold to disappear. Neurosis is just as physical as a cold. If there is any doubt of that, ask any neurotic how much his body hurts when he is anxious.

Enjoying widespread popularity today are the conditioning therapies. These therapies concentrate on the removal of symptoms, often by the use of mild electric shocks administered each time a person has an impulse to shoot drugs or take a drink, for example. I believe that conditioning methods enjoy such approval because they are part of the establishment thinking which believes that repression is the best way to get rid of problems.

Shocking patients so they no longer show unsociable behavior simply drives feelings deeper and makes the patient sicker in the long run. So the addict stays off drugs and dies from a heart attack at a young age. Meanwhile the conditioning therapist can point to therapeutic success because the patient's behavior was "good"; i.e., he stayed off drugs for a long time. What has happened to his body during all this? Do we really think we can shock away the need for a kind father or a warm mother? Can we shock away years of living in an institution early in our lives?

The conditioning therapist (often called a Behaviorist) looks at *behavior* and makes conclusions from his observations. Ten years off drugs, two years without homosexual contact are statistical truths. Having no inner drives producing those behaviors is a biological truth. Lack of inner tension is the key index, irrespective of the behavior of the subject. There are many men and women who would like to have homosexual contact but do not dare due to their moral structure. Though their behaviors are impeccable, their bodies may be ravaged by unrelieved tension. The Behavioristic approach is superficial. It takes things at face value. It does not question the "why" of behavior. It does not probe the complexities that drive each bit of conduct in a neurotic. Addicts who are off drugs but who have not resolved their inner tension are *more* sick, not less. They are just as repressed as they always were, without the outlets that would provide some relief.

We must understand that statistics are not synonymous with science. Too often we rely on statistics to try to prove what we can't feel. We fail to understand that feelings validate—that feelings are not something to be shunted away as irrational and unreasoning; if something feels right to a feeling person, it is likely to be right, especially when we are talking about human endeavors. Statistics measure quantities, not qualities; and feelings are *qualities* of being.

Clearly, neurotics and normals can behave exactly alike. They both may be highly efficient on a particular job when measured on a rating scale. But one is loaded with tension and the other is not. In doing the same amount of work, one may burn much more energy than the other. We could never tell by the behavior whether the efficiency was neurotically motivated. A person may seem well-adjusted and productive. He may be functioning socially while all the time his body is disintegrating from neurotic tension. The normal doesn't pay a price for his functioning.

If we deal only in biologic states, then the notion of what constitutes cure can be cross-cultural. An Eskimo who hunts well and is the leader of his tribe is still sick if his body says he is—if his body is suffering from a psychosomatic ailment. Even though he may have no notion of psychosomatic illness, his body screams his pain. So, any talk of cure must be a *human* cure and not a culturally circumscribed one.

Again, why is there only one cure? Because neurosis is the inability to feel (and integrate) Pain, and its cure involves feeling specific Pains and nothing else. We may quibble about techniques used to get people to their Pains but not about the Pains themselves—they are the sole property of the patient. In conventional therapy patients often expect to feel "better," with only a vague idea about what "better" is. Therapists and theorists who get caught in the trap of helping patients get "better" end up having to posit some norm (such as happiness, productivity, social adjustment) against which to measure their patients. If they understood that there is no "better," only getting real, which means becoming you, then they would automatically be led to the kind of therapy that would lead the patient into himself. There is no "better" than "you."

Patients in conventional therapy too often hope to get well and stay in that struggle with their therapists because they don't know what they're after. They never feel really well because they are continuously tense, no matter what their adjustment, so they stay in therapy, setting new goals of wellness—finding a mate, a better job, etcetera. People who have left their reality behind cannot fully trust themselves. They will give themselves over to someone else's ideas and theories just as they gave themselves over to their parents' ideas and values. They have forgotten that they are the sole holders of the truth about themselves. They may even become suspicious when they are asked to trust their own judgment. They would rather trust others (because they have buried the self they could really trust), and unfortunately, there is no dearth of experts willing to shoulder that trust and offer sage advice.

The Primal contention is that no one can bestow a truth on someone else. No one can interpret another's behavior or his dreams. There can be no valid field of "interpreters" of human behavior. Truth is the reality of experience. If a mother's abrupt leaving early in a child's life produced anguish, that is the truth. If her leaving was *experienced* as a relief, *that* is the truth. No expert can contradict that feeling. The key phrase, of course, is, when someone is feeling. When someone is *not* feeling, he is up for grabs, and any interpretation might ring true for him. There is scarcely a way to make a mistake with Primal patients, just because they are feeling. They would not want an interpretation from a therapist, but if one were offered, they would know immediately whether it was right or not. It is the patient in Primal Therapy who keeps the therapist straight—quite a switch from the usual therapeutic situation.

What is a cured patient like? Is he content and happy? When there is something to be content and happy about, yes. Primal Therapy does not erase the past. Thus when one thinks about one's early life later on, there is bound to be sadness because that was the reality—life was sad. But there will be no Pain, which is blocked sadness. Having felt the Pain, there will be no neurotic acting-out.

Nor can Primal Therapy erase the present. When we live in a cruel and unreal world, that world is bound to be most difficult for Primal patients. There is nothing we can do about that except help make a better world.

Because Primal Therapy deals in the overthrow of a sick personal system, it is revolutionary in concept and method. I believe that one reason we have not come upon a revolutionary theory before is due to who is doing the theorizing. Psychologists are not often drawn from the working and oppressed classes (it is only recently that more than a handful of Blacks and women have become psychologists). More often they belong to the White middle-class "liberal-intellectual" segment of society, and are more likely, in my opinion, to come up with "liberal" reformist theories and therapies such as psychoanalysis. It would be illogical to expect revolutionary theories from middle-class reformers. It would be more illogical to expect middle-class psychotherapists to embrace such a theory. They are comfortable with reformism because they have made their peace with the system. It is more comfortable to think in terms of dialogue, communication, and confrontation—more comfortable to be the kind therapist than to turn a patient (a system) inside out. What we now need is to stop communication and dialogue with neurosis and create the only thing that is meaningful—an inner dialogue.

A person who grows up in an educational system that is based on teaching by rote and drill instead of through personal experience may well come to think that drilling new habits into someone is the way to improve him. An educational system that thrives on dialogue and communication shapes its trainees so that they would not be likely to discount such approaches. An educational system that treats learning blocks apart from the effects of an early home environment is missing something. Freud was so close to the truth about what causes neurosis because he wasn't a Freudian. He observed and learned. He studied early childhood. He did not superimpose learned theories on his observations. This is why he could grow and change as a theorist. Why he wasn't stuck in the early Freud.

One last reason why we have not trusted the patient's experience is our professional stake in being "experts." Primal Therapy is the first psychotherapy for the masses, in which one spouse will be able eventually to help the other, where parents will be able to help their children. This eliminates an elitist corps of experts, holders of special knowledge with their own private patois. It is rare, indeed, when an elite proposes to do away with itself, and our field is no exception. The M.D. and Ph.D. are symbols of achievement, brilliance and expertise. These symbols will not be relinquished easily. But the goal of medicine should be to eliminate the doctor.

2   *Incident in Henry's Therapy*

This chapter and the one that follows were written by two Primal patients, two very different people with dissimilar backgrounds, yet united, as we all are, by Pain. Pain is the same in Henry's Germany as it is in the American WASP enclaves exemplified by Bill. The language to express it is different, but the bodily processes are the same. Both men hovering around fifty years of age indicate the power of Primals even in older persons. Their stories are eloquent testimony to the persistence of Primal Pain—it never leaves us. Too, they tell us graphically about the feel of a Primal and what it does to and for us. What makes Henry's chapter particularly edifying is that many of his Primals are in Yiddish. The fact that Primals occur in the native language, the one spoken as a child, is evidence of the "reliving" quality of the experience, as opposed to the acting "as if." In other words, memory is a total phenomenon, not just something we do with our minds. We don't recall with emotion—the Freudian abreaction—we relive. Recall and "remember" are mind phenomena; relive is a total neurophysiologic one . . . and that is the difference between abreaction and Primals. One of the clearest examples of this difference was in a case reported in my previous work, *The Anatomy of Mental Illness*. A birthmark, gone since just after birth, returned in a woman who was going through birth Primals.

41

Could one say that the return of such a large red mark was abreaction? Hardly. It was part of an encapsulated memory circuit which preserved *all aspects* of the original experience intact. One of the aspects of that memory circuit is language; and so we have Primals in the native tongue.

Bill's case is instructive in many ways. There have been so many approaches to alcoholism, and Bill has tried nearly all of them. In a very short time (some four or five months) he was rid of it—because he was rid of a great load of Pain. As he says, alcohol is the medicine for Pain (what a simple yet profound idea) and with little Pain, why would there be a need for the medicine?

Bill wasn't just an alcoholic. He was a pill-head. He took every kind of pain-killer and tranquilizer imaginable, indications that Pain was the basis for it all. We have no special name for someone hooked on tranquilizers (because half of our nation seems to be on them), but we do make out that alcoholism is some special disease, which it isn't. It is just a nongeneralized way of easing one's hurt. Those who take tranquilizers and aspirins have escaped the opprobrium of a label.

Both Bill and Henry are excellent writers, and I can't think of any better descriptions of Primals than theirs.

TENTH SESSION OF INDIVIDUAL PRIMAL THERAPY

As soon as I am on the couch I started to tell Les about "group" last night, which he did not attend. I was telling the group about my reactions. I explained how much I had always wanted to understand my fear-response toward any kind of group involvement. For instance, just then, when I had been asked if there was anything I wished to say, in other words, when my safe anonymity had been torn away from me, I had instantly broken out in profuse perspiration, my throat had become constricted so I could hardly speak, I was breathing laboriously, and I felt generally horribly uncomfortable to the point of faintness . . . My reactions to situations of this type had always been very puzzling to me, since they would occur even when I was with a group I liked very much or a number of people I knew well individually, so there certainly was no cause for anxiety when we were all together . . . It was, in short, a terrible social and professional handicap.

The reason I describe this incident during last night's group session in today's entry is the fact that the "insight" in this entire problem popped up most unexpectedly in this morning's regular private session with Les, at the same time shedding light on what I feel very deeply might have been my "Major Primal Scene" as described in *The Primal Scream* by Dr. Janov.

After telling Les about the anxiety reaction I had last night, he suggested that I try and locate a very early situation in which I had a similar sensation in a group scene.

I was quiet for a while but suddenly was eagerly relating about a very strange and powerful feeling, just a single feeling, which I once had in a group situation during my early adolescence, and which, for some reason, I would vividly remember every few months in all these many many years . . .

I went on to explain that this happened in Cologne, Germany, when I was no more than ten to twelve years old and tightly pinned in a mass of celebrating, joyful, and near-hysterical people . . . I never missed a chance to participate in mass-celebrations because of the dreadful choking and sickening air of deepest depression, bitterness, and resentment that hung over our home at all times. I was always waiting for carnivals, parades, festivals, and holidays, and since these were the early days of the Nazis rising to power in Germany in the thirties, all such celebrations had a highly anti-Semitic and ultranationalistic overtone . . .

I was only vaguely aware of all this and as far as I was concerned, these were the only times when life was exciting and fun . . . I would march along happily or stand packed in with the exuberant spectators, rejoicing in the mad noise, the sense of belonging, the closeness to hot, pulsating, living humanity around me and also strangely aroused from the intimate warm body contact, which I never experienced in our totally love-dry home . . .

It was in such a setting that suddenly, without warning, I was electrified by a brain-twisting, chilling, very clear realization that I was in the midst of a fantasy, a dangerous illusion, that I didn't really belong!

I remember this happened on a main street called Hohestrasse, in Cologne. One moment I was literally in orgiastic joy as the vast human mass tossed me about and pressed me against the voluptuous buttocks of strong perfume-drenched females, and in the next moment I felt an icy claw grip my heart with the crystal-clear realization that these people didn't care for me, that they hated me, that they didn't want me and would gladly see me die, if they knew that I was Jewish! !

The music kept blaring away deafeningly, I continued to be carried along like a helpless embryo in the embrace of the vibrating, restless throngs of people, but suddenly I knew that my safety was the result of my anonymity and that my feeling of belonging was a terrible and dangerous daydream . . . I was utterly bewildered and paralyzed with this sudden unbearable view of reality, that these people were united in their intense hatred for me for a reason that was not quite clear to me, except that it had something to do with my parents being Jewish . . .

That, I told Les, was all I could remember of that day. As if the day consisted just of this particular moment . . .

As I have learned to expect, Les responded by urging me to go back to that scene and let that feeling take me in completely . . .

I fall instantly into an abyss of excruciating despair . . . I am back in that incident as if sucked in by a powerful vacuum machine . . . A feeling of utterly unbearable pain seems to tear my heart apart . . . I start to sob, then cry, and finally scream: "There is nobody . . . never anybody . . . in this whole fucked-up world! Nobody listens . . . nobody cares . . . nobody loves truly," and I become incoherent even to myself and simply drown in tears and endless agony.

I finally notice myself calming somewhat, and I hear Les ask very quietly, "Who isn't there . . . ?"

"Nobody." I erupt again and repeat the single word with increasing intensity as if stuck on it . . .

Les persists: "Who is it, who is it that isn't there . . . ?"

A great gale of frightening, horrible, terrifying deadly pain begins to rise from my guts, up and up and up and nothing can
hold it back as it finally explodes from my throat in a truly monstrous chain of piercing screams. I remember only little of it,
except that it seemed to go on forever and that my whole body,
every nerve and fiber of me, seemed to be involved in it, gro-
tesquely convulsing and pulsating with the agony of it . . . Most
astonishing of all, right in the middle of it I became very intrigued
with a growing awareness that somewhere within me I was also
calmly, even happily, witnessing this with a certain amount of
"scientific" curiosity, wondering at the incredible amount of ex-
plosive power that I must have contained in my system all these
years . . . There was a distinct sensation that the waves of
screams were not produced by the throat system alone but seemed
to burst directly from my bones, tissues, and skin . . . Soon the
cries contained an increased number of coherent phrases.
"Mummy . . . Mummy . . . where were you always . . . why
did you never, never, never come to me . . . love me . . . oh,
please love me . . . pick me up . . . hold me . . ."

Control is entirely impossible yet and hysterical cries wrack
through my body like merciless machine-gun bullets. I really become terrified at my inability to reduce the intensity of this scene,
and I begin to wonder if this is going to be the end of me . . .

A long time passes until I finally find myself lying there, more
exhausted than I ever would have thought possible, and watch my
mind gradually resume function with a strange, new, very very
clear lucidity . . . I pay it attention with rapidly growing amazement, as if I was looking into a special, secret, oh-so-long-hidden
compartment of my brain for the first time . . . There, flowing
easily and effortlessly, unfolds the orderly, compiled step-by-step
explanation of the nature and cause of one of my major anxiety
syndromes!!

I am so astonished and delighted, I feel positively intoxicated
. . . I start to grin and then laugh in tremendous relief . . .

"What's going on?" Les wants to know.

Starting to get up, because I simply can't lie still now, I say:

"Les, I suddenly understand my mysterious fears of groups and my lifelong loneliness and depression . . . I'm so overwhelmed with a new sense of understanding and insight that just simply crowds into my mind, I hardly know where to begin."

Encouraged by Les, I continue slowly and carefully. "Just a little while ago I was screaming for my mother with every fiber of my being, in terrible need and longing. I had only very vague awareness of being here, on this couch . . . No, I was right back there, in my infancy . . . For her to come to me seemed to me, really, in every way, a matter of life or death . . . But the fact is, this sick, unfeeling, uncaring woman never came, she never, never, never came. Naturally there were many reasons for this. Grown-up reasons, sensible reasons, practical reasons . . . All of them vastly overshadowing my unbearable ache for her attention . . . Each time I died a little, gave up a little more hope, until I stopped screaming altogether. To survive, I became a good little boy, my real needs and pains pushed deep into myself, out of sight even from myself . . . With this pretense of life I fought myself through early childhood, precariously balanced over the terror of utter despair. The reason I managed to do this was that somewhere within me I still had not given up all hope. Sometime later, somehow, a miracle would happen and salvation would come. Love would come, tenderness, feeling, and a sense of being wanted . . . Daydreaming, the little boy kept on waiting for all these things and, inside, crying for help, day after day and year after year, and from the outside it was visible only in my perpetual depression and sadness at absolutely all times . . . Everybody was always staying away from me and avoiding me, for I was literally dripping sadness and loneliness . . .

The "miracle" I longed for of course never happened, until one day I discovered the marvelous warmth and joyful "togetherness" of crowds, of masses of people . . . I was hooked immediately and eagerly developed this new hobby of mine, this compulsion to sink with delicious self-abandon into the warm, powerful, life-radiating feeling of "mother-mass." After all, my unconscious self must have reasoned in its animalistic logic, flesh is flesh, skin is skin, and feelings are all feelings . . .

I had discovered a beautifully effective tranquilizer for my pain, a marvelous pacifier. No heroin addict ever longed for a turn-on more than I longed for another crowd, another parade, another carnival . . . I used to really be on a wild trip, when the mad masses would nearly squash the life out of my little body, when they would crush me and grind me against hot, throbbing female arses and I would cling to these tall, powerful, lusty bodies entranced and in absolute ecstasy . . . Perhaps most of the overheated and hysterical bodies of the spectators were there for much the same unconscious needs, for I remember clearly a sense of very enthusiastic semi-sexual "group involvement" within these shrieking throngs of people, and this did not distress me at all . . .

Until that scene on the Hohestrasse, which I described before . . . Suddenly the significance of the happy, catching marching tunes that proclaimed the joy of seeing Jewish blood drip from the Aryan daggers hit home. Suddenly I knew my being Jewish as a real fact and that I was bitterly hated and rejected by my joyous "playmates." At the height of my euphoric happiness the danger and stupidity of my delusion suddenly whipped through my ten- or twelve-year-old brain in deadly intolerable clarity.

And indeed, then I died and I, what had remained of my true self, withdrew for good. Never since then did I know myself . . . Often since then would I look into a mirror and stare at this sad, tormented stranger, not quite knowing what to make of him. I just dragged on with the listlessness, hopelessness, and ineffectiveness of the doomed . . . Like a derelict in the gutter I would occasionally meekly beg for a little pseudo-love, would experience a little pseudo-happiness or sit around with other deadly sick people, struggling weakly for something neither of us had to give and neither of us had the health to accept . . .

And as to my fears and anxieties in group situations . . . ? After all, it was in a group that my death scene took place . . . Who would want to face rejection-death again and again and again . . . ?

SABBATH PRIMAL AT HOME

Dear Vivian and Art,

Home from that "staff meeting," I just barely manage to close the door behind me and my brain explodes, I fall across the room into my bed, barely stifling a devastating scream in the torn, dirty pillow, watching it all in utter amazement because a few seconds before I felt "cool and aloof" and I am suddenly, without the slightest advance notion of it, cut to shreds, the head one big open wound, sore and in wild shock, the body convulsing and in horror of itself and one of my many split-off disorganized and bewildered selves watching it all, trying to understand but feeling so incredibly stupid, mystified, because it wants to "comprehend," but there is nothing but unbearable, excruciating animal pain, pain so horrible, so deadly, I know I really want to die, please let me out of here, let me sink into the earth and be devoured by scurrying, blind, busy worms, let me get out of this agony . . . and there it comes again as I write this, why am I writing this shit, why am I always writing, not saying it, writing it when no one is around, then sneaking, sort of illegally, sort of "I hope no-body sees me" to a mailbox, to tell Mommy and Daddy how it hurts, how I want them to tell me it's all right to live, "there, there little boy, we won't kill you after all," but still, just to make sure, I better not risk my bodily self, "got to survive at any cost, you know," but I'll let them know from this "safe distance," I'll let everybody know how I burn down here in this dungeon, in this hell that is all I ever knew, oh I will write and write and write, until the great miracle happens and somebody comes, for no reason at all, just comes and loves me for what I am, the innocent, rejected, hungry little boy inside who cannot and will not stop searching for a way out into the world, who in all these many long long years has not for a minute given up the promise that he will yet live, will come out of this prison into the sunlight. . . .

Still on the bed and coming out of the sudden seizure of seemingly inexplicable pain, I feel above all bewildered, what the hell was all this about . . . I never had a Primal like this, without the slightest theme to it, just plain agony and pain and an unbearable sensation of general floating frustration devoid of definable content, and then I notice the position in which I am lying there after all the tossing and wild convulsions of the intense Primal. . . . I am mostly on the floor near the bed, only my head on top of it still pressed into the old pillow and my hand clinging to the edge of the bed top, just like a tiny boy, still too small to get on the bed by himself but trying, trying . . . And suddenly I go tense, hit by a high-voltage shot that jolts my brain into amazed alertness, I see clearly a scene I never never had in my consciousness since ever then, I see myself happily, playfully run up to the oncoming tall figure of my father, eager and excited to tell him some childish happy thing, and as I reach him, stumble into his knees, he casually and in deep preoccupation with something "more important" reaches down and pushes me aside toward the old-fashioned sofa on the door-side of the living room, I can smell the rancid leather smell of it, I half fall against it, my little hands on the edge of the soft top, my head pressed onto it, just exactly as I am now and I explode in a bitter tantrum of tears and screams, I feel so stupid and horrified and helpless, I don't understand, I can't ever understand why nobody ever, ever, ever will listen to me, just stop once and listen to my little secrets and simple worries and questions, just listen once, see that I am here, it's me, so small, so eager for somebody, anybody! ! ! Then I am in the Primal all over again, only this time it definitely has meaning, *"Taate!"* I scream in Yiddish, and again and again, *"Taate! Taate! !* Father, Daddy! ! ! You old heartless, miserable, blind, stupid son of a bitch . . . I hate you, I hate you, I will always hate the memory of you as long as I live! You looked so tall to me then, you little grotesque nothing of a selfish, frightening animal. All you needed to do is grant me a few minutes of your stupid attention, just this to save me from a lifetime of burning, merciless hell . . . You and that confused, sick, bewildered bitchy wife of yours . . . ! What have you done to me . . . what murderous, subhuman abominations was I born to!" I am crying and screaming and choking with anger and revulsion. I go on until my voice is gone, all strength has left me, and I lie there like a wet rag and rest and slowly begin to think again and then I sit up as understanding dawns . . . yes, yes, yes, I whisper.

THAT'S WHY . . . I write these endless letters all the time, because all the "grown-ups" seemed to have no ears, never, never listened to me, so I write, maybe they can SEE me with their eyes, if they can't hear me with their ears and THAT'S WHY I have such trouble speaking up in groups, because I will only get pushed away, it is no use, they will kill me every time, and THAT'S WHY I cannot stop talking when I have somebody "helpless" on the floor, a MOMMY or a DADDY, and here is my chance to be heard, listened to . . . or on the phone "he wouldn't dare hang up on me," or alone anywhere, where they "MUST" listen . . .

Finally I get up from the floor and I am so happy, I am so happy, I think I will surely go crazy . . . On the other hand, I will write you this letter.

THAT will make you listen! ! ! I love you!

What on earth is happening with me! The thing is, hell, I don't know how to put this into words at all, I mean, what is going on since about six hours ago is that I am having this wildest, outrageous, most unbelievable kind of orgy that ever took place on this sick planet or maybe on any planet in any galaxy . . .

I woke up, went swiftly and impatiently through my usual ritual of thinking how lonely I am, how forsaken, for heaven's sake, how I have not worked in five months and am running out of things to sell, how I am getting old and brittle, bitter and obsolete, and decided to go and waste a whole dollar and a half on having breakfast in the Pancake House with the mini-skirted stupid-cute waitresses and, yes, smoke some damn cigarettes, anything, anything to stop dying like this, stop hurting like this, just somehow get away from me . . .

I drove down Sunset Boulevard. I drove looking for the usual cop to give me a ticket for something or another and kept feeling a gnawing sensation that something was wrong . . . It took almost the entire distance to figure out what the hell it was. God, honestly, it would take a real real writer to describe this with some kind of coherency . . . What was "wrong" was that I did NOT feel miserable, I did NOT feel depressed (perhaps for the first time in forty-nine years), in fact, I almost felt like I have a right to live and driving down this street was perfectly all right . . . I looked about me and the trees were simply very quiet and happy trees and the sky was gray and cloudy but sort of looking like an okay sky . . . I thought suddenly that I must go on a diet, because my stomach is beginning to look ridiculous . . . I was feeling how it bulges out, but then I realized that I was really FEELING it! And my toes too and my legs and my thighs and my chest, with the heart pounding away inside, the lungs on an oxygen spree, gulping it up like there was no tomorrow . . . I looked about me some more, curious now, and the outlines of things were almost painfully clear, the people shuffling along with hateful, worried, confused eyes, and the traffic lights blinking on and off like Martians on guard duty, and then I was laughing like a shmuck, just couldn't stop laughing, just couldn't get used to this new way of being awake, meanwhile hurriedly passing the Pancake House, glad to escape all that poison just in time, driving all the way down to Wilshire Boulevard, looking, looking and not believing how I was feeling, thinking maybe some creep slipped me a bit of LSD, but then, no, I was feeling great, like somebody, I mean like actually a person, *homo sapiens* waiting for the next step of evolution, and then I was back home again, biting into a big slab of Swiss cheese for breakfast and drinking a glass of milk that tasted just like the one my mother never gave me and pulling out a tape I once made up of Bach, Sarasate, and Tchaikovsky, still half crazed and becoming positively intoxicated from that voluptuous milk, I put the music into the recorder at full volume, and when the music starts I really flip, I am beside myself with excitement, I start to scream and sing and laugh, completely out of control, I want to climb up the wall, stand on my head, fuck somebody, anything, including soda bottles, marmalade jars, and medium-sized keyholes, I roll on the floor, jump up and turn on the TV set just to see how it will go with Sarasate, then I go and take the wildest, maddest kind of a shower ever, exuberant and ecstatic in the water, and come back, naked and wet, a joyful ape whom I like, oh I will never let go of him, I love him, "Tchaikovsky," I yell, "you hear, you old son of a bitch, I looooooooooove me!!!!" and I go on and on, even after the music ends, and then I tremble a little, because I know all this can not really be, having been in therapy only a little more than two months, and still have a long way to go, probably, but I keep thinking how I love you two forever and ever and that I must write this to you, right now.

3   *Alcoholism–Bill*

Dear Art,

Six or eight weeks have passed since you asked me to put to paper my reactions, an "alcoholic's" reactions, to Primal Therapy. My wastepaper basket overflows with discarded beginnings. I had thought it would be a fairly simple, straightforward task but I can't seem to accomplish it. At least not in the form of a report. My failure is not due to a lack of effort but rather to my inability to cope coherently with the sheer mass of emotions, thoughts, and impressions released during my thrice-weekly Primal sessions. The man who sits at my typewriter this morning is not the man who sat there yesterday. Yesterday's notes are limited by yesterday's understanding and tomorrow's notes will make today's obsolete.

My mistake, I think, was in trying to "get outside myself" in an effort to write the definitive study of an alcoholic from a detached, Olympian perspective. I know the libraries to be well stocked, even overstocked, with such examinations, but I felt I could outdo them all in the accuracy of my observations and the brilliance of my insights. What nonsense. The Olympian view is, by its very nature, a limited perspective. It has the honesty and clear delineation of a good photograph, and it is as limited. It is mindless and soulless. It cannot see really pertinent detail. A snapshot of a child smiling "for the camera" does not show the welts on the child's backside nor the angry face of the photographer.

What, then? I give you Primals on paper, as far as I am able. They were written at blood heat and I wept as I wrote them. I felt pain as I wrote of pain. I do need my mommy and my daddy and I cry as I write these words. I have inserted some material and done some rewriting in the interests of clarity. I hope you will find these pages of interest. I believe writing them has helped my therapy.

With gratitude and affection,
Bill

AUTOBIOGRAPHICAL NOTES

I am fifty-one years old and am now in my fifth month of Primal Therapy. Prior to Primal Therapy I had two years of psychiatry and nearly eight years of psychoanalysis. I have twice been hospitalized as an alcoholic. I have been divorced for eighteen years. I have attempted suicide both knowingly and unknowingly in automobile accidents. I have been incapable of a continuing relationship with a woman and have satisfied my sexual needs by picking up women in bars. Until I entered Primal Therapy I daily, every day, took aspirin for headaches, Librium as a tranquilizer, Tofranil as an antidepressant, and chloral hydrate as a sleeping potion. Since starting Primal Therapy I have not used so much as an aspirin.

AN INTIMATION OF PAIN AT SIX MONTHS

I awaken and I am alone. Mommy? I turn my head as far as I am able but she is not there. Mommy? The smells I smell are not my mommy's smell. Mommy? My eyes search the ceiling for my mommy's face. Mommy? My ears strain for my mommy's sounds. Mommy? My body hungers for my mommy's milk. Mommy? How can my mommy be gone? Mommy? Is she not my mommy and are we not one? Mommy? As my lips shape themselves for her nipples do not her nipples shape themselves for my lips? Mommy? As she is my food am I not her hunger? Mommy? As I cry for her milk does her milk not cry for me? Mommy? As I ache for the touch of her hands do not her hands ache for me? Mommy? Are we not one? Mommy? If I hurt does she not feel pain? Mommy? If I smile does she not laugh? Mommy? If she sings do I not hear? Mommy? Have I not known the beating of her heart? Mommy? Are we not a single person? Are we not inseparable? Are we not indivisible? MOMMY! MOMMY! MOMMY! MOMMY! MOMMY!

PAIN AT TWO-AND-ONE-HALF YEARS

My crib is near the window and I am awakened at dawn by the light of the rising sun. I am alone. I am completely alone. I am here and I am separated from my mommy. My mommy and I cannot see each other. I sleep in my room and my mommy and my daddy sleep in their room. I sleep alone and I am lonely. I sleep alone and I have nobody to touch and nobody touches me. I hurt with my need to be touched. I would scream with my hurt but I have been warned to be silent . . . ordered to be silent . . . conditioned to be silent. I open my mouth and stopper it with my thumb. Why have I been exiled? How can this be? What has happened? What did I do wrong? I am not ready to be alone. To be alone is to be a separate person. I am part of my mommy and my mommy is part of me. I hurt. If my mommy knew how much I hurt she would take care of me. She would touch me with her hands and I would be blessed.

I lovingly extrude my shit into my diaper. Now my Mommy will "change me." I will feel the touch of her. My mommy will look down at me and we will laugh. My mommy will tell me I'm a good boy. My mommy and I will be together and we will not hurt anymore.

I stand in my crib, my hands gripping the railing, and I listen to the silence. My mommy makes no sound. I shiver in the morning cold and I am lonely. I know my mommy is out there, and I know where her room is. My mommy's room is out my door, and down the hall, and past the closet, and past the bathroom, and open the next door and that's my mommy's room with the big bed and the mirror on the closet door. My mommy's bed is always warm. I listen. I hear only silence. My mommy's bed is big and warm and it has mommy and daddy and wonderful smells.

I climb over the crib's railing and slip down to the floor. I will surprise my mommy and daddy and they will laugh. I giggle as I hurry down the hallway to the door of their room. I hold my breath as I open their door. I can hear the soft purr of my daddy's snore against the measured ticking of the clock. I cross to the foot of the bed. I can smell my mommy's sweet, comforting odor and, too, the more acrid smell of my daddy. I can see the shapes of them under the blankets. I suppress my excited laughter. Was ever a moment more wonderful than this? Am I not surprising them? Are we not going to be reunited? Are we not going to love each other?

I climb upon the bed and quietly, slowly crawl between their sleeping bodies. My daddy's snore becomes louder. Now I can hear my mommy's breath. I pull down the blankets just a little bit and ease myself into the small opening between my mommy and my daddy. The warmth surrounds me like a hug. The sense of security, of homecoming, is an ecstasy. I have found the center of the universe.

I look at my mommy. I can feel the heat radiating from her body. Her eyes are closed and she is breathing through her mouth. I put my finger between her lips. My mommy murmurs in her sleep and shakes her head. I laugh. I push my finger up my mommy's nose.

"Billy, for heaven's sake!"

I laugh aloud. My mommy is awake and now we will love each other. The raw, still bleeding wound of separation will be healed and— But my mommy grabs my hand and slaps it. "Don't you ever do that again!"

I begin to cry. My daddy struggles from his sleep. "What? What's the matter?"

"Billy got in bed with us."

"Oh, Christ."

My daddy looks at me with his sleepy eyes and I look back at him through my tears. I want my daddy to love me. I want my daddy to laugh his loud laugh and hold me on his chest with his big hands and let me feel the exciting strangeness of the whiskers on his chin. My daddy makes a face and turns away from me. "Jesus, he stinks. Get him out of here."

My mommy hefts my shit-filled diaper with an impatient hand. "Billy, you're a bad boy. What's the matter with you? Why didn't you wait and go to the potty? Now, go back to your crib and stay there until we call. Understand? If I hear one word out of you you'll get a good spanking."

I leave my mommy's warm bed and, crying, return to my room. I climb into my crib but I do not lie down. I stand facing the door and holding onto the railing. I suck my thumb and I wait for my mommy.

The shit in my diapers is losing its body heat. It becomes uncomfortable, cold, and damp.

I don't understand.

I AM FIVE AND I IDENTIFY THE ENEMY

I am alone. I have been sent to my room as punishment for playing with the pots and pans and leaving them on the kitchen floor. My mommy says I am a bad boy. I lie on my back on my bed and look at the ceiling. I try to find a face in the cracks in the plaster. I look for my mommy's face. My mommy doesn't love me. My mommy held me by the shoulder and struck my bottom with the back of a hairbrush. I tried to protect myself with my hands and now my fingers hurt where the brush hit them. I want my mommy to be nice to me. I want my mommy to love me. I want my mommy to touch me gently. I want my mommy to take away the hurt. I want my mommy to hold me on her lap. I want my mommy to hold me in her arms and tell me I smell good and that she loves me better than anybody. I want my mommy to tell me I'm the best boy in the whole world. But my mommy doesn't love me. My mommy says I'm a bad, messy boy. The enemy is me.

I AM SIX AND MY DADDY TAKES A NAP

When my daddy takes a nap it is on the davenport in the living room and I must be very quiet. My daddy lies on his back, his hands clasped across his chest, his mouth open, snoring. On his upper lip is a short, brown moustache that is prickly to the touch. I am on the floor wearing my brand-new school shoes and playing with a blue balloon given me by the shoe store. It has a picture of Buster Brown and his dog on it. If I rub the balloon with my fingers the balloon squeaks, so I do not rub it. My daddy has already warned me once. I am afraid of my daddy. I am afraid of his anger and his strength. When my daddy hits me he hits to hurt. When my daddy naps he dominates me with the mere sound of his soft, intermittent snore. I make no sound. I lie on my back on the floor and tap the balloon with my fingers to keep Buster Brown's face floating in the air above me. I want my daddy to love me. I tap the balloon harder and Buster Brown soars nearly to the ceiling. I want my mommy and my daddy to love me. The balloon drifts down again. When I hit it this time I do not quite hit it in the center. The balloon flies away from me and strikes the shade of a standing lamp. The pull cords jangle against the base. My daddy stops snoring. I look toward my daddy just as my daddy looks toward me. I stop breathing. My daddy points his finger at me. It is as threatening as a club. "Get that damned balloon out of here."

I hurriedly grab the balloon and leave the living room. I go through the den, through the downstairs hallway, up the stairs, along the upstairs hallway, and into my room. I close the door behind me. I am in my limited sanctuary. I lie on my bed and tap the balloon into the air. Buster Brown touches the ceiling with a small *boomp* and floats down again. I bounce the balloon against the wall, *boomp,* and it returns to me. I tap it first with one hand and then the other. Buster Brown always returns to me. Good-bye, hello. Sweet pain, sweeter joy. The balloon and I continue our game against the wall.

From downstairs I hear the sound of a thud and then the sound of my daddy's hurrying feet. I am immediately frightened. I hug the balloon. Can I have disturbed my daddy again? I hear my daddy running up the stairs. Can he have heard the *boomp* the balloon made? My bedroom door explodes open and my daddy enters. His face is contorted with anger. I am now standing by my bed. My daddy grabs the balloon with his left hand and bursts it. With his right hand he slaps me on the side of the head, knocking me to the floor. I look up at my daddy and my daddy looks down at me. I am crying. My daddy is trying to contain his righteous anger. His hands clench and unclench. His mouth works. His eyes narrow. I shrink back because I am afraid of my daddy. Afraid of his anger, his hatred. "I *told* you to be quiet," he explains. My daddy goes away, leaving my bedroom door open, my sanctuary razed. I hear his footsteps go down the stairs, across the downstairs hallway, through the den, and into the living room. Then silence. My daddy is taking his nap.

After a while I pick up the pieces of balloon from the floor. Buster Brown's face has become mere ink on rubber. On two pieces of rubber. My daddy doesn't love me. I have been bad again and he doesn't love me. I bothered my daddy while he was taking a nap, and he doesn't love me. He doesn't love me because of the bad things I do. I have done many bad things my daddy does not know about. I have stolen cookies and candy. I have taken money from my mommy's purse. I have broken things and then hidden them. If my daddy knew all the bad things I do he would hit me until I was squashed. He would hit me the way he hit Tuffy and I would whimper and my eye would be hurt.

I want my daddy to love me. I want my daddy to smile when he sees me. I don't want to be afraid of my daddy. I need my daddy. I want my daddy and me to do things together. I want my daddy to take a walk with me so that Bud and Jim will see us and know that he loves me. I want my daddy to show me how to catch a ball so I won't drop them all the time. I want my daddy to show me how to swing a bat so I can hit them a mile. And I want my daddy to hold me. I want to smell his tobacco and feel his whiskers. I want my daddy to tell me I'm a good boy. I want my daddy to tell me he loves me. I want my daddy to give me a squeeze. I want my daddy. I need my daddy. Oh God, I want and need my daddy.

I don't know how to do anything and if my daddy doesn't show me, how will I ever know? My daddy doesn't show me because he doesn't love me. He doesn't love me because I am bad. I am even worse than my daddy knows. If anybody gets to know me they will find out I am bad and they will not love me. I am not a lovable person. I am a bad person. I hate myself and I love my daddy.

MY FIRST REPORT CARD

When my teacher gave me my report card she smiled and squatted down beside me. She smiled and she told me she was going to keep me with her for another semester because she thought it would be better for me. Then she gave me a note to give to my mommy. I know my teacher loves me and I feel warm and happy.

I give the note and the report card to my mommy and after she has read them she looks down at me with anger in her face. "For heaven's sake, Billy, what's the matter with you?" I don't know what to say. I don't understand her meaning. My mommy will not talk to me all afternoon.

When my daddy comes home from work my mommy is fixing dinner. I am on the kitchen floor playing with my baby sister. My mommy hands my daddy my report card and says, "Well, he flunked." My daddy looks at the report card and then looks down at me. His mouth works. "What in hell's the matter with you?" My daddy reaches for me with both hands. I shrink away from him. My mommy watches with silent interest. My daddy grabs me by the upper arms, lifts me, and jams me into the seat of my little sister's high chair. "There. That's where you belong." Then my daddy goes into the living room to read the evening paper.

I look at my mommy but she will not look at me. I don't understand. What did I do wrong? Why don't my mommy and my daddy love me? I look at my baby sister on the floor. She is laughing to see me in the high chair and crawls toward me. I love her very much and I start to cry. My mommy says, "Oh, shut up." I climb out of the high chair and I feel very ashamed. I need to be loved so much I hurt with it.

A HIGH SCHOOL REPORT CARD

It is Monday morning before breakfast and I must get my daddy's signature on my last report card. I have a C, two D's, and a failing grade in French. I have not shown the report card to either of my parents. I have not mentioned it. I have been terrified all weekend. I have tried to keep out of sight. I have tried to be invisible. I have been comforting myself with masturbation. And I am ashamed of that, too.

My mommy is in the kitchen fixing breakfast. My daddy is in his bedroom, dressing. I go to the bedroom door and ask him to sign my report card. He grabs it from my hand without speaking. He reads it, then hits me on the jaw with his fist, knocking me down. "What in hell's the matter with you?" I am crying as I get to my feet. I tell him I don't know. "Look at me," he yells. I look at him. His mouth is working and I can see his teeth. "We're going down in the basement and fight this out, man to man." I refuse. I tell my daddy I don't want to fight him. My daddy's face is twisted and his eyes are filled with hate. He knocks me to the floor again. I am afraid to get up. My daddy is looking for an excuse to kill me. He tells me to get up, but I will not do it. My mommy comes up the stairs to find out what the noise is all about. My daddy gives her my report card. My mommy reads it and then looks down at me. "For heaven's sake, what's the matter with you?" I tell her I don't know.

I hate my daddy. My daddy doesn't love me, and I hate him. I hate him because he hurts me. I hate him because I am bad. I hate him because I am weak and stupid. I hate him because I am hate-filled and hateful. I hate him because he has made me hate myself. I hate him because he has placed me outside the limits of loving. I hate him because I need my daddy to love me, and he does not. I need my daddy. I need to be loved. Please love me, Daddy. Please tell me I'm a good boy. Please hold me in your arms and love me.

MY FIRST DRINK

I am eighteen or nineteen and have come to a bachelor-party picnic being given for a fellow employee of the bank where I work as a messenger boy. It is a BYOB party, and I have brought Coke. After an hour or so it is decided that we will make a punch out of the various drinks. Bourbon, Scotch, gin, rum, Coke, whatever, is mixed in a large kettle. I drink from a jelly glass. It is a vile mixture which tastes bad and burns going down. I retch on it. My friends laugh at me. I drink more. Just to be a good sport. For the adventure of it. For the good fellowship. What nice friends these are. How good. How wise. How wonderfully funny. And how loving of them to include me in this party. I refill my glass. What a beautiful spot for a picnic. What a lovely day. How warm the air, green the grass, and shimmering the lake. And what good stuff this drink is. It cheers the soul and the glow of it lightens the gloomy corners and cheerless dungeons of my personality. I laugh. I make jokes. I know peace. I don't hurt anymore. The perimeters of my awareness contract until there is nothing beyond this picnic ground. I continue to drink. There is nothing except the drink and my friends and the enormous love I feel for them both. Stop drinking at this point? Out of the question. Only a madman would willingly risk exchanging this present bliss for the horror of reality.

As I drink more the contraction of awareness continues. The picnic grounds disappear. I am only aware of the friends in my immediate vicinity, and these drift in and out of my perceptions until all at once they are gone and I am alone. There is only me. I have no friends. I am neither liked nor respected. I am laughed at. I have no hope. I am worthless. I am shit. I am in pain and I can endure no more.

I scream and run to a pier jutting into the lake. I go to the end of it and jump into the water to drown myself. I swim toward the middle of the lake. Two of my friends swim after me and pull me to the beach. I vomit my self-loathing into the sand. My friends look at me with mingled pity and contempt. I cover my face. I try to die. I will myself to die. I want nothingness. I want oblivion. I want separation from myself. I want to do violence to the monster I have become. I would mutilate the very concept of me. I would murder my soul.

If I die, will not my mommy and my daddy be sorry? If I kill myself, will they not see I hate myself as much as they do? If I hate myself as they do, can't they then love me just a little bit?

Love me, mommy. My sweet mommy, hold me. Let me suck your breast. Look into my eyes as I look into your eyes. Let me feel your hands on me. Touch me, Mommy, touch me. Tell me I'm a good boy. Sing to me. Sing me a song of love.

Love me, Daddy. Be strong where I am weak. Be wise where I am unknowing. Be gentle. Bless me, Daddy. Love me. Hold me as you would be held. Love me, Daddy. Let us ease each other's pain.

With this last episode I have brought my life's story to a point where the intimation of future alcoholism seems apparent and there I arbitrarily end my story. I had hoped to put my Primals on paper, but I have failed. I have given you the raw materials of my Primals but they are no more Primals than a load of lumber is a house. The missing Primal ingredient, as I'm sure you've long since realized, is Primal Pain. I don't know how to put that kind of Pain on paper. Perhaps you have felt some degree of Primal Pain drawn from your own store of memories as a result of read- ing these pages. But your Pain cannot exactly equal mine. It may be greater, or lesser, but it cannot be the same.

What is Primal Pain and what does it do? I wrote the following lines after my fourth session of individual Primal therapy.

> Suddenly I am sobbing and begging my parents not to hurt me. Enough. I can take no more. Help me, don't hurt me. I am wracked by sobs that go on and on. Sobs that picked me up and carried me and rocked me back and forth in loving solicitude and I cried and I cried, and I am crying now, and when finally I was done, I cried some more, and then a sense of peace surrounded me. I asked Les for some tissue. My body was limp, exhausted. My legs had fallen into awkward, but comfortable, positions as a child's legs in sleep.

And still you cannot know the actual quality of my Primal Pain, nor I yours. At best, perhaps, we can agree that Pain is a four- letter word and that experiencing it hurts and heals. Heals, there's the thing. The volume and intensity of the Pain experienced by Primal patients during a group session is astonishing. The Pain becomes a palpable substance. And it heals. When a session ends we sense it in each other. How quiet we are. How gentle and lov- ing. We are at peace.

Does Primal Therapy cure alcoholism? I don't know. I have concluded I don't know what an alcoholic is. I know the cliché definition: an alcoholic is a person who drinks compulsively. By that definition I am an alcoholic. I drank heavily for many years and eventually reached the point where I was consuming a quart of vodka a day. Every day. I had to have it. Compulsive. I ruined my health and my career. I was hospitalized as an alcoholic. I went through delirium tremens. I almost died. I went through an agonizing withdrawal from alcohol. I stayed clear of alcohol for about a year, then fell off the wagon. I was back to a quart a day within a month. Within a few months I was again in a hospital. But am I an alcoholic?

I am a man who has known Pain. Alcohol kills Pain. To call me an alcoholic is to call me by the name of my medicine. I had no desire for the taste of it; it's a frightful drink. I didn't enjoy the social aspect of it; I usually drank alone. Alcohol didn't help my career; when I drank I couldn't think clearly enough to work. Alcohol doesn't help one's physical condition; alcohol almost killed me. And it saved my life.

Alcohol dulls psychic Pain. It blurs the edges of grim and chilling reality. It narcotizes the endless hurt. It turns consciousness into sleep and sleep into nothingness. Nothingness was the most desirable of states for me. If I had not been able to find it in a bottle of alcohol I would most surely have found it in the barrel of a gun. Or in a dive off a building. Or in total insanity. I had to somehow escape my Pain.

In Primal Therapy I have faced my Pain. I have felt my Pain. I have sought out my Pain. I have examined the substance of my Pain through the magnification of my tears. And now I hurt less. I am more open to life. I dare to be vulnerable. I dare to love and risk not being loved in return. And I do it sober. I have no desire for a drink containing alcohol. I want no dullness of outline now. I need no narcotic. I no longer flee life. I hug it and I glory in it.

I realize I still have a long way to go in Primal Therapy. Primal Therapy isn't a quickie cure; it is a way of living life. It is a way of being open to love, and of loving. It is the way I shall live the rest of my life.

4 *The Difference Between Tension and Feeling*

The differentiation of feeling from tension is a most important one, for often, what looks like feeling is really tension. Neurotic tension is the physiologic segment of painful feelings severed from consciousness. It is the "energy" of feeling. When a feeling is repressed out of consciousness due to its great load of Pain, what we experience is that energy . . . tension. A birth trauma that cannot be integrated becomes residual tension when the organism shuts down, just as being humiliated produces such tension. If a child could fully feel the birth event or the humiliation and answer back, there would be no "Pain-memory" which lingers in the form of tension. The specific antidote for neurotic tension is connection: to make a sensation into a connected feeling. A fully feeling person is not tense . . . and a tense person is not feeling. He is suffering from amorphous sensations that have lost their specific mental roots.

The body is the first line of defense in each of us. Before we have an intellect, we have Pain; and we must defend against that Pain by deadening our bodies. If the trauma is catastrophic enough and occurs early enough, the body will become lifeless and unavailable to the person. If, for example, there is strangulation by the cord at birth, it may well shut down the body. This shutdown may be an important factor in later frigidity. That is, if there is an overlay of puritanical attitudes by a woman's parents, there may be little or no sensation in the vagina. The body, then, will be unavailable to her.

Generally, we can tell how close a person is to his feelings by whether or not he suffers from some of the usual sensations in neurosis—shaky hands, butterflies in the stomach, dizziness, trembling, etcetera. If a person has none of that available to him, we tend to think that he is far from his feelings, and furthermore, that the problem lies very early in his life.* With this kind of patient, the first indication we have of improvement is the appearance of shakiness or trembling. What I am saying is that bodily sensations are the physical components of feelings, and their absence in neurotics may well indicate the degree of repression.

Each feeling of Pain that cannot be integrated adds to the tension. What happens to this tension is that the person is forced to find ways to ease it. Since the only real way that tension can be erased is to have the *feeling*, the person must do the next best thing and seek pleasurable *sensations* to soothe himself. In this sense, pleasure for the neurotic is the successful anesthesia of Pain. The sensations that he seeks will depend on several factors. First, the areas of initial trauma. If an infant was orally deprived, weaned too early, not allowed to suck for the proper length of time, he may become fixated around his mouth and lips—the result is a compulsive smoker. If the area of initial trauma (the focus for original tension) was in toilet training, then the genitalia may become the focus for pleasurable sensations.

The second reason for the choice of area of focused sensation is what was allowable. If food was the central family focus, then food (and the mouth) will be the fixated area of satisfaction. The aim of the sensation exchange, in which we substitute a good

---

* In our Research Laboratory we are beginning to develop a neurophysiologic profile of repression which thus far has accurately indicated how deeply repressed a person is, i.e., how far he is from his feelings. We hope through the development of this repression profile to scale degrees of severity of neurosis and thereby be able to predict therapeutic improvement.

sensation for the bad (tense) one, is to quell tension. Therefore, the neurotic will focus on those areas of his body with the greatest nerve supply. And this is where the confusion comes. For he will "feel" hungry, when he is really tense. He will "feel" sexual, when he has simply eroticized (transformed) tension. What looks like great feeling is in reality great tension. When a homosexual *feels* his great need for warmth from his father and also the need to suck his mother's breast, then he is no longer compelled to cruise in search of a penis to suck. His compulsive need for that *sensation* has been eliminated. So long as he cannot feel his true need, he is stuck with sensations.

Because the neurotic is trying to fulfill a feeling with sensations, he cannot get enough. To fill a feeling (emptiness of one's life) with food is a vain effort, for all the food in the world cannot fill the void. A person who has automatically converted his tension into sex cannot tell the difference. He will truly feel sexual when something has made him anxious. Why the sexual area? Why not hunger, for example? The choice of outlet depends upon our very early experience, earlier than we might suppose. In the last two days, I witnessed two Primals that are relevant to this discussion. The first involved a man who relived the rather pleasant experience of being diapered in the crib. It became a Primal when he felt more than simple pleasure; he was being overstimulated. He felt the warm diaper being brought from underneath him, rubbing against his testicles as it was pulled tightly toward his belly. At the same time, he remembered wetting his diapers often because his doting mother would rush in as soon as he was wet and change him, producing the warm sensation on his testicles. It wasn't that his mother was seducing him or deliberately overstimulating him; she was simply anxious about his being wet. The experience, however, was sexual, or at least focused in a sexual area. This area became the focal point of any tension.

A similar Primal in another man had to do with the tension, very early in life, of having to urinate, and the fear of displeasing his mother by wetting his pants. He discovered that when he had to urinate badly his penis became erect, to shut off the need to urinate. So in a complex interplay, an erection became a defense against losing his mother's love. Later, in unconscious and automatic fashion, any tension or fear turned into an immediate erection. Erections (and later sex) became the central defense.

If one were to have asked either of these men before therapy about their sex lives, I'm certain they would have said they simply were highly sexed—had a lot of sex feelings. The truth was that they had few sex feelings, only tension eroticized. During the early part of the treatment, as tension reduced, the sexual drive diminished significantly.

There is some research that helps clarify the difference between tension and feeling. Subjects were put into unpleasant situations that produced fear and anxiety. Later they were hypnotized and made to forget the episodes. Still later, these subjects were asked to volunteer for another experiment. This experiment was similar to the first uncomfortable one, although none of the subjects could remember it.

These subjects were then given a battery of physiological tests even before the unpleasantness began. All of the measures of tension were raised during the second situation, even though there were no memories to go on. The levels of tension at the beginning of the second situation were significantly higher than the levels recorded during the peak of discomfort of the first situation.* If there were no memories to go on, how could we explain the higher tension levels before the second situation even got under way? Subjects in a control group did not show elevated tension levels. Clearly, memories linger below the level of conscious awareness, and tension can be reactivated simply by putting the person in a situation similar to an earlier "forgotten" one. The tension could not be resolved because there was no conscious connection to origins—no feeling.

Hypnosis here was an externally derived process of repression. That is, critical, evaluative consciousness was lulled so that

* E. E. Levitt, *Clinical Research Design and Analysis in the Behavioral Sciences*, Charles C Thomas, Springfield, Ill., 1961. As cited in *The Psychology of Anxiety* (same author), Bobbs-Merrill, Indianapolis, 1967, pp. 40-41.

the subject responded to the cortex of the hypnotist instead of to his own. The result was the blockage of memory. Primal feeling *is* a memory which remains as tension because it is not a conscious one. That is why memory returns after Primals; to bury feeling is to block memory—and vice versa. Hypnosis is able, through suggestion, to divert awareness. Thus, a subject can be conscious (of his surroundings) but unaware. Because of this diversion, it prevents the kind of connections that would transform tension into feeling. Feeling is the only solution for neurosis just because it is the only way to resolve tension.

Having established that a feeling is an awareness of sensation —a *correct* awareness—we are faced with the question as to how many basic feelings reside in man. In the early twenties it was believed that man had three basic feelings, rage, fear, and love. Later, psychologists added trust, revulsion, and disgust. Others believed that self-esteem and confidence were basic to man. I think that the feelings basic in man are those which arise endogenously—without outside stimulation—hunger and thirst, for example. Each of the endogenous feelings revolves around need. Because I do not think that self-esteem arises endogenously, I do not classify it as a primary feeling.

I would classify anger and fear as secondary feelings—those requiring outside stimulation. Secondary feelings overlie basic feelings and serve to block them. For example, when a baby is dropped, he has a fear reaction. The fear results from a threat to the child's safety—a more basic feeling—to feel protected and safe. The distinction between primary and secondary feelings is more than semantics. Rage is not something endogenous in the Primal context. It occurs when basic feelings are thwarted. In Primal Therapy, if we were to stop probing after the expression of anger, we would miss the basic need underneath it. If our theory posited anger or rage as endogenous, then we would simply be content to have a patient express that rage and mistakenly believe that we were helping him resolve the problem.

Let us take an example: A woman in therapy is discussing how her father molested her sexually when she was young. She rages at him during the Primal. But as we push further, the rage fades into need—"Why can't you be my good daddy?" she shouts and cries. The reason we must take care to distinguish the primary feelings from others is that only the experience of primary feelings can resolve.

Perhaps this becomes clear when we discuss the more obvious secondary feelings such as self-esteem or feelings of being important. If a patient comes in and recalls an incident which made him "feel" "unimportant," we always pursue the matter and arrive at something more basic—hurt. We find that some of these secondary feelings are really not feelings at all, in the Primal sense, but mental labels for hurt. And this hurt covers the need. For example, a child gets up to recite in class. She loses the glass out of one side of her eyeglasses. The class laughs at her. As she retells it, she says that she felt humiliated and unimportant. As she gets into the *feeling* of the experience, she begins to shout, "Don't hurt me any more, please!"

So we have this polarity—a single basic feeling, need—the need to experience all of oneself, which only a relaxed organism can do; and the countervailing force of blocked primary feelings which produce hurt. If fear were endogenous, then when the blocks are removed in Primal Therapy, pure fear should arise. But this is not the case. Fear hides the more basic feelings, and when we push through fear we get to them. The problem is complicated, however, since fear can be blocked. For example, a child is scared at night and his father tells him not to be such a sissy, that he doesn't need the light on. Here the night fear covers Primal feelings and then even the fear is forced back.

The child might develop a new feeling—pride. Every time he bucks fear he "feels" proud. And professionals have come along and labeled this symbolic, derivative feeling as something basic—a need to feel "proud." But when we get below pride and into the feeling, we discover it is something quite different. In this case, it might be "Daddy loves me because I showed him that I'm not a sissy."

Unnatural man has blocked his basic feelings and so it is logical that he has mistaken the symbolic ones for real ones. Unnatural man may be so far removed from himself that he no longer feels the basic survival feelings of hunger; or he may no longer feel sexual or feel the need to be touched. Pain has blocked correct awareness of the bodily sensations and shunted that awareness into other channels. If we think about wild animals, it becomes more lucid. Mother animals aren't telling their young that they are really important. They aren't convincing them that they are loved. These mothers are simply doing what is natural. The young don't say to themselves, "I feel loved or I feel important." They just experience themselves and what is happening around them. They act automatically in terms of how they have been treated. The idea of a young loved animal having a genetic drive toward self-esteem is a bit ludicrous. What the animal will want is not "to be important." Rather, it is to have his basic needs fulfilled. A child who is loved, caressed, protected, talked to, listened to, looked at, has no need for importance and does not feel "important." He feels himself, and the concept of "importance" would not enter his mind.

Neither would he feel "loved." He would have no need for such a term. "Love" was invented by those who felt unloved. Love is often confused with need, because needing people want it. As man becomes real, his so-called basic feelings (such as rage) diminish or evaporate. His feelings become pure and uncomplicated, and it is then that he discovers how few are the basic feelings of man.

To summarize: All of us defend against Pain first by repression—an automatic process that disengages consciousness from bodily processes. All of us differ as to what we then do with the remaining tension. Some of us smoke. Others drink. Others talk incessantly. The symptoms of tension are both voluntary (nailbiting) and involuntary (tics, bedwetting). The defense outlet depends on two central factors: first, the underlying feeling or need (sucking to smoking); and second, the early environment. The solution arrives when we reunite the bodily processes with correct consciousness.

5 *The Struggle*

Denying feeling is what makes the neurotic act-out symbolically; that is, he "acts-out" the feeling instead of feeling it. That is why the struggle never ends—the feeling is never resolved. Instead, there are always symbolic solutions.

For example, a girl is constantly beaten and threatened by her father. She becomes afraid of men, especially their touch. She becomes involved with weak, nonthreatening, passive men, often homosexuals, who will neither touch nor threaten her. In this way, she symbolically tries to resolve the fear of her father. But she is foredoomed to misery because she deprives herself of affection, of a real man—a real human being who could care for her. Her struggle, then, becomes one of trying to make these men care about her. But they cannot; they are too passive, too weak, too much in need of a caring parent themselves. If this woman, married to a weak man, should get a divorce, she will still unconsciously seek weak men, because her underlying fear of men is unresolved. She will be in a constant struggle to make her weak mate strong, and fearful that he will be.

If this woman could have felt her fear specifically with her father she would not have generalized it to all men. The problem is that her need for a good father remains and drives her constantly to find one, while her fear from the past pushes her to avoid strong men who could offer her protection and caring. She dominates the men she becomes involved with, not to "castrate" them, but to keep them from becoming the "bad" daddy, someone who could hurt her again. Finding a weak person is the symbolic solution. And she will go on finding weak men until the two feelings from the past—the need and the fear—are resolved.

Another example. A man has a compulsion to dress up secretly in women's clothes. His mother wanted a girl and tried to mold him in that direction, while his father demanded a "normal" all-American boy. There was no way he could be both. So he acted normal for his father, and secretly tried to become the girl his mother wanted so that he could feel loved. His ritual was perpetual and would remain so until he could *feel* what he was acting-out. It isn't enough to *know* why he did it, since he had learned the why of it years before in psychotherapy, with no results. He had to *feel* all the ways that the events, scenes, and experiences molded him.

One of the ways patients in Primal Therapy get to their feelings is to watch the ways in which they act-out, since they know they are always acting-out specific Primal feelings. One person, a compulsive sunbather, learned that he tried to extract warmth from the only place it was available—the sun. Another person with the same need tried to get it from God.

One patient was always starting new projects—starting afresh. The feeling being acted-out was, "Give me one more chance, Dad." There are thousands of symbolic struggles. Joining clubs to get the family you never had; organizing parties so you won't feel left out; constantly being on the go to keep from finding out that there is no place to go; delaying payment of bills as a way of getting others to take care of you; getting everyone to give you advice as a way of saying, "I'm lost, take care of me"; studying history as a way of finding out about your past; buying old houses or cars as a way of resurrecting yourself; constant talking as a way to avoid the feeling of not being worth listening to; acting badly to give people a reason for disliking you; getting sick as a way of being taken care of; constantly saving money to feel safe; always being in a rush so that you are never "all there";

acting dumb as a way of saying, "Explain it to me, Mommy." You fill in the blanks with your own struggle. This may be difficult, because acting-out usually keeps one from being aware of what he is doing. It is automatic and unconscious, because the feeling is unconscious. When a person is constantly sweet, as if to say, "Be nice to me, Daddy," he usually has no separate awareness of his so-called personality. He began acting this way from his earliest years, and his "personality" is second nature.

Acting-out is always against the feelings—a way of keeping feelings down. The aim of acting-out is to produce what could not be felt and said. The solution is to feel and say it in therapy.

6 *The Nature of Consciousness*

One of the requirements for the experience of Pain is consciousness. If one is not conscious of Pain, then there is no *experience* of it. This does not mean that Pain will not register itself in the system. There is enough evidence to indicate that the brain registers high evoked potentials when noxious stimuli are applied to the body even though the person is not conscious of it, as, for example, in hypnosis. The same is true for elevations in blood pressure and pulse rate.

For there to be an *experience*, there must be consciousness. Consciousness is the awareness of the processes of the body. That is, real consciousness represents the integrated interrelationship of the body and mind. Consciousness is not to be confused with activity by the cerebral cortex. LSD, for example, is called a "consciousness-expanding" drug. But what expands is not consciousness; rather, it is the activity of the cortex *away* from the feeling processes of the body. What one achieves with psychedelics is pseudoconsciousness—merging with the universe—cosmic consciousness—at one with infinity.

Neurosis is a state of partial unconsciousness. The neurotic is unaware of certain experiences that have impinged upon him during his early life. The only way he can expand his consciousness is to feel and *experience* those Pains. Feeling Pain is a consciously connected experience. Pain is its own definition; it expands consciousness by "telling" it where, what, how much, and often "why." Without consciousness, there is no definition . . . no sharp delineation of experience by the mind.

One of the ways we can understand the nature of consciousness is by examining the hypnotic state, for in hypnosis we often have pseudoconsciousness—a seeming awareness of one's surroundings (of the investigator) accompanied, often, by a total unawareness of Pain the body is undergoing. In hypnosis, there is a vast "constriction of awareness . . . and a degree of automatism."* This is very much how one would define neurosis. And perhaps one reason why we have been unable to find specific physiologic correlates for the hypnotic trance state is that it is not qualitatively different from the neurotic one. It is a transient neurosis, only more so. I believe that it works on particular kinds of neurotics because they are already split from their own consciousness and more attuned to the conscious will of others. That is, they will repress their own consciousness in deference to a suggestion by an authority figure. This may, in part, help explain the mass unconsciousness (and therefore unfeelingness) of the German people during the Nazi era.

If we look again at the definition of a feeling person—someone who is consciously connected—then we see that a feeling person cannot have his consciousness severed by any act of someone's will. It is interesting that many of the characteristics of the hypnotic state are also characteristics of the fascist personality— denial, (attention focused away from reality) literal-mindedness, automatism, passivity, rigidity, and a lack of spontaneity and initiative. Where would we look for the physiologic correlates of hypnosis? In the same place we would look for them in the fascist—in measures of tension, which indicate severe repression.

One of the conclusions of a study that showed that the brain responds to Pain whether or not the person is hypnotized was: "No part of the loss of sensation in hypnotic anesthesia can be attributed to attenuation of the sensory messages in the afferent

* A. M. Weitzenhoffer, quoted in T. X. Barber, *LSD, Marijuana, and Yoga,* Aldine Publishing Co., Chicago, 1970, p. 237.

pathways on their way to the cortex."* Reduction in the conscious experience of Pain, then, is due to "processes going on at the highest cortical levels of the central nervous system."† What this means is that the *sensation* of Pain is being processed below the level of conscious-awareness, even when there is no consciousness of it. This, again, is exactly what happens in neurosis. We are in Pain and are unconscious of it. The degree of Pain determines the amount of unconsciousness. "Total" Pain means psychosis—a great amount of cerebral cortical activity and no awareness of what is going on inside.

One can have a high degree of *selective* consciousness; that is, one can memorize all the dates and figures on past wars, baseball games, etcetera, and still be very unconscious. Consciousness in neurosis is attuned to only those outside events that do not lead to the Pain. That is why fascist denial is so complete; nearly all reality must be snuffed out. "If you can't say something good, then don't say anything," becomes transformed into, "If you can't *think* something good, then don't think anything." "Why do you always see the bad in things?" is another fascist-style slogan. It is a slow process of hypnosis in which we learn through our parents to attend to the "good" and ignore the bad. The hypnotist works faster to make us unaware of Pain.

Being diverted away from what is painful leads to the kind of unconsciousness where a parent cannot see the psychological anguish of his child before his eyes. Though he may see that child every day of his life, not once does the recognition of the child's Pain reach the parental consciousness. The parallel is tacitly pointed out by August, who stated, "Hypno-anesthesia results from directing attention away from pain response towards pleasant ideas."‡

Hypnosis is an encapsulated neurosis and, because of this, offers us a clearer understanding of the nature of consciousness. For

* *Halliday and Mason.* Found in T. X. Barber, *op. cit.,* p. 242.
† *Ibid.,* p. 242.
‡ R. V. August, *Hypnosis in Obstetrics,* McGraw-Hill, New York, 1966. As reported in T. X. Barber, *op. cit.,* p. 243.

example, through suggestion a person can be rendered deaf—he cannot consciously perceive sounds. Sophisticated tests indicate that this is not a faked experience. There is an absence of startle reflex to loud sound, and when sounds are fed into earphones while the person is speaking, there is no interference with speech as there is when a non-hypnotized person is trying to speak while listening to his voice played back on a second's delay through earphones. External stimuli (the hypnotist and his suggestions), then, affect and diminish conscious perception. This is no more than what I maintain about neurosis. No act of "will" could expand the hypnotized person's consciousness; that consciousness has been circumscribed by another person.

Repression of what is real produces a false consciousness. So we have two consciousnesses—one real and one unreal. Intellect (discussed in depth later) is often a false consciousness because it is not in accord with real consciousness—awareness of inner reality.

I have pointed out in *The Anatomy of Mental Illness* that the split in consciousness may take place in the limbic system of the brain—our ancient cortex. Recent work indicates that the split is not only between higher and lower brain centers but that it also occurs within the right and left hemispheres of the brain. There seems to be a comprehending, intellectual side of the brain and another which is more feeling (the feeling side being the less dominant hemisphere). In right-handed people this (the intellectual) is the left (major) side of the brain. What split-brain research indicates is that there are two kinds of consciousness or two separate consciousnesses—a feeling one and an intellectual one. For example, musical sense belongs to the minor hemisphere. And it is musical sense that is inextricable with feeling—tone, timbre, rhythm, all are expressive of feeling. It is no accident that music can set off very deep feelings in us. A number of nonverbal functions are associated with the minor side. Minor-side consciousness is more gross; there is a general awareness of feeling—the major side supplies the specifics, the scenes, the exact memories. The major side symbolizes information from the minor side.

The proper functioning of both hemispheres is essential to psychological integration. Even though the minor hemisphere has largely to do with feeling, it also is involved in intellectual functions. But the more complex and abstract of these functions seem to be the property of the major side. So the minor side can be conscious of a feeling, but the *insight* into that feeling state is supplied by the dominant hemisphere . . . a consciousness of consciousness.* It is very much like having a feeling during a dream and being aware of that feeling, and then being conscious that the awareness is taking place during a dream. Perhaps a better example is having a hallucination or crazy idea and "knowing" that the idea is crazy.

Proper integration means, *inter alia,* that there is conscious access to feelings, an ability to introspect and connect. This integration is what I call Primal Consciousness. Neurotic consciousness is having intellectual insight into one's feelings but being powerless to change them (and neurotic behavior) because of lack of fluid integration between hemispheres (and also between higher and lower centers of the brain). "I know I feel inferior and yet act superior," one might say for years without changing behavior because the knowledge comes from disconnected consciousness. An inordinate development of the intellect seems to help mask awareness of feelings; or, better put, blocking of feelings helps produce inordinate development of the intellect (given a certain intellectual environment) so that the hemispheres are "out of synch," not properly balanced and coordinated. It is the job of the major side to properly symbolize the feelings of the minor side. In neurosis, it improperly symbolizes. In persons who have had a commissurotomy where the connections between hemispheres (a mass of connecting nerve tissue called the *corpus callosum*) are severed, there is often a loss or diminution of dream life . . . a severing of the symbolic functions.

The commissurotomy splits consciousness so that there is no

* For an excellent discussion of this, see W. A. Lishman, "Emotion, Consciousness and Will after Brain Bisection in Man." *Cortex* (a journal), June 1971, Vol. VII, No. 2, 181-191.

information transfer from one side to the other. In neurosis there may be a functional commissurotomy; one side is feeling Pain and the other side is thinking pleasure, or is in some way incorrectly symbolizing the feeling. Thus, there may be a dual kind of neurotic split—from higher to lower, and from side to side. Many patients report going dead on one side during Primals, or are cold on one side and warm on the other. The *corpus callosum* may have an integrating function between hemispheres, so that when we speak about the integrated conscious person, we shall keep this in mind.

New evidence about the nature of the relationship between hemispheres comes from Finland, where a neurosurgeon named Lauri Laitinen has done brain surgery on eleven intractably tense patients. He destroyed part of the front end of the *corpus callosum* and in so doing eliminated the patient's tension. He found that tense patients showed excessive nerve activity along the pathways connecting the two hemispheres. Again, what we are seeing is how tension results from the collision of feeling with the forces of repression. Further, that tension is part of continuous activating forces in the brain. All of the implications of this surgery are not clear as yet, but it would seem that consciousness is both a vertical and horizontal (across hemispheres) process in the brain. Surgical interference in either direction—either a lobotomy or a commissurotomy—seems to reduce consciousness of inner states. Nor is surgery necessary to produce this state. Laitinen found that high frequency electronic stimulation of the *corpus callosum* eliminated tension. It may be that overload of these circuits produces the same kind of non-feeling state as an electronic overload of the limbic system—the system which mediates higher and lower brain centers.

The split in consciousness is particularly evident in an event such as birth Primals where a neurologic sequence is run off with no conscious control. Yet there is a simultaneous here-and-now dim consciousness that such an experience is taking place in a therapy room. So there is a nonverbal consciousness of an old experience and a simultaneous one of a current experience—that experience being the consciousness of reliving an old event.

The major hemisphere seems to dominate the minor one, and perhaps this is one reason why we can use intellect to repress feeling. Once that repression is done, there is the job of inventing a new consciousness—of rationalizing, figuring out and explaining. A person involved in rationalizing may seem very alert and conscious, yet he is the victim of pseudoconsciousness, and in this sense is really unconscious. His brain is working, but he is not truly aware.* This state of affairs may well be true of the philosopher who ponders the most profound intellectual questions about the nature of the brain and consciousness.

The degree of consciousness, in Primal terms, means the degree to which we are open or aware of stimuli, either outside or inside. The more free and open we are as an experiencing organism, the greater is our outside consciousness, and the more perception and insight we have. Real consciousness, then, is not a "runaway" cortex. Rather it means a properly integrated brain where there is an easy access among the various structures. It may be well to reiterate: a conscious person is a feeling one.

* For an excellent exposition of split-brain work, I refer the reader to Joseph Bogen, "The Other Side of the Brain," Bull. of the L. A. Neurological Societies." July 1969, No. 3, Vol. 34.

7 *Homosexuality*

The following chapters were written by former homosexuals, both educators. What is clear in their writings is that there is no "homosexual." There are people in Pain who, because of life circumstance, act-out with members of their own sex. They quell Pain with sex much in the way that an addict shoots heroin. Both suffer without their "fix." Some individuals know they need love and go after it symbolically in the form of homosexual acts. Others deny the need for love, suffer because they offer themselves no outlets, and need to kill the pain with drugs. In this sense, one might say that homosexuality is a defense against addiction, and conversely, addiction is a defense against homosexuality.

What is a homosexual? It is a person who has sex with members of his own gender; or at least wants to. The reasons are diverse, as I have discussed in the chapter on Why There Can Be Only One Cure For Mental Illness. In the case of males it can be a repressed need for father love or a fear of mother (and then women). In the case of females, it can be due to never having a warm mother, or avoidance of men due to fear of incestuous feelings toward father (and later men). The reasons for homosexuality are idiosyncratic. There are those who believe that the cause of homosexuality is hormonal. But why would a need for a kind father have a hormonal basis? The fact that there is a *homosexual* reaction to the lack of a father is usually because it was the only avenue left open to the child who was given nothing. It was "safe," as odd as that may seem. A frigid, man-hating mother may unconsciously want her son to be a girl.

It is possible that hormone balance is rent askew during gestation, because progesterone, androgen, and estrogen levels can change due to neurosis in a pregnant mother. This may ultimately affect the fetus and help shape the direction and manner in which environmental factors (such as the lack of a father) are reacted to.* But this is not a cause of homosexuality. In some cases it might be a contributing factor; but it would make as much sense to believe that hormone imbalance causes homosexuality as to think that a repressed and unrecognized need for a father—latent homosexuality—would have a hormonal basis. Or what if a person acts-out with animals. Surely, this is a sexual deviation. Could this be hormonal, as well? Unlikely. The fact that homosexuality is reversible in Primal Therapy should help us lay to rest notions about the hormonal basis for its occurrence. There was a recent study of homosexuals where hormonal imbalance was found to be a factor. Later, when they tested physically ill persons, they found this same imbalance. Thus, individuals whose systems are "out of whack," may all suffer from physiologic changes.

What is evident about one kind of homosexual is that he has made "daddies" out of other men (in the case of some male homosexuals) and acts-out symbolically as though *they* were the sought-after love object—since the real daddy, perhaps, was unobtainable. But don't all neurotics do that? Don't we make the boss a father and act-out our fear of him by mollifying behavior, for example? Is that less perverted? The homosexual's symbolic trip is for the attainment of love—now sexualized. The non-homosexual neurotic may try to get love from this same kind of father figure by more circuitous means such as achieving for him. Whether the acting out is sexual or not will depend on the

---

* This point is discussed in detail in a forthcoming book of the author to be published by Simon and Schuster, *The Feeling Child*.

neurotic's life circumstance; but in any case, we should not consider homosexuality some special disease just because it is *sexual* acting-out and not some other more acceptable form.

It isn't just some scientists who think that homosexuality is a natural state (in keeping with a peculiar kind of physiology). Many homosexuals believe it. It is part of the credo of The Gay Liberation Front. They have slipped into homosexuality "naturally" in their teens, have made a "good" homosexual adjustment, and see themselves as unneurotic. They may be "well adjusted" because their defense works, just like any person whose defense holds him together. Homosexuals who are not comfortable with their state are more apt to come for therapy—not so much for their homosexuality, which they accept as a "given," but to find relief from their aggravating tension. What they get in the bargain is eradication of their homosexuality.

What follows from the above is that there can be no experts on homosexuality. Each individual homosexual is his own expert. When he begins to feel in Primal Therapy, he will unravel the mystery of his homosexuality as no psychiatrist ever could. Indeed, there can be no expert on any form of psychopathology.

For example, a lesbian patient had a birth Primal regarding her premature expulsion into the world. This left her with an unconscious residual feeling of being sent away from her mother before she was ready. While reliving the birth trauma, her body attached itself like a vise to the warm body of the female therapist. The epiphanic insight at that moment was that her homosexual acting-out had been in part due to the need to attach herself to a female (mother) at birth. This insight never could have been made by a therapist, no matter how acute.

Another example is a lesbian who went to visit her mother back East at Christmastime. During the afternoon she became edgy and had a desperate need to seek out her female lover. She had a Primal that day in which she felt that she was never going to be loved by her mother and desperately had to find some female who *could* love her.

Homosexuality, at any rate, is not a *sexual* deviation. It is what a human being does who was not allowed to be himself totally early in his life. The homosexual has found a sexual outlet in much the same way that the "clown" finds a comedic outlet and the intellectual finds his academic outlet.

ROGER

As I began therapy seven months ago, I thought it would be so simple to unlock the key to my homosexuality. Such was not to be the case. The structure around that particular defense is undeniably complicated. Those who think that people are born homosexual *are wrong*, but not by far in my case. The foundation for this defense was laid within me by the time I was six months old. Because of its complexity, I am convinced that there is no universal pattern as to why some neurotics act out their defense homosexually, any more than there is any universal pattern as to why some other neurotics act out their defenses by smoking, drinking, compulsive fucking, or running off at the mouth. Before entering Primal Therapy I had dozens of "insights" as to why I was a homosexual. Each "insight" satisfied me for about six months. They did nothing to change my behavior, nor did they make my life any easier—only crazier. By the time I entered Primal Therapy I had convinced myself that I wasn't really an overt homosexual. I preferred to say I was a bisexual with strong feelings of hostility toward women. By acting-out occasionally in a heterosexual fashion, I was able to "convince" myself I was not really "queer." All I really knew at the time I began therapy was that sex of any kind did not meet my needs. Orgasm with women was so intense as to be painful; orgasm with men was unfulfilling—ten minutes later the tension level was so high I was again on my quest for another partner.

Thirty-four years ago I was born in New York City of Irish-Catholic immigrants. Excluding my twin brother I had three older brothers. My mother was sent to a sanitarium because of tuberculosis when I was six months old, and we were left in the care of nurses for eight months until my mother returned home. Because of her fear of transmitting the disease, she took the precautions of not ever touching us and of maintaining the house in as sterile an atmosphere as possible, e.g., all bedclothing and dishes were boiled. She was a semi-invalid until her death fourteen years later.

After my mother came home from the hospital we moved to the country. My father remained in New York City for the next eight years and visited us occasionally on weekends. My oldest brother, Bill (nine years older than I), tried to assume the role of father. Early in therapy, the Primals in which I started to feel the need for Daddy, Bill tended to replace my father. One night in group I felt a strong sexual attraction toward Jerry, my therapist. As Jerry worked with me I let that feeling overtake me and I went back to a time when I was horsing around with Bill. I wanted him so much to hold me and love me. I wanted to "blow" him—anything to get his attention. As I went further into the Primal my crying out shifted from "Bill, love me!" to "Daddy, love me! Daddy, love me!" After feeling this, the insight came that in my homosexual acting-out I was nearly always attracted to anyone who reminded me of Bill—tough, supermasculine, and athletic.

My childhood was one of rapid transition from babyhood to adult responsibility. Mama, capitalizing on her sickness, was unable to assume much of her role as manager of the household, and she trained me to take over. By age eight I was responsible for all the cooking, shopping, budgeting, letter writing, and much of the cleaning, laundering, and ironing. Most of this I did willingly. Mama gave me enough praise and encouragement to keep me going. She was sick, and my cross to bear, as her good little Catholic boy, was assuming all that responsibility. As I pondered on this over a period of time, it became very clear that I had become Mama's mother—her creation designed to meet her need, since she really was a sick, helpless little girl. By keeping busy in this role I didn't have to feel my great need to be mothered myself. This same role has repeated itself over and over again in my life. I paid my way through college by being a "housemother" and cook to a fraternity of twenty-four men. Later I married a woman who was virtually helpless as a housekeeper and I had to take over. At various times I had male roommates that I could mother. I am saddened by the craziness of my struggle. What a stupid fool that made me into, just so I wouldn't have to feel my pain.

My first homosexual experiences were with my twin brother and started long before puberty, continuing with him up to the time I left for college at age seventeen. My next experience occurred in my junior year in college with a fraternity brother. From that time until entering therapy, I was extremely promiscuous. There never seemed to be enough cocks in the world to meet my need. Always, however, there was the hope I would find the magical one that would make me content.

At age twenty-seven I became sexually involved with a woman for the first time. She was ten years older than I. The affair lasted for around a year, during which time I also had frequent homosexual contacts.

My second heterosexual experience occurred at age thirty-two, and ended in a brief and disastrous marriage. Both experiences were felt as ones of entrapment and being smothered. As much as I enjoyed the company of women, I was always terrified that they would get too close. To be casually touched by a woman even with no obvious overt sexual motivation was enough to make me freeze with fear. When I did permit myself to get physically close, it was always counterphobic. I would quickly talk myself into believing "I'm not really that scared."

After my tenth week in therapy, I became sexually involved with Barb, a thirty-year-old divorcee. Out of this experience came several very important insights and a feeling of confidence that my sexual neurosis was well on the way to being cured.

Each time that I have had sex with Barb the arousal has started in my body. There has been no need for my head to "talk" my body into becoming sexually aroused, as had always occurred in the past. My homosexual experiences were always a "head trip." Most of my prior heterosexual ones were too, but not always.

Many of my orgasms that have occurred with Barb have led directly into Primals. It is from these Primals that the insights result. As I "come," I start screaming "Mama, Mama," and I become the helpless child crying out for the fondling and love that I never got. From these particular Primals it has become clear to me that I have never hated women. My need for them was too great. What I thought was a fear of them coming too close to me was really the fear that *I* might get too close to them and then have to feel the pain of needing my mama. In short, I have been a *latent heterosexual.* As an adult, of course, I still had a need for sexual release. To attain it with males was simply less painful than to do so with women. At the same time I was fulfilling part of my need for the father who literally and figuratively made me twist myself out of shape to get any attention at all from him. One day I relived the time when to get even a nickel for an ice cream cone from him I had to beg, and beg I did. Later in life, sexually I preferred to degrade myself by getting on my knees and sucking cock. Perhaps then Daddy would pay some attention to me.

All my life I have been ashamed of my penis. I have always felt it to be too small and inadequate. Even at night I could not sleep without a sheet covering it. Unerected, there were times when I thought it would disappear. Erected, it is larger than average, but I wanted a larger than average unerected penis, particularly if I was to compete in a homosexual world. It is clear now that my mother did not want a boy—rather she wanted a sexless, angelic creature. One day in therapy I remembered a scene as a little boy in which I saw my mother's cunt. I saw her terror and shame. It was contagious and I caught it. I had completely blocked the event from my memory. As she was ashamed of her sexuality, so was I ashamed of mine. She always disapproved of my older brother's interests. I read the cues and became the sissy she wanted. But enough of the *real* sexual me remained even though it acted itself out in an unreal fashion—

homosexually. And because of that, my mother did not succeed in getting me into the seminary to become the truly sexless priest she wanted.

For me to ask for most things has always been very difficult; to ask for love, impossible. To get, I have always had to be devious. By hinting, perhaps people would see my need. Not the real need for love, which even I could not recognize, but some symbolic need, such as a loan or a compliment, that would camouflage the real need. Asking involved directly taking the risk of not getting, which would be too painful. To ask for love would reveal my vulnerability, and then I would be left open to real hurt. My sexual Primals that begin with asking Mama to love me usually end with begging Mama not to hurt me.

One night I had a Primal in which I was lying in the crib as an infant, feeling smothered. As this feeling enveloped me, so did the feeling of needing my daddy. The pain of wanting so desperately and not getting became almost unbearable. I realized that I was dying. My body was attempting to shut down; if I could stop breathing I would not have to feel the pain of not getting my daddy's love. At the point in the Primal I thought I was going to die, I could feel myself go numb. I curled up into the prenatal position and put my fingers in my mouth and started sucking. This felt good.

The next night in therapy I again sank back into the infant scene. It took on a new dimension. The back of my neck started aching. As this pain grew, I realized my head had slipped between the bars of the crib, and I started crying out in fear and pain. After what seemed an eternity, my daddy came and pulled my head back through the slats. I could sense his anger and annoyance with me as it was registered on his face and in the rough way in which he handled me. More than anything in the world I wanted him to fondle me and reassure me everything was all right. Instead I got nothing except his anger. Again my only defense was to curl up in the prenatal position and start sucking my fingers.

As I came out of this Primal I was flooded with insights. Later in life, whenever anything brought me close to feeling the pain of not getting Daddy's love, I had a compulsion to start sucking. Whether it was a cigarette, food, or a cock didn't matter—they all felt good. They all numbed me. No longer do I feel compelled to smoke, or to overeat, or to suck cock. When the pain starts to rise I can feel it rather than act it out. Today a man is only a man—not a symbol of someone who has something—a cock to make me "feel" better.

That night I wrote in my journal: "Tonight it became clear that Hell is here on earth inside of me. By not giving me as an infant what I needed most—their love—Mama and Daddy placed within me the living *hell* of struggling *not* to feel that need. It's as if they locked the gates of hell within me and then threw away the key. Only through Primal Therapy have the gates been unlocked so the real me could start to emerge. No longer can I be their 'nice,' fear-ridden, neuter, depressed, simpering little unnatural pawn. I am who I am, neither elated nor depressed, merely existing—for that is all there is."

It sounds all so simple. And the feeling is really so simple—"I need their love." Being there, feeling that incredible want, is such a relief. Getting there is such a painful struggle. Sometimes I'd rather go completely mad than feel that feeling. And why not? For that is what I have done all my life—struggled to avoid feeling. The adult me can handle that feeling. The infant me would have died. I cry even now as I write this because it is so clear to me what a nightmare my life has been when they could have made it so wonderful—so easy. Just a little love—"Mama and Daddy, was that really too much to expect?"

Not feeling the need and want is the *universal* underlying homosexuality—and every other neurotic defense.

TIM

My name is Tim. I was born in the Great Lakes region thirty-three years ago. I have two older brothers and one older sister. My oldest brother and sister are alcoholics; my sister has also been addicted to drugs. Both have spent time in jail on felony charges. My other brother was a Trappist Monk for a number of years; he is a college graduate. Since he was graduated from college he has lived mostly as a Third World dropout.

My father and mother were raised in families where one or both parents were deceased. Their emotional deprivation is readily evident to an observing eye. My father worked as a dental technician for thirty-four years. My mother was a simple housewife.

Before entering kindergarten I felt strangely different from other boys. I thought it was more important to be a nice, quiet little boy than to run about with unbridled enthusiasm. My parents often remarked that I could entertain myself with the simple household wares. My favorite game was to create my own little world, using a blanket and a couple of straight chairs.

Elementary school was a trial for me because I was retained in fourth grade due to numerous illnesses. In many ways the school grew to be an extension of the home, a place where little people were blamed for not acting like adults. Praise was always at a minimal level, while blame was continuously used as a thrust to motivate better work and maintain a deadly social order. My world was like being reared in a giant mixmaster.

When I was in junior and senior high school I was a likable neurotic. My demands were few; all I asked was that people not kick me or make me fight. I had seen enough of that at home. My scholarship in school was above average when I had accepting teachers, and poor when I was faced with severe, clinical personalities.

My college years began with a flair. I participated in a student exchange program and grew to know many of the "in" people on campus and in the business community. My entire family was thunderstruck by my performance. My junior year of college, I moved to the campus because my parents would not adjust to my late hours and girlfriends. This is when I first faced the fear of not being able to have a meaningful relationship with a girl. I began hanging around the Catholic Newman Center,

discussing religion with the parish priest. Going to Mass and saying prayers didn't ease my tension. Finally, out of exhaustion, I
gave in to a homosexual proposition. Slowly, I slipped into a
gray twilight zone of nonexperience and nonfeeling.

The following describes in capsule form my unreality made
real by acting-out through father substitutes. Being queer is not
a simple condition that can be distilled into a few simple phrases.
It is a whole constellation of nonfeelings, emotions, impulses,
and compulsions that is thrown together in millions of different
combinations. I am convinced that there are as many combinations as there are queer people. With this notion in mind, then, I
am much more brave in discussing my own condition because
I know I will not mislead my readers.

For me, being queer meant living my life around a search for
cocks. My search began the night my daddy beat up my sister
because she called him a bastard. I was not yet five years old. I
knew at this early age that my father was capable of killing my
sister, and it followed that he was capable of killing me if I
didn't toe the line. The daddy that I once loved and depended
upon suddenly became a monster out of a nightmarish Hollywood production. Like a snap, I was swept over by feelings of
insecurity, powerlessness, contingency. My mother was no refuge for me; she always seemed abrupt in her handling of me.
Her remarks always denied my feelings as a child. "Don't you
dare look at me like that, or I'll give you something to cry about."
"Now what do you want? You have to be after something all the
time." "What you need is a darn good thrashing, and I'm just
the one to do it."

These remarks sound so incongruous now because I was never
given a spanking in my childhood that I can remember. The
reason for this is that I made sure that I was always the good
little boy/girl that my parents wanted.

Although I was never dressed as a little girl or rewarded for
acting like a little girl, I was also never permitted to play with
little boys because they were "outlaws."

My search for a big strong daddy brought me to my brother,

who is six years older than me. Both my parents idolized him, claiming he was just like their side of the family. It didn't take long for the message to sink in that maybe if I were more like him, then I would reap the same affection and attention. My struggle to remake myself in the image of my brother began before I was in second grade. I allowed him to tease me, and I made myself compete with him, hoping one day that a magical spell would be cast on me and take me out of my miserable condition. As I grew weary in my struggle to get my parents' attention, I also became aware that my brother gave me more affection and security than they did. Soon I became fixated on my brother. I grew sullen when he would leave me home with my parents. I wanted to be with him always, even in the bathroom. I admired his athletic build and his large cock and balls. One day I saw him masturbate in the bathroom. At the time I didn't understand what he was doing, but I knew I wanted to play with his cock and have it for mine. As the years passed and I entered my teens, I continued to feel inadequate compared to my brother. I was not athletic and handsome, nor did I attract friends who were "in" as he did. Instead I felt weak, dull, insecure, and frightened of most new experiences.

When I was eleven years old, my brother enlisted in the Navy. It was like a loving daddy running off and leaving me to the wolves. I was miserable immediately because there was no one to take me places, play with me, and give me the affection I needed.

Many years passed without my brother, because he entered a Catholic monastery upon his discharge from the Navy. All the while I never accepted my father as a loving figure. I despised him for being mean to my sister, for always muling and puling about his illnesses, for always shouting and acting out in crazy unbelievable behavior. I continued to reject my mother because of the bind she always put me in: "Whose side are you on? Decide who you are going to be loyal to right this minute!" I thought many times that she was poisoning my food. Frequently I would refuse to eat meals because I thought she wanted me to die. I became so insecure and neurotic that I masturbated every day, and I would have orgasms in my pants if my schoolteachers became angry or impatient with me.

While I was in high school, I never had any kind of sexual contact. I felt so inferior to my peers that I would not dream of touching a girl or boy unless I was directed to do so by a teacher. My father reinforced my feeling of worthlessness by informing me that I was a mistake and that my birth accounted for all his misery. He told me he had a vasectomy two weeks after I was born to insure no more mistakes. This news shut down the last available line of communication with my father. An important part of me died that day. I relived that Primal Scene that happened when I was less than five years old, when my father beat up my sister. It became clear to me that I was nothing but a burden to both my parents.

I kept my needs under control until my junior year in college. One day a pleasant fellow began staring at me while I was in the student union. He reminded me so much of my brother because of his athletic build and full smile. After a number of days he struck up a conversation with me. It didn't take long for him to spot my insecurity and overall interest in him. That day he gave me a blow job in a telephone booth in the student union. I liked it a lot, I liked his attention. It was like having a big strong daddy who made me feel good all over. I saw this fellow around campus on two or three other occasions, and then he evaporated. Soon, my tension level began to skyrocket again, and with it my need for a fix—another man, another father substitute. When I look back upon all my "tricks," it's almost like a trip through a house of mirrors. All the images have something in common, but all of them are slightly out of focus. All of the men I have been attracted to were distorted reproductions of my brother.

When I graduated from college, I used my teaching as a bromide. My students became my captive audience, a ready-made suck. I was all-powerful—I could determine their life changes with a flick of my grading pen. My needs quickly became unmanageable. Soon I was organizing outside activities for my students in order to fill in my lonely hours. I had to be with my "family" constantly so I could reassure myself that I was needed and loved. Later, my need grew in even greater proportion; this time I zeroed in on committee work and curriculum planning. I liked to see my name in print because this reassured me I was smart and would not be left behind in important matters. How true the gay saying, "There is no gravity, the whole world sucks."

As my professional career launched me to new heights, I became proportionately more insecure. I was frightened to death of people outside my sphere of influence. I was on alert at all times, fearing that someone would unravel me and find the little boy/girl inside.

Tired, weary, and exhausted by my struggles, I finally turned to pot, LSD, mescaline, and other assorted mind-benders to ease the pain and allow me temporary relief. The drugs put me in contact with people who were accepting of my needs. Gradually I began to take suicidal risks. One day I went to school freaked-out on LSD and played the piano and directed a play in front of several hundred parents. I began to smoke pot with my students and lecture while I was stoned. My ability to control my behavior under stress was incredible. My superiors showed confidence in my ability by assigning me additional responsibilities that gave me control over important campus programs.

On weekends and vacations I would go on wild sex binges. My favorite hangouts were the Y.M.C.A. and the steam baths. I wanted to watch other guys have sex as much as I engaged in it myself. My "tricks" all had to be bigger than life . . . large builds and big cocks. I disliked pretty queers, so I avoided gay bars and other places that attracted them. One time at the baths I was so stoned and worn-out from having sex that I collapsed in the shower room and had to be carried to my room.

About nine months before entering Primal Therapy I decided to consult a doctor. I guess he thought I was a lost cause, because he gave me an unlimited prescription for phenobarbital, to take four times daily. Some days I felt more like a living corpse than a functioning human being.

After ten weeks of Primal Therapy I am well on my way toward cure. I thought I wanted a boyfriend or a girlfriend for a lover. What I needed was to feel love from Mommy and Daddy. Now that my mind and body are functioning as a system, a new world is opening to me. Heterosexual experiences are fulfilling. My vision is improving, and my hands and feet are growing. Now that I'm off drugs, cigarettes, and booze, I feel healthier and cheerful. My taste in music, art, films, literature, and friends has changed. Shopping is even fun now because I actually look at the merchandise instead of seeing the salesman as a sex object.

These many years before therapy have been spent as a sexual neutral. I acted out the homo trip with men, but it was devoid of experience. Now I have found an alternative to acting-out my childhood fantasy. At the moment I am a latent heterosexual.

To get where I am at in therapy did not mean getting electroshocks, being probed with critical remarks, or being told that I must face reality and be reasonable. My therapist helped me to face my pain by being kind, a behavior that I have no defense against.

8 *Heterosexual Perversion*

It seems to be a contradiction in terms to call a heterosexual a "pervert," but we must take care not to equate heterosexual acts with normalcy. Normalcy is not a matter of an "act"; it is a matter of the nature and quality of internal experience. Otherwise, someone who acts normal would have to be considered normal, whereas we know that some of the sickest people can put on the best act.

The heterosexual act can be perverted in many ways. It is my clinical experience that the latent male homosexual often prefers cunnilingus to intercourse. Though he is having sex with a woman, the experience can be the *avoidance* of penetration. This avoidance can result from many causes. He may be having symbolic incest, for example, and the lack of penetration is the way to avoid the taboo act. We have frequently seen this in men who have had seductive mothers. These women have aroused their sons in many ways (not wearing panties and opening their legs so that the son can see it all), setting up a situation in which the now-grown son finds himself attracted to mother figures but never consummates sexual relations. Or, if he does, finds himself impotent.

The heterosexual act can be perverted by fantasy. A woman can imagine that she has found the ideal loving person in each sexual encounter, only to feel let-down and disappointed after each encounter, because it was not "Daddy." The woman can fantasy dominating the male, taking away his penis and keeping it for herself—so she can be the "strong man." One woman had the same fantasy during sex, of taking the penis away from her partner. In her Primal she felt what it was—castrating her husband so that he wouldn't be big and powerful and hurt her, as her father had done. Certainly this is a perversion of a supposedly one-to-one loving relationship. In this sense, the "act" is not heterosexual, even though it appears to be. One homosexual, for example, always had the feeling while blowing men that he was castrating them by taking their power away—symbolically making his father less of a threat. Though he was engaged in a homosexual "act," the experience was something else again.

In short, "experience" is not simply what the body does. It is a mental-physical connected event. Shut-off people can have many sexual experiences and feel nothing; that is, they have not truly *experienced* the sex act. Thus, neurotics do not learn from experience because they do not experience. Experience is not where we've been and what we do; it is what we feel. When a person cannot fully feel, he must be perverted in some sense. He must pervert experience in the service of his need. Thus, his sexual encounters will not be straight. His heterosexuality will not be pure heterosexuality. It will be a search to fulfill a need (for love) through an "act."

Is it not a perversion of a pleasurable act to feel pain instead of pleasure during sex? Sensations that were meant to feel good yet feel bad? A woman can be heterosexual, or trying to be heterosexual, yet feel repulsed or in pain during sex. This is hardly heterosexuality.

Just because a person acts-out feelings in heterosexual ways rather than in homosexual ones doesn't make him any more healthy. If he is acting-out, trying to get the warmth of a parent symbolically through sex, he is still neurotic. Society happens to approve of heterosexual "macho" behavior, so we tend not to see that it is sickness. Unfortunately, if he acts out the need for a parent of the same sex, he can be put in jail; if he acts out the need for a parent of the opposite sex, he can be a hero—the Namath syndrome. We should be just as concerned about the rise of neurotic heterosexuality as we are about neurotic homosexuality. Both are indices of a sick society.

We need to understand that sex is a feeling experience; that there is no pure sex feeling that exists apart from other feelings inside us. The ability to feel anything, including pleasure, has all to do with whether we will feel sexual or not. The sexual dimension is obviously something added to the feeling base, just as taste is the dimension involved in eating good food. That is to say, feelings can be discriminated both mentally and physically. We see a sex object, feel aroused, certain hormones begin their secretions, and our mind points the way for the focus of that arousal. If we grew up normally, with no inordinate need for love from the parent of our own sex, and with no inordinate fear of the parent of the opposite sex, then the focus of our arousal will be heterosexual. If, however, there were distorted relationships to the parents, if they demanded certain kinds of behaviors before they would approve of the child, then those distortions will somehow find their way into sex, because sex is part of the entire feeling experience. If a parent expected a child to be "dead" and lifeless in his general conduct in order to get by without punishment and disapproval, then that person is likely to be lifeless in sex.

Even the choice of the heterosexual partner is significant. A man too much into the "macho" game, too interested in being the "big man," yet with longings for love from a father, may choose a woman who is really a man. In this way, he can claim to be heterosexual while having an essentially homosexual experience. Tough, masculinized women may choose effeminate men for the same reason. It is not exactly a conscious choice. It is simply that need drives one into those exact places where one has to go to fulfill oneself, irrespective of what the mind says. If by some error the neurotic marries a fairly straight person, he will then have to convert him or her into something that fits the neurosis. The straight partner will somehow have to become part of a fantasy or a game that the neurotic person must play time after time, year after year. That game is a perversion, as perverted as homosexuality or exhibitionism. Only the form of the perversion is different. The straight partner may have to pretend to be someone else, or may have to act-out being commanding and strong, giving orders to the neurotic person.

Sometimes the neurotic can keep that perversion inside. He can fantasize and keep the fantasy to himself during sex. But he is still perverted because the *experience* is a perverted one, even though nothing overt and external is going on that looks like a perversion.

The whole idea of teaching neurotics sexual techniques must be seen as fallacious, because knowing where to put one's hand, or how to lie and in what position, cannot alter the *experience* of the sex. We know that Primal feelings determine the nature of our dreams and daydreams and our fantasies. We can put the body through all sorts of correct motions as per the sex manual, but the Primal feelings determine the mental experience. Techniques rarely have to be learned by normal people, and when they are learned this way, they are really most helpful for normal people who can feel.

THE SECRET CRAZINESS OF NEUROTICS

A football hero leaves the game and goes to exhibit himself in an alley before a little girl. A lawyer wears his wife's panties to work, while a sociologist is hooked on sniffing his girlfriend's panties. A judge is a chocolate freak and consumes an average of ten candy bars a day while on the bench. A knighted actor is a child-molester; a well-known business manager changes his name, adopts the Christian Science religion, and refuses to allow his daughter to have needed surgery. A teacher goes home and masturbates his dog; an orthodontist insists that a woman watch while he and his wife have sex. The list of secret crazinesses is endless. All of the above are facts, not fantasy.

I believe that in every neurotic, by definition, there is some kind of secret craziness—some hidden sickness that erupts. The psychotic is "up front" with his insanity. He can't hide and put on a good social face. But the neurotic has learned to do just that; he acts. The act is perfected and unconscious. But the early thwarted needs and impulses find devious routes for egress. And each route has an idiosyncratic meaning. The panty-sniffer remembered that his mother worked all day, and her clothing and their smells were the only important reminder of her he had to hang onto. He had no father, and desperate as he was, he developed a so-called "perversion." For the judge, it was simple. Reared in a righteous religious home, where the family were "Renunciates," no pleasures were allowed. So later, he kept giving himself some kind of allowable pleasure that would not evoke overwhelming guilt. The exhibitionist felt like a little boy. He tried to be "macho" on the football field, but even that defense wasn't enough. He had to prove himself to little girls.

There are always convoluted reasons for any perversion; and not all perversion is sexual. One can pervert the eating response —and eat candy from morning to night. One's system can be perverted so that it doesn't function properly; a smooth facade may hide agitated colitis inside. We might say, in general, that when a value system (the parental brainwash) does not even allow for a *secret* craziness to erupt, then the "craziness" will remain deep inside, and psychosomatic disease may ensue.

The neurotic *is* a pervert. His natural feelings have been suppressed and perverted. The form they eventually take is of little consequence from a Primal point of view.

9 *On Nudity and Sex*

One current approach in the field of psychotherapy is nude therapy. One aim of this kind of therapy is to free sexual inhibition. Implicit in this goal is the notion that there is a necessary relationship between nudity and sexuality. The fact that the two are related in a psychotherapy is more a reflection of the puritanism of the therapy and the therapist than it is an indication of liberation. It is possible to cavil and say that the object of nude therapy is much more than sexual liberation—total freedom of one's body, perhaps. But if that is the goal, why is it necessary to strip in front of others? Why can't one dance naked at home and achieve freedom? Obviously, it is showing one's body to others that would seem to be crucial.

One must assume that showing one's body to other group members in nude therapy will help one to be less ashamed of one's body, and, ergo, sexually more free. We shall have to harken back to the Primal theme: Problems that take years in their formation, that derive from early experiences, cannot be solved in the here-and-now. Frigidity, for example, is the end-point, a symptom of possibly thousands of experiences that have gone before. These experiences need not have been sexually repressive. Simply quelling a child's exuberance time and time again helps shut him or her down to any kind of spontaneous excitement. A neurotic's body is the sarcophagus for *all* kinds of re-

103

pressed feelings. For one patient, to feel anything meant to feel the terror of imminent death, of being strangled by the umbilical cord. To think that shedding his clothes would help him feel sexual, when he had actually shut down at birth, would be to take an unnecessarily insular view of sexuality.

To undo a sexual symptom such as frigidity or impotence, it is necessary to resolve those critical feelings that underlie the symptoms. So therefore any nakedness in therapy must be experiential—it must flow from a feeling and not be a mechanical gimmick that one does out of context. There is nudity occasionally in Primal Therapy, but that nudity evolves from a particular feeling, and more often than not, that feeling has little to do with sex.

For example, one woman stripped to show her "fat ass." She wanted to show her "unacceptable parts" because she no longer felt that being loved hinged on having a perfect body—for mother. Another patient stripped at the end of his therapy, saying, "This is all that's left of me but it's me. I'm not afraid of me anymore, Momma." One woman showed her breasts while deeply into a Primal. She kept shouting, "I'm not George, Daddy, I'm Georgia. I can't be a boy for you anymore." She had hidden her breasts since puberty out of fear of losing her father's love—he wanted an athletic boy. Another woman had a Primal about hiding her breasts since she was fourteen because she sensed that her father, who had finally taken an interest in her, was really only sexually interested. Trying to be unsexual was her way of making her father love her as a father. One man finally let himself achieve an erection, shouting, "It's all right, Momma, it's all right. It's not dirty to be excited. I'm not bad, I'm human."

So we see that nudity had special meaning to each of these people. And that meaning was historic, not current. Those Primals alone did not liberate their bodies nor solve their sexual problems. But those nude Primals, along with many other feeling-liberating therapeutic experiences, did liberate them. Sexual feeling is part of feeling. It is not an isolated compartment unrelated to a general ability to feel.

What is significant is that these nude Primals were unrelated to anything or anyone in the here-and-now. They would have been just as important and liberating if they had been done at home alone. Nudity in Primal Therapy was a triggering mechanism to reawaken those specific Primal feelings associated with nakedness. Nudity may reawaken in one person a memory of being diapered on a bassinet and being treated roughly. For another it may set off the old feeling of being ridiculed for running around naked at home. In puritan households it is often opprobrious to show one's body. The first time one may do it openly is in sex. In this way, the body becomes transformed from a natural object into a strictly sexual one. In a strange dialectic, it is sexual repression that makes the body solely a sex object, while sexual freedom allows it to be something human.

Normal children who grow up in a free and unsuppressive environment would not become automatically aroused sexually at the sight of a body. Their heterosexual relationships would be between two people rather than between parts of people. Sex would be embedded into a relationship rather than existing as a viable isolated entity. Sex would be something human instead of antihuman, as it is for so many neurotics. Therapies that concentrate on the body alone, whether it is simply showing one's body or giving instructions for sexual techniques, are compounding the problem by making sex something apart, something not human. Indeed, nudity in a neurotic may not only be nonliberating but may contribute to one's defensiveness. This can easily occur when nudity is done as a mechanical gesture, thereby increasing one's shame and fear. Inner liberation, then, must always flow from inside out and not outside in.

Primals related to nudity are often complex. For example, one woman kept having the impulse during a Primal to take off her clothes but would back off each time. Finally, during one session, she began to strip, crying more and more as she shed each article of clothing, until she was finally totally naked, which pushed her into an agonizing, writhing Primal where she was wailing, "Daddy, I know you won't like me if I'm a girl but I have to be me!" Showing all of herself made her feel the brunt of his rejection—something she had avoided by always being well covered with blue jeans. What she was showing of herself that day was not simply her body—she was showing her feelings, and that was the meaning of showing herself to Daddy.

The insights that flowed from this Primal are instructive. In her previous analysis, she learned that she had "penis envy." She did, indeed, wish to have a penis. She had promiscuous sex in order to get a penis inside of her, with the fantasy that it was really hers. But that penis envy was not basic. She felt in her Primal that to be a girl was to be unloved. She somehow connected early in her life with the notion that to have a penis (as her "loved" brother had) would make her loved. Finally feeling the unlove she had experienced as a girl freed her from the so-called penis envy and eventually from her frigidity—each sex experience had reminded her that she was what she did not want to be, a girl. She had to fantasize being a boy during sex so as to feel loved, even momentarily.

Now it is quite clear that for this woman to shed her clothes outside of this feeling-context would have been a meaningless exercise that she could have repeated to no avail for the rest of her life. In fact, what really brought up the feeling was making her dress—in frilly, feminine clothes.

The point of all this is that you cannot "teach" sexuality. One does not teach instinctive behavior—infants do not have to be taught to suck. Sexual problems derive from a thwarting of naturalness in every area of functioning. "Teaching" naturalness is too often more of the thwarting process.

10 *On Perversion and Bizarre Murder*

Almost every bizarre (as opposed to planned) murder and perversion is an encapsulated Primal. The denied feelings are not felt but are acted-out directly in symbolic form. They are rituals, temporary insane states in which present reality is submerged by the past feelings on the rise. Consciousness is diminished and what is unconscious takes over. The intensity of the compulsion or ritual is commensurate with the intensity of the unconscious Pain. The compulsion is the drive away from feeling, but the energy behind it is the feeling itself. Thus, the need for a man to exhibit himself will depend on how much of his maleness was thwarted, how many outlets for male activity (sports, sex, clothes) were blocked, and how many demands were made on the child to "act like a man." If a boy's maleness was robbed by one parent while the other demanded adult "manly" behavior, he may later reach a neurotic compromise by attempting to "show" his masculinity. If the boy was made into "mother's little angel," sexless and passive, then, given the right circumstances, he will have a built-up drive to prove his maleness. The force behind his exhibitionism is the reality of the need to be himself. This is what every natural organism strives to be. No matter how life perverts that natural real self, the drive to be oneself will be there, energizing the compulsion. If this were not so, then "mother's little angel" would simply be that, without any Pain or any drive toward exhibitionism. The force, then, is always to be real, and the strength of the compulsion depends on how far a child has been taken from his reality.

Bizarre murder is no less a ritual than sexual perversions, except that the force takes violent, as opposed to sexual, forms. Whether it takes the violent form or the sexual one will depend on the life-circumstance of the child. If the child is given nothing, beaten and humiliated, and allowed no sassing, he may well develop a fountain of rage to be discharged later against people in his environment—strangling women while degrading them, for example. If, on the other hand, the child was subtly seduced by his mother, he may become homosexual to flee the incestuous relationship.

Because the real feeling is suppressed, the ritual in both the violent and sexual forms will have to be acted out again and again. This is because the ritual is symbolic and nonconnected to its true source. That is why jail solves nothing in regard to any kind of perversion. To put an end to the problem, it must be hooked up with its Primal generating source.

What happens in bizarre murder is that a Primal Scene is thrust upon the person, reawakening all the latent power of the Primal feeling, which then drives the person to act-out. For example, a girlfriend being unfaithful may trigger an unconscious memory of mother being unfaithful and abandoning the children. Though the actual scene-memory may be unconscious, the overpowering feelings are set off, and murder is the result. The killer becomes lost in the Primal feelings, present consciousness is dimmed, and the girlfriend-mother dies. The girlfriend was but a symbolic stand-in for a reality never faced, felt, and accepted.

If we strip the act of murder from the event and treat the person while those feelings were on the rise, he would go into a Primal instead of externalizing his feelings. Murders occur when the person has no idea what he is feeling; he has no help with those overwhelming feelings and succumbs to their intense pressure.

Perversions are not just sexual in nature. One can't pervert the sex drive, because it remains pure. What does get perverted is the person himself, in order to be loved, and the sexual ritual is just one more way he shows it. A person can't be all healthy except for his sexual habits. His sexual habits express his problem perhaps more eloquently than anything else about him. Someone who has to tie himself up in order to engage in sex may be trying to say, "I've made myself rigid and immobile in order for you to love me." Or, "I'll punish myself ahead of time in order to feel any pleasure"—because he really did have to struggle to be allowed any pleasure around his parents.

The perversion is the exact message. All that has to be done is to have it decoded by the feelings of the person. It can never be decoded by anyone else. The feelings form the base of the elaborated symbolic ritual, and it is futile to attempt to untangle the meaning of the ritual, because feelings do it all automatically. This is more clearly understood in terms of dreams. The symbolism is the same. The feelings ascend and a story is made up at night (and acted out during the day). In both cases, the dream and the perversion, there is a loss of hold on reality in deference to the symbols.

What, then, is the difference between those with fantasies of perversion (which are prevalent in the population) and those who act it out? Most perverts begin with the fantasy, but as feelings build they overtake more and more of one's organism, so that the head alone cannot control the impulse and it generalizes to the whole body. The measure of sickness, then, is how much of the person is encompassed by the underlying need. A good number of people have violent fantasies, but only few act them out totally. And those people are adjudged insane because they could not control what the rest of the population controls. Their feelings were too overwhelming. In a dialectic process, the perversions represent a breakdown in the first-line neurotic defenses and bring the person closer to his feelings. That is why perversions are easily treated, in differentiation from the fantasy-dominated intellectual, who has everything (including his perversions) in his head.

Several years ago a Hollywood character actor was found hanged in his bathroom. He was over sixty years old and enjoyed a reputation as a cultured, intellectual, and humanitarian person. He had written brilliant essays on art and politics. Yet, this man was driven to kill himself in the most bizarre way—handcuffed and chained, wearing a woman's clothing. His intelligence could not save his life. I am sure that he knew he had an aberration, but with all his intellect and reason he was powerless to stop it. It was as though his need lay encapsulated inside for all those decades, and because he could not feel his feelings, he was forced to twist and warp himself until he killed the needing self. His perversion was unaffected by his intellect, so that he was forced to reenact a strange ritual over and over, trying to gain some kind of satisfaction and surcease from his tension. The unreal, perverted, and twisted self finally became total and preeminent; with that the real self died.

Actually, the neurotic's whole life is a ritual of trying to be loved. The pervert has narrowed it down into something specific.

The true societal insanity is the way we treat perverts and those who use violence. We jail them—or, if they are lucky, we hospitalize them. The magical notion is that after five or ten years of incarceration the person will have learned his lesson and go straight. In this morning's newspaper is the story of Bertram Greenberg, shot to death like "a mad dog" in the desert after raping and killing a little girl and murdering three others. He had been in and out of prisons and mental hospitals for years. He had been violent many times before, yet his latest psychological report indicated that he was making a "good adjustment." He had had individual and group psychotherapy, counseling, and the help of probation officers—one of whom saw him the day before he killed the little girl. His case is most instructive: the tendency to use violence or to be sexually perverted does not go away, ever, with incarceration. There must be recidivism so long as the reverberating Primal circuits exist. If there isn't a return to the crime, it is an accident, or salutary social conditions are holding things in check temporarily.

It would be the same kind of thinking involved if we jailed someone with recurrent headaches and then expected the headaches never to return after his release from prison. I feel certain Primal Therapy could have saved not only Bertram Greenberg but all his tragic victims as well.

11 *Violence and Murder—Fred*

The following chapter was written by someone who knows violence intimately. Most of his family have been in prison for murder, and he has served a term for accessory to murder. His family life has been serialized on "Gangbusters," and the murders committed by his family were the fare of the crime magazines for months. I think he is most qualified to discuss violence, and what he is really saying is that violence comes from having violence done to yourself—not just in the sense of beatings and whippings, but in more subtle ways, where the child is never allowed to be, never allowed to feel safe and protected.

His first Primals dealt with the obvious hurts (beatings with a whip) and moved from there to the more subtle "psychological" ones, such as having to fight when he didn't want to and living with a variety of "fathers" who didn't love him.

I can always remember something violent happening in my life. When I was two or three years old, my mother had a fight with another woman. They were pulling hair, punching, scratching, screaming. My mother fell backwards and the other woman was on top of her and really punching her. Other people stopped the fight. My mother's nose was all bloody. I was scared and was crying. I didn't want my mommy to be hurt. I wanted to hit and hurt the other woman for hurting my mommy.

Many times later, I had to fight for Mommy. I think my brother, Dick, killed two men in an effort to keep from the feeling that Daddy really hated him.

Being angry is a survival thing for me. The opposite of being angry is being passive and submissive. Daddy never wanted me to get angry. That was something they reserved for themselves. It seems if you don't get angry, you will die. The feeling that people will insult you, walk all over you, make fun of you, cheat you, make you seem foolish, are ways they have to hurt you. It's easier to do those things to other people yourself than to feel the hurt when they do it to you. The feeling that they think you're stupid, dumb, incompetent, are similar threats. Getting angry is all you have left.

Daddy said I was a bad boy and beat me for it. He chose to be violent toward me. My acts of misconduct were not violent. I didn't hurt anyone or inflict pain. He decided to and inflicted pain on me.

My dad came to the house on 4th Street. He knocked on the door and I came to see who it was. My mother, who was upstairs with Sid, said not to open the door. I was only four or five years old, but I knew Mom was doing something she shouldn't be doing. My dad hollered through the mail slot, pleading, "Come on, Freddie boy, open the door for Daddy." Mom screaming, "Don't open the door." Sid, now dressed, I suppose, came downstairs and out the back door. My dad saw him through the mail slot and broke down the door. He caught Sid going over the back fence and pulled him down and beat him. I remember seeing my dad, now sitting on top of Sid, pull out his pocket knife and try to open it. I think my mother hit my dad on the head with a soda bottle. Everything was kind of hazy after that.

I think that a person being violent is giving some release or expression to their pain. The form the violence takes and with whom is directly related to the scene of the original pain. The degree of violence (murder being more violent than a beating) may be proportional to the amount of pain an individual has within him. Someone who has had some means to get off some of the pain will not be as violent as someone who cannot. My brother, Dick, killed two men and I never killed anyone. The difference—opportunity? circumstance? I may have been able to get off a little of my pain from time to time. Dick had no means at all to express any shit. He just kept it in until he got sick enough to kill.

The person you are chewing out, fighting with, or murdering is not the true and intended victim. The men Dick killed were just stand-ins for Daddy. Kill Daddy and be free. He can't hurt you if he's dead. The real tragedy in murder is that all the wrong people are being tried. I never felt that Dick was to blame for what he did. He was just a little boy being bad. It was Daddy who taught him how and Mommy telling him he could do it. Since I don't know exactly why Dick was a killer and I was not, it could just as easily have been me who killed.

I was about nineteen or twenty when I got out of prison. I bought a .38 Smith and Wesson revolver in a hock shop. I carried the thing around with me. Once I went to see Jules, who was still in prison, and showed him the gun. Imagine carrying a gun into prison. I felt more powerful, stronger with a gun. I really felt so afraid that I needed something to protect me (protect me from Daddy). One night when I was feeling bad, I put the gun in my pocket and went out walking. I felt alone, angry, really pissed off. I felt like hurting someone. I purposely bumped into people on the street and stared angrily at everyone, saying in my head, "Don't mess with me, fuck with me—give me some shit and I'll blow your fucking head off, you lousy bastards." I was hoping that someone would push me around; then I would pull my gun on them. They wouldn't be expecting that and would really be surprised. They wouldn't be so fucking tough then. I just point it at them and tell them I was going to kill them. Make them beg me not to kill them. Make them beg like I had to.

I never found anyone to do that to. At the same time that I wanted to find someone, I also didn't want to. I was really too afraid.

The only reason Daddy could hit me and get away with it was

because he was physically bigger than I was, and stronger. He was threatening and dangerous to me, and always too big and strong to resist. The only way to stop him would be to kill him.

A beating is a violent act. An open and obvious denial of approval, love, and the affection a child needs from the parent. It hurts so much when you don't get love.

You'll do most anything to keep from completely facing and feeling that denial of love. If something provokes the feelings, gets too close, the only thing you can do is eliminate the provocation—kill yourself or the person in front of you.

The child could be killing one or a dozen people in a Primal frenzy. What he is really trying to do is kill the pain inside of him. The consequences aren't even there, like getting arrested. They're not even in the picture. The Primal is overwhelming. You have no control, you're completely into it, and you're just hacking it out, and you could murder somebody—it's that simple. The difference between somebody having Primals or some aggressive action to somebody else . . . murder, is very close, you know. My brother and I lived together, we went through the same shit together, and somehow I got off more easily . . . and he went to prison when he was seventeen, and except for a few years, he's been in there . . . and will be in there for the rest of his life . . . and that's what he got out of it. And I just feel so fortunate to be out and not to be in prison . . . and to find some way of getting release from the feelings of what happened. Like the thing with my father and my mother just seems so monstrous . . . like nobody can be that fuckin' mean . . . how can anybody be that goddamn cruel?

I've never been really conscious of feeling murderous. It's like something you carry, without complete knowledge of how to express itself. To walk around with the feeling inside you that . . . I mean, I am a person, I deserve some right to live and some degree of safety, and my mother and father fought each other, and they beat me, they hurt me, they did things on such a monstrous level to violate me in just my very act of being . . . and that's too much . . . I mean it's just too much . . . and you're angry

. . . just . . . Jesus, like you're just so fuckin' angry. . . . I bought a gun, you know, and carried that around, waiting for somebody to hurt me, or do something to hurt me so I could hurt them . . . You know I really want to be violent, it's like you gotta get out of you in a violent way . . . you gotta get the pain out. It's so close and always up on the top . . . it's so big, you know you're always choking it down, you're always choking it down . . . you go through your whole life that way . . . and you're looking for a way to get off your pain. You can go to the Primal Institute now, and get it off . . . it's a place to go and get it out. When you're living outside, in the real world kind of thing . . . there's nothing to do . . . there's no way to get it off . . . the only acceptable way, it seems to you, to get off your pain is to be violent . . . it's an acceptable way of doing it . . . in our society, being violent is acceptable . . . you know, you can go get drunk and get into a fight, and the police seem to think well you shouldn't do that, but we understand. You can do that . . . beat up your wife, or get into a fight or something and say oh I'm sorry, I was feeling bad . . . people will forgive you. It's really weird. You see it all around you. My father was violent . . . he got it off on me . . . he got it off on my mother . . . and it was acceptable. . . . A violent person is somebody who is brought up in a violent way . . . and saw around him that violence was an acceptable way of getting it off. The whole society is violent. They go to wars and fight all the time. So, it's how you get it off. Being violent is a way of getting your pain off; it lets the pain out . . . and you can relax. Probably the most relaxed person would be a guy after he's murdered a few people. . . . You know like a guy like Speck, who chews up maybe five or six or seven or eight women, you know. . . . Or this kid in Texas, you know, who could blast people, or a guy in Vietnam with a machine gun. I guess after he does all this, he can probably relax and go to sleep. It's really the way it is. You might be afraid of what you did after you realize it, but then, you know, it doesn't hurt so much. There's nothing they can do to you that's gonna hurt so much, even if they put you in the gas chamber, or hang you, that hurts as much as the hurt that's in you. And so it doesn't matter. Now maybe somebody who can't find a way . . . now maybe I found a way of getting it off somehow . . . so I always let a little out. I didn't let go and kill somebody, I always felt like I wanted to . . . like if I could do it, if I could really hurt somebody bad, then I wouldn't hurt so much. And it seems like I have a right to do it. Somehow . . . there's something, like something's owing me . . . and maybe to my brother and other people. Something's owing to you, and what you got to get is some violence . . . you know somebody beat the shit outta you, you were hurt, and it's only fair that you gotta give it back, that you're allowed to give it back, all you gotta find out is how to do it, you know. I did it through my women, getting married and hurting women.

I suppose I've been in more situations where I wanted to kill myself, which is really quite the same thing . . . it's really quite the same thing . . . you know that you hurt so much that you have to get it stopped . . . and you can get it out on somebody else by beating the shit outta them . . . doing something physical like hurting them, or you can do it yourself . . .

The hurt is . . . the part of it is, you want your Mommy and Daddy to love you, that is . . . what you want to feel is safe, you're afraid, you're frightened . . . or you don't feel safe . . . that Mommy or Daddy or both are there to put their arms around you . . . and to hold you close and just say, everything's all right . . . you don't have to be afraid . . . it's okay and we love you. They never did that . . .

Mommy and Daddy are there to take care of you and to keep you from being afraid . . . and to make the world a place where you're not gonna get hurt. It's like with my child now. I think I've always had these things, you see . . . I've gone through my life with those feelings but never expressing them. The things that my father did, sitting there and making a whip to beat his children with. You know that's gotta be a monstrous insane situation. And so I just assume that he didn't just happen to make that up . . . He just wasn't born like some kind of a monster, he was made a monster. But it really doesn't matter. I can't excuse him or forgive him because it happened to him. It doesn't do me any good. Let him get his own therapy . . . I gotta do mine. So fuck, I still have to blame him . . . I have to blame him . . . it's my anger . . . and I think any violent person's anger comes out of the fact that they really blame their parents. They really blame them for hurting . . . they blame other people . . . they see their parents in other situations, their boss, or their wives or even their children or their mother. They blame them for what's going on, they blame them for their hurt, you're supposed to love me, you're supposed to take care of me . . . you're always supposed to feel safe, and I never was, I never did, I never was safe. I was always scared.

I shouldn't have to work like hell to be someone lovable, some-one really great so my mom and dad would love me, that's ridiculous. They were supposed to love me and didn't and they just hurt me and I just had to live with that hurt. I didn't feel that as a child, I just never knew what was going on. I was just some kind of dumb freak, and I probably deserved being beaten . . . It was just the way I lived . . . I never could do anything right. My father really didn't love me—what difference did it make? I think the only time he really paid attention to me was when I was bad, you know. Sometimes even now I think that I was bad on purpose, to get his attention, to get the beating, to reinforce the idea that I wasn't worth a shit, I'm just not worth it and I de-serve a beating . . .

You finally really need to totally feel—that way you're acting anger out. I am bad in order to be criticized and punished, maybe be beaten, therefore it really happens. I deserve to be beaten and nobody loves me. The trial was in Norfolk and lasted for three months, a long time. I helped bury the men, the ones Dick killed. I still can't feel everything that happened that time. But that night my mother told me—the next morning you have to bury him. I never questioned anything, you know, I was just an obedient kid . . . it was just something you had to do. My mother said, oh that Mr. Kinney, he insulted me today. He said something to me. So I'd put a blackjack in my shirt and go over and talk to him . . . I'm gonna beat him up. And if my mother ever told me to kill somebody, I'm not sure what would happen— it's really scary, you know. Dick did. I was afraid of her, terrified. After the first killing, no not the first killing . . . Dick and I buried this man in the pigpen . . . we were living on the farm then . . . and buried him in the pigpen. And then we just went on living our lives like the normal thing.

My first Primals were related to my father and the things he did to hurt me, like killing my cat. We had a canary, and one day the cat tried to get into the canary cage. The housekeeper screamed and my father got angry and grabbed the cat and kinda squeezed it. The cat was howling. I just thought he was gonna chase him off. My father was angry, and you gotta be care- ful and get out of his way. He grabbed the cat by his tail and just slammed him down on a board. The cat went all limp. It was broken inside. I was ten years old. It wasn't so much that it was my pet; it was that in a moment you could be dead. That's how I always felt living with him. I could never relax because I was always terrified; at any moment he could beat me up and kill me. If at any time he wasn't cheerful, I had to be careful. When I was getting a beating I thought he would never stop. I thought, What's gonna make him stop? Pleading that I would be good wouldn't do it. Maybe he would never stop. There was something inside of me that held on, that wouldn't give up, that kept hoping. If you give up, you're gone. You'll never be yourself again. It is like I retain a piece of my sanity.

I was more afraid of my mother because she could and did kill; she was more insidious. She was unpredictable. She used me. She didn't love me. We had to kill for her. Jesus!

I've finally found a place where I can feel all those abusive in- sults perpetrated on me. I'm feeling the most monstrous thing that can happen to anyone—being an unloved baby.

12 *On Drugs and Drug Users*

There is a monomania on drugs and their use in our society to-day. The Establishment's crusade against drugs is tantamount to being against sin, and a man's moral fiber seems somehow to be related to how strongly he can put down drug use. We need to ask ourselves whether this monomania is valid, sincere, and necessary. Are drugs the number-one problem in society today? Or have we made it the number-one problem for reasons sequestered? I plan to discuss these questions, first, from the viewpoint of the effects of drugs on our systems, and second, in terms of the war on drugs and what it means.

I am not going to discuss the biochemical effects of drugs in any great detail. There are literally thousands of books and booklets on the subject already.* I shall point out, however, how a variety of drugs either enhance or suppress feelings, particularly painful feelings. Generally, I shall classify feeling-suppressive drugs as Downers, and feeling-enhancing drugs as Uppers.

* See Annual Review of Pharmacology for listings and research. Annual Reviews Inc., Palo Alto, Calif. (particularly Volume 2, 1962). I would recommend also, H. E. Lehmann and T. A. Ban, *Pharmacology of Tension and Anxiety,* Charles C Thomas, Springfield, Ill., 1970. Also, John Marks and C. M. B. Pare, *Drug Therapy in Psychiatry,* Pergamon Press, London, 1964.

THE DOWNERS

1. cigarettes
2. alcohol
3. tranquilizers
4. sleeping pills
5. muscle relaxants
6. addictive painkillers, such as Demerol, heroin, and morphine.

Cigarettes

The principal drug in cigarettes is nicotine, and nicotine has widespread effects on the entire system, depending on the dosage. It is a most toxic drug, with about twenty to thirty milligrams of nicotine in each cigarette. It is addicting, both psychologically and physiologically. I shall discuss the nature of addiction in a moment. Generally, smoking relaxes the system through the nicotinic suppression of feeling; the blood vessels constrict, the pulse and heart rate increase (the heart must work harder to pump blood), and there is an increased secretion of adrenalin, a stimulant. Adrenalin is a stress hormone that aids in activating the system for defense. Its secretion, together with increased activation of the brain, helps mobilize our defenses to suppress. Smokers automatically reach for a cigarette when under stress or when feelings are coming up. The very drawing in of the smoke seems to help push back the feelings.

Nicotine helps slow down the transmission of impulses from one nerve cell to another so that the brain is no longer zipping along at breakneck speed. While we may feel relaxed with a cigarette, we are, in reality, putting our bodies under more stress by allowing feelings to accumulate and stay unresolved. This can lead to heart disease, gastrointestinal disorders, and many other diseases. One of the reasons the neurotic must smoke more and more, why he seems to build a tolerance for nicotine, is that the reservoir of unresolved feelings grows with each cigarette-suppressed feeling.

Neurosis is the natural tranquilizer of the system. Under Pain, it does what cigarettes do for us—constricts the blood vessels, activates the brain, and stimulates the secretion of stress hormones. Cigarettes are called upon when neurosis falters in its job. Indeed, it is the tranquilizer of choice if temporary calming is needed because it seems to produce less Primal rebound than the commercial tranquilizers.* Ambulatory psychotics in Primal Therapy find cigarettes to be of help in the initial stages of therapy (something forbidden for neurotics in therapy) because their Pain levels are so high. Once therapy has drained enough Pain, cigarettes are no longer needed or desired by these patients.

Alcohol

The brain is most strikingly affected by the use of alcohol. The effect is repression. Though many areas of the brain are involved with the use of drugs, there are three essential sites that must be affected by the Downers: the reticular activating system, which arouses the brain in a diffuse way and provides for the "intensity" of feeling; the limbic system, which organizes and stores feeling and might be said to supply the quality of feeling; and the frontal cortex, which provides fine discrimination and conceptualization of feeling. It would seem that the greater the number of key feeling sites affected by a drug (and the more intense its effect on the site), the more addictive it can be.

Alcohol depresses the alerting centers of the brain, resulting in the loss of fine discrimination, judgment, memory, and insight. Alcohol decreases our *reactions* to pain; because we have less ability to be hurt, we tend to be less afraid to be hurt. We can, therefore, be more aggressive, more warm and sexual, and more open as human beings. Clearly, it is Pain that closes us down and keeps us from being the warm, open, affectionate persons we can be.

---

* The onrush of built-up pain into the system after continued chemical suppression.

A Downer such as alcohol taken in small doses can produce an Upper effect because it inhibits the inhibitory centers, thus liberating what we have been holding down—even the ability to laugh out loud.

Alcohol is often called "the liquid that dissolves the conscience." It seems to dampen socially acquired inhibitions. Too much dampening produces sleep, unconsciousness, or death.

The Other Downers

It is not my intent to discuss each drug in detail. Downers differ in their effect on the various brain sites. There is a wide variety of effects even among the tranquilizers. The two major classes of Downers are the barbiturates, such as phenobarbital, and the tranquilizers, such as Thorazine. Barbiturates depress many brain functions, including the higher centers, so that with them thinking tends to be clouded. They reduce the activity of the RAS, block arousal of higher brain centers (as shown by reduced EEG activation), and diminish the excitability of the hypothalamus, the somatic effector center. With less stimulation of our physical system by a lessened hypothalamic output, we have a greater physical sense of ease. In short, barbiturates are powerful because they have a broad-range effect on vast areas of the brain. This is generally the effect of the sleeping pills, which suppress so much consciousness and activation that unconsciousness results.

Tranquilizers have a different effect. Many kinds of tranquilizers depress the limbic system, the system responsible for repression. In this way, a load is taken off the limbic system, and past emotional behavior that had been punished is given access. Thus, a tranquilized person is less worried if he is rude or if something is upsetting. His socially acquired concerns and inhibitions are diminished. Tranquilizers also depress the alerting system so that we respond in a lesser way to the usual anxiety-laden situations, and hence feel more relaxed.

Heroin and Morphine

The ultimate in Downers are heroin and morphine. They depress a broad range of brain functions, often produce sleep or near-sleep in the latter stages, and finally, with a large enough dose, death. There seems to be a continuum from full consciousness to narrowed consciousness, through unconsciousness and, finally, death. The hard, addicting drugs seem to blot out more aspects of consciousness than the tranquilizing ones. They produce, therefore, a more severe Primal rebound when the drugs are removed. There is vomiting, great pain, shakes, and the sweats—very much like what we see when a person is being flooded with Primal Pain that he cannot integrate. I think that this is in part due to the degree of repression of Pain by the drug, and because a heroin or morphine user is, *de facto,* someone in great Pain.

The effects of morphine sometimes resemble the effects of a prefrontal lobotomy. It seems to delay transmission of impulses from the frontal lobe to lower centers where Pain is processed. Hypothalamic stimulation is also decreased with morphine so that the system is less agitated. Morphine depresses EEG arousal to painful stimuli, though sensitivity to other sensory stimuli seems unaffected.

It is interesting to note that nearly all of the so-called anxiety-reducing drugs actually attenuate Pain, again indicating that the central ingredient of neurosis and anxiety is Pain.

Scientists describe addiction to these drugs in terms of "narcotic hunger." They believe that the addict has a need for narcotics, and they have attempted to find so-called nonaddicting drugs to handle that hunger. Therefore, the preferred mode of treating heroin hunger is with methadone, itself a mild narcotic. Because methadone is legal, it stops all the crime involved in getting money for the illegal drugs. It also seems to satisfy many addicts. However, methadone, or any drug or chemical, is hardly a cure.* The cure, I submit, is in the removal of Pain—the reason for the drug use.

I don't think it is "narcotic hunger" we are dealing with, any more than there is an "alcohol hunger." We must always keep in mind that it is "love hunger." That is, the need is for a mother's or father's love. That need, impossible to fulfill, becomes transmuted into a new need—for alcohol or drugs. The energy or drive for that drug or drink is still the central love-need, which does not disappear simply because it has been altered so that it is no longer recognizable. To treat drug or alcohol "hunger" is to treat the *derivatives* of the real need. That is why *any* treatment that does not deal with the underlying feelings cannot succeed. Using mild electroshock techniques as part of Conditioning Therapy on an addict or alcoholic may drive away the open need for drugs or alcohol, but the result is more tension and *enhanced* (though latent) addiction or alcoholism.

I suppose one reason that there is financial support for the shocking of addicts is that it is but an extension of a general philosophy that they are criminals and must be punished; even with the fancy term "behavior modification," it is still an attempt to punish away the impulse to shoot up. It is part of a general approach of sweeping overt problems under the rug and pretending they are solved, which stems from a psychological orientation of self-deception—of repressing disturbing thoughts away and pretending they do not exist.

One wonders what fine line our society draws that enables us to jail heroin users and approve of "official painkillers" such as the tranquilizers. Don't we realize that addicts are often suppressing violent tendencies? That they are keeping hallucinations and delusions at bay with their unofficial medicines? Would it be better to have no drugs and have streets full of actively hallucinating individuals, or individuals who can no longer repress

* Perhaps one reason why a heroin addict needs less of the drug after a withdrawal period is that he has felt a great deal of Pain and is less suppressed for a period of time. In any case, I believe that what makes a drug truly addicting is the high level of Pain that must be narcotized continuously, until it is resolved and liberated permanently.

their impulses? Why won't the government take a hand in helping some of its constituents with their Pain? Because Pain isn't recognized by the government nor by many of the mental health people involved in drug treatment. But that is a redundancy. How can people who won't recognize their own Pain understand the suffering in others?

Sometimes, the suppression by drugs becomes quite subtle and sophisticated. Recently, a group of psychiatrists at Stanford University announced a major breakthrough in the treatment of agitated, suicidal depressives. They discovered that these patients have a low serotonin level (a key chemical agent involved in repression), and that by administering a serotonin precursor—what the body uses to make serotonin—there was dramatic improvement in the patients. What was *not* reported was whether those patients would have to spend the rest of their lives taking serotonin precursors. There was no hint as to *why* serotonin levels were low. It may well be that depressives exhaust their store of serotonin in keeping feelings down. The injection of more serotonin aids in more repression.* The result can be a *less* feeling human being.

I would say, in general, that the Downers are the middle-aged "adult" drugs, while the Uppers are the drugs of youth. Of course, substantial numbers of youth are on Downers, so that no strict categories can be set up. By and large, adults turn against feeling and the youth turn toward it. And when I say, "turn against feeling," I mean that in the more general sense of turning against the show of feeling, the value of feeling, the necessity of feeling.

UPPERS

Marijuana and LSD

There are people who use Downers to achieve an Upper effect. That is, inhibitory centers are further depressed so that repres-

---

* Psychotics also have depleted serotonin levels.

sion is lifted and feelings emerge. However, most young people go directly to repression-lifting drugs, such as marijuana and LSD. There is a brain system that either permits feelings into consciousness or suppresses them, depending on their load of Pain. Inhibition of the hippocampus is expected to enhance feeling. Both marijuana and LSD do exactly that, marijuana to a much lesser degree than LSD. The effect is to lift some of the repression under which neurotics labor.

Marijuana or LSD experiences can either be pleasant or bummers, depending on many factors: first, the dosage; second, the amount of Pain being suppressed, and the efficacy of the defense system. With marijuana, feelings seem to be enhanced, food tastes better, colors are more vivid, and the nuances of music are heard. Thoughts often contain insights. Generally, marijuana is taken in a social atmosphere where the emphasis is on *current sensory input*. Taken in a Primal atmosphere, the result is most often Primals. The effect of marijuana seems to be in large measure tranquilizing, often more effective than any commercial drug. I think that this is accounted for by the fact that when repression is lifted, sensations that are the physically blocked part of feelings become more intense or feelable. There is less of a feeling of pressure that repression (repressure) brings. If a neurotic is well-defended, he may have no reaction to pot at first. Later on, with continued use, he may have pleasurable effects. Still much later on, as the repressive lid weakens in a more permanent way, bummers may be the result. Because marijuana (like LSD) is a serotonin antagonist, the chief result is the liberation of sensation. So it is no wonder that marijuana "intensifies" sensation. Actually, it only allows the neurotic to see, hear, and feel what the normal already can do without drugs. Anything more than real sensation is unreal sensation.

Because under marijuana sensory input can have facilitated access to the frontal cortex, a dual process exists. Competing for access to the frontal area where sensations are conceptualized is the reservoir of Pain. In a well-defended person the pain is filtered out or, more likely, its energy is transmuted so that the person may laugh hysterically over practically nothing. This laughter is a neurotic reaction. It is the Pain converted by the defense system. A person in Primal Therapy would have an undiluted Primal under the same circumstance.

A person not "keyed in" to marijuana, who doesn't know how to react to it, may, on his first trip, have either no reaction (if well-defended) or an anxiety reaction (if less well-defended). What is happening is that the Pain is beginning to be liberated, albeit in diffuse form, and a vague anxiety takes shape. The aim of the chronic user is twofold: one, to relax; and two, to feel. To really feel, however, means Pain first; so the neurotic is caught. He may feel just enough to be less tense temporarily, but not feel enough to become a liberated, permanently feeling person. (See *Anatomy of Mental Illness.*)

LSD

I have discussed LSD in *The Anatomy of Mental Illness.* LSD opens the limbic gate, the cortex is flooded with Pain, and the person must then symbolize heavily. The complexity or bizarreness of the symbolism depends on the dosage of the drug and the amount of underlying Pain. Such factors as the setting where the drug is taken, the kinds of people close by, the pre-drug mental set are all lesser factors in the overall reaction to the drug.

The tragic results of the use of LSD is seen in the newspapers every day. Recently, a young man was arrested for murdering his girlfriend while on an LSD trip. He stated that he had been sucking on her breast when she suddenly became his mother (when the need and Pain gained undefended access to consciousness). A feeling of overwhelming Pain overtook him, and his infantile anger surged forth on his unsuspecting friend. LSD unhinged the inhibition that kept his early maternal deprivation at bay—the same inhibition that kept him neurotically acting-out, trying to find mother substitutes. Unable to understand what his feelings were or even that he was having old feelings—in short, unable to have a Primal—he acted-out the infantile rage against a symbol who became his momentary reality.

It is really unfortunate that LSD research has been hampered because of fear engendered by a lack of understanding of its therapeutic effects. LSD can be of help in clinical situations where patients are so completely blocked from their feelings that needless months are used up in getting them to any feeling at all. LSD can only be useful when it is used in a Primal framework where its effects are thoroughly understood. Otherwise, I believe it can be harmful. I believe in what is natural. By and large, it is only the rare patient who would need LSD to start him on the road to feeling. One key danger of LSD is that it evokes painful feelings out of their natural sequence of ascension, so that an unsuspecting patient is flooded and cannot integrate his experience. If we understand that the chief effect of LSD is the liberation of feeling, perhaps we can see that it is not dangerous in and of itself; it is the premature liberation of feelings that is the danger.

We are now seeing just how dangerous the uncontrolled, non-Primal use of LSD is. We are seeing patients who had many trips from two to five years ago; some of these took LSD as part of university-sponsored research programs. One is a well-known author on the subject of LSD. All of these patients have never recuperated from the LSD-engendered Primal onslaught. They have never integrated the dredged-up feelings, and so suffer from either periodic serious depression, bouts of hallucinations, delusions, and depersonalizations, or from continuous psychosomatic ailments such as ulcers. Finally, in Primal Therapy we are going about the business of helping them integrate each bit of feeling slowly and systematically; we are reversing their problems at last.

Other Uppers

The most common Uppers are caffeine and the amphetamines. We tend to overlook the fact that nearly all of the adult population is hooked on the drug caffeine. These Uppers generally stimulate the cortex; thinking is initially sharper and the feeling is mild euphoria (when taken in small amounts). Uppers stimulate the reticular activating system and get us "keyed up." The blood pressure generally rises (to defend against ascending feelings) and the bronchioles dilate so that respiration is changed. Generally, the function of these Uppers is to break out of the "deadness" that complete repression brings. Paradoxically, too much of the Uppers produces a shutdown by the limbic system and a Downer reaction, just as too much of the Downers suppress inhibition and produce an Upper reaction. For a thorough discussion of the Uppers, in particular the amphetamines, I suggest reading Journal II, Issue II of the *Journal of Psychedelic Drugs.*

I have already pointed out how the brain amine, serotonin, aids repression. Anti-depressant prescription drugs are usually monoamine-oxidase inhibitors. They block the production of serotonin. By blocking serotonin the system is less repressed and more energized. The person "feels" happier. Here again we see how depression is the handmaiden of repression and that by chemically lifting repression we also ease depression.

One final comment about drugs and Primals. Over the years, a few patients have experimented with drugs on their own, sometime during the therapy, and have found some interesting phenomena. They can get to Primals very easily with marijuana, but often just as easily with painkillers such as Percodan. It depends on how much Pain they are holding down and at what stage of therapy they are in. Some patients holding back a birth Primal with its great load of Pain find that by bringing the Pain down a bit with a painkiller, they are finally able to feel and integrate some early catastrophic event. Others go the other route. They try to ease the lid of repression with marijuana so that buried feelings may ascend. We have noted that drugs, when used properly, can be therapeutic, and not at all addictive. There has been such hysteria about drugs of late that even to mention the word evokes panic. We do not use drugs in Primal Therapy, mostly because they are

* Edited by David Smith, M.D., and published by the Haight-Ashbury Medical Clinic, 1969. See also Donald Blair, *Modern Drugs for the Treatment of Mental Illness,* published by Charles C Thomas, Springfield, Ill., 1965.

not necessary. But in rare cases they are necessary in order to avoid a protracted therapy time. A lot of what we have learned about drugs has been due to serendipity. Patients on Demerol and Percodan after surgery began reporting constant Primals. Others who smoked marijuana before therapy would go back for one more try during a party and find that it was not fun any more; it was Primal time. So long as we study drugs without reference to the kind of person who takes them, we will not understand their function. It is in the study of the interaction of specific drugs with individuals with certain Pain levels that drug reactions will be understood.

DISCUSSION

The function of the drugs I have been discussing is consciousness-alteration. Certainly, cigarettes and alcohol can affect the brain just as much as marijuana can. How is it that legislators can rail against the use of marijuana and LSD while ingesting drugs such as alcohol and nicotine freely? Why has there not been an outcry and legislation passed against the use of tranquilizers, which seem to be the all-American drug? Is it truly concern on the part of the Establishment for the welfare of youth? I rather doubt it, since much more time, energy, and money is spent in arresting and jailing drug offenders than in treating them. I know from my own professional experience how difficult it is to get any governmental appropriations for the outpatient treatment of drug users. Usually it is left to free clinics to handle, and they are often without sufficient funds to do an effective job.

I believe that the war on drugs is part of the overall suppression that occurs in a neurotic society. The first reflex of unreal systems, both personal and social, against change is suppression. Drugs that aid suppression, which allow for accommodation to a suppressive mode of life, are considered "safe." Drugs (like people) that tend toward liberation, toward feeling and toward acute insights, are the threat. There is much more evidence of the harm of cigarettes, evidence that indicates the ingestion of the nicotine drug over a period of time can be fatal. There is far less evidence that marijuana causes any harm. Why, then, do users of marijuana go to jail? Why is it all right for a person to get smashed on alcohol, endanger lives while driving drunk, and only have a driver's license suspended, while a person in possession of LSD can go to prison, for decades in some cases. I don't think that these are fortuitous events. They are the result of living in a suppressive society where feelings themselves become a threat. Indeed, feeling people would not accommodate to an unreal society, nor would they go out and kill their fellow men. Feeling people are indeed the threat to the business-as-usual group.

In a sick society, people are driven to strive and achieve. When they go to bed at night, these same people cannot turn themselves off, and they turn to drugs to help out. There is little in the mores of current society that allows for rest and relaxation. It is all done artificially with drugs, and this artificial relaxation has the societal stamp of approval *when* one can continue to produce and work. To take a drug such as marijuana and then lie about doing nothing but relaxing has no such social approval. This is not to indicate approval or disapproval of any consciousness-altering drug, but only to point out why some drugs are acceptable and others are not. I am suggesting that the youth and youth drugs are a threat because they are pro-feeling.

Unreal systems produce subsystems in their own image. Thus in medicine, almost the first reflex against the "hysterical," emotional patient, the patient who cannot cope with society, is to give tranquilizers. If the patient feels "down," then Uppers are given. How often is there an attempt to talk to the patient about the causes of his problems? "No time" is the answer most often given by physicians. That is not an answer, it is an excuse given by professionals who contrive (often unconsciously) to keep themselves on the run, away from themselves. How could they stop to help someone else get into himself? Unreal systems do not allow time for reflection, for investigation into the "whys" of things. Suppression of symptoms is the first order of business.

Medical specialists become specialists in symptoms and their "management," a fancy word for suppression. The notion of cure is often not even considered.

Suppressive drugs keep an unreal society together. Imagine today if there were no such drugs. Imagine if we were all sleepless and continually anxious and unable to work. Imagine if a great percentage of us were breaking down. What would happen to our society then? Drugs allow us to continue the sham, to go on pretending and adjusting. They keep the unreal system functioning. What would our medicine men do if they could not "manage" their patients' emotions, their ulcers, colitis, and headaches. They might have to dig deeper and find cures. They might be led to the knowledge that unreal systems orchestrate symptoms by their very nature.

Why is it that "behavior modification" is the most accepted psychological approach today? Why does behavior modification psychotherapy enjoy such financial and research support by the Establishment, while LSD research is practically nil, and indeed, is outlawed? I think, again, that feelings become the center around which we may understand these phenomena. The control of feelings fits into the cultural mode and will be supported. Any approach that neglects history and underlying causes, and that treats symptoms as viable entities, accommodates itself to that cultural mode.

It is men—neurotic, suppressed men—men with an oversimplified mechanistic view of the world and its problems who pass on appropriations for research; the same men who pass on the laws as to which drugs may be used and which may not be taken. There are law-abiding drugs and outlaw drugs. Middle-age, middle-class America has its drugs delineated: drugs that parallel the kinds of TV programs that are allowed—opiates where reality never intrudes—opiates that keep the unreal system safe and unquestioned.

13 *Psychosis*

The following chapter, written by a patient, illustrates psychotic reactions to the use of LSD. What we see here is that with the repeated use of LSD, a person ordinarily having "neurotic" trips may begin having psychotic ones, and sometimes these trips are not just transient states. The transition from neurotic symbolism to psychotic symbolism with LSD comes about for two basic reasons. First, repeated assaults on the repressive systems in the brain cause more and more flooding of Pain, and the Pain that cannot be integrated becomes symbolized. Second, whether there is psychotic symbolism at all will depend on the amount or strength of the underlying Pain. With great Pain, it would not take many LSD trips to unhinge whatever repressive forces were still operable.

Life circumstances can cause the same kind of flooding of Pain as a massive LSD dose (the death of both parents for a young child, for example). The fact that LSD "caused" psychosis does not alter the fact that it is psychosis we are dealing with. What matters is that LSD-induced psychosis is more often reversible than a psychosis that began in early childhood. LSD psychosis means that the person at least enjoyed a marginal neurotic adjustment prior to the drug trip. Treating a person who has been psychotic most of his life with Primal Therapy is another matter. Primal Therapy cannot undo a shattered and totally deprived existence. We cannot give a lifelong psychotic back a lost child-hood. We can only help a person feel that childhood deprivation *when* there is some strength somewhere to experience that Pain and integrate it. This does not mean that non-drug-induced psychotics are not treatable. We must keep in mind, however, that the treatment is more difficult and depends on the reservoir of inner resources of the person.

If we think of consciousness as but a small aperture that can only accept bits of Pain at a time, then when something such as a drug experience or catastrophic life happening floods that aperture, the "excess" nonintegrated Pain must be diverted into symbolic (and often psychotic) spillways. If there is a low reservoir of Pain, then the spillway is more apt to be neurotic rather than psychotic. If the Pain residue is high, then it drives the symbolism further away from the reality of inner feelings into the realm of delusions and hallucinations. I recall once when a patient was getting into feeling like the totally lost little boy that he was. He became impatient with the Pain he was in and wanted to get the Primal over with. He took LSD and came in the next day explaining to me that he was actually the *lost* chieftain of an Indian tribe and that he was going to move back to Arizona to find his native tribe. He had already made preparations for the move. The LSD drove him right over the connection of the feeling into something symbolic. Instead of feeling lost and the need to find his mother who had abandoned him (a Pain too great to face all at once), he became the lost chieftain looking for his tribe (more easy to accept). This delusion lasted for many weeks, because the drug had liberated the feeling and it had to be dealt with in some symbolic way continuously. That same overload can be somatized (absorbed by the physical system) with the result being ulcers or colitis. LSD is particularly dangerous to someone opened up with Primals. Indeed, marijuana produces almost a literal LSD trip in advanced Primal patients.

Once the floodgates are opened artificially by drugs, the symptoms, both mental and physical, can last for months. The dam, once opened, is not so easily shut down again. We are neurotic for good reasons. Nothing should abruptly rob us of our neuroses, or psychoses may well be the result.

Psychosis means that memory becomes the total environment of the body. External reality no longer exists. The psychotic has regressed to his past without any separate awareness of that regression—without any feeling of it.

We shall have to think of perception in new ways to understand the point. For, in a dream, when we "see" people and "hear" noises, are we actually seeing and hearing with our sense organs? Obviously not; we are perceiving with our brain. And this is what the psychotic is doing when he hallucinates—he is seeing with his brain, with the Pain inside it. He does not see outside reality, he sees a symbolically transformed and externally projected inner reality which he cannot fully and nakedly recognize. His Pain suffuses all of reality and makes his perceptions obviously bizarre; whereas the neurotic simply misperceives or distorts reality so that his sickness is not so obvious.

The fact of a hallucination or nightmare while asleep means that underlying feelings are nudging their way into consciousness —a healthy sign. The psychotic is close to reality and that is what drives him so far away when there is no one around to help him face it. The problem is that the neurotic and psychotic really do believe they see reality (because they are seeing their own reality symbolized) and get reinforced by their own misperceptions.

We note here that the Primal view of health—broken down defenses which permit for reality—is different from conventional views, which posit strong defenses as the sine qua non. At some time in their therapy, Primal patients feel as if they are going crazy. It is when much of their defense system has crumbled and when heavy Pains are on their ascent. At this point they are similar to the psychotic who first enters Primal Therapy, except that the advanced patients know what they are going through and can let it happen.

Hallucinations, delusions, dreams, and ritualistic perversions all have something in common—they are circumscribed symbolic events. The symbolism has a "fixed" quality to it. As Pain begins its ascent into consciousness and takes a specific form, symbolization becomes more delineated. The person may fixate on a certain bizarre idea. The example cited previously was of a man about to feel how lost and abandoned he was as a child. By externalizing the feeling that he was part of an Indian tribe there was something he could now do about it. He could travel to find his "loved ones" and believe that he could belong somewhere. Not to have symbolized would have meant to feel the utter hopelessness of never belonging, of never having a family.

Before the delusion began, this person was having bad dreams about going to an old city where he grew up; where suddenly everything was different . . . he was a stranger, lost and alone. What drove that dream into a delusion? The inability to repress the powerful feeling even after he had awakened and regained conscious controls.

A critical event can unhinge the controls—a severe illness that depletes one's strength, or a spouse leaving and getting a divorce, or the loss of a child—many things can intensify the situation so that normal wakefulness can no longer hold back the Pain. The delusion then becomes an extension of the dream; the transition is made from feeling a stranger in a dream to feeling part of a lost Indian tribe in the delusion. The same feeling drives both phenomena. Had the person with the "lost tribe" delusion been given tranquilizers, the delusion might well have disappeared, because the painful feeling would have been chemically suppressed for the moment. We see here how nightmares are the way-stations to insanity. The only thing that separates them is the ability of consciousness to hold down the feelings.

The hallucinations we see during the aura in (psychogenic) epilepsy is another example of the point. Feelings which begin their rise produce, often, the same kind of premonitory symbolization—hearing a certain song, for example. This hallucination portends a Primal feeling; but before it can be connected, consciousness is obliterated by a seizure.

Symbolic behavior, such as exhibiting oneself in public in the same way day after day, is the diverted channel of the feeling and serves to drain off the energy of the feeling temporarily, again, in a circumscribed way. In other words, fixed symbolic behaviors do release tension, and the closer the feeling is to consciousness, the more the symbolic thought or practice must be pressed into service.

I pointed out in *The Anatomy of Mental Illness* that Penfield's work indicates the possibility that symbols become more specific the closer they are spatially in the brain to the feeling site. So, an epileptic hallucination may be, "I'm scared because robbers are after me," while the real feeling close by in the brain may be, "I was terrified when my brother held a real gun on me."

One more example: One patient believed in flying saucers and thought he might have seen the lights of one in the sky—a not uncommon notion. In Primal Therapy he had a birth Primal and felt himself blinded by the strong light of the delivery room. He then felt the connection to why he had seen lights in the sky. The reason he remained symbolic and fixated on flying saucer lights before was that there was no way for him to properly conceptualize his ascending Pain, and so it got diverted each time. Seeing the lights of a flying saucer was a fixed delusion—a continuous symbolic acting-out mentally of the Birth Pain.

A hallucination is the perception of a transmuted historic Primal feeling. The symbol is idiosyncratic for each person, and there can be no universal symbol. What determines the choice of symbol—how primitive and abstract it is—depends on many factors, including the age at which the Primal feeling occurred. A color can be very abstract and be several steps removed from a feeling. Color as an abstract form is rather primitive and infantile —commensurate with an infantile trauma. Thus, when an early feeling becomes too difficult to handle, the child experiences it in terms of color. In a child's mind, manipulating the color, avoiding black, may be a way to control the feeling. The Freudians recognized this in their play-therapy techniques, where a child forced to toilet-train too early would be encouraged to slosh brown paint on a paper and fingerpaint with gooey brown textures.

These techniques, of course, were just as primitive and symbolic as the magical manipulation of color by young children. They were also, therefore, as noncurative.

For the psychotic, people can become as symbolic as colors. The psychotic projects magical notions onto people (that they are secretly laughing at him) and believes that the manipulation of others is a way to stave off evil spirits—as we shall note in the chapter written by Ted. Thus, a neutral person, just like a neutral color, can take on inordinately fearful meaning.

The selection of a specific symbol (as Freud pointed out in his *Interpretation of Dreams*) is a condensation of a cluster of events linked together by a specific feeling. A lifetime of being helpless in the hands of one's parents might later be symbolized in the paralysis of one's hands or in the feeling of being manipulated by unseen evil forces. LSD accentuates the symbolic reaction by opening the Primal floodgate. But we do not need LSD to be symbolic. We dream in symbols very nicely without LSD, and we act-out symbolically in our neuroses without the use of drugs. We can see in the chapter by Ted how the progression of symbolism took place with each succeeding LSD trip—how a nightmare became extended into a permanent reality because Primal flooding had taxed the repressive mechanisms beyond their limits.

LSD and sleep are similar in producing symbolism because both allow for Primal flooding—sleep accomplishes it by easing conscious control, and LSD does it by artificially "blowing the lid" of conscious control.

I have recently had a conference with Primal patients who were formerly psychotic. They generally agree that insanity is "the inability to fake sanity" in the way neurotics can. In psychosis, *the feeling is right but the thought isn't*. The feeling—they want to hurt me—is an ascending memory for which the mind provides a current story . . . "Those people on the corner are trying to hurt me!" This is exactly like a dream where the feeling is right but the story is a fantasy. When we dream out loud, we can be put away as crazy. If we can keep our dreams to ourselves, we're neurotic. We must not think that memories are only consciously remembered events. Reliving a birth is a pre-verbal memory of an event stored in the system and "remembered" by the organism as a totality. It is still a memory, as any Pain is a memory.

What the ex-psychotics agree upon is that, unlike neurotics who can repress the Pain until they do not know it exists, they were too loaded with hurt to successfully escape from it. They had to "deal" with it constantly, usually by projecting the feeling externally—*"They* are doing this or that to me." I think our systems are only capable of so much abuse; that is, we can only repress so much Pain. When life-circumstances, deprivations, and assaults are inordinate, there are going to be leaks in the repressive lid.

As the level of Pain rises, behavior becomes more generalized and abstract. It is one thing to be angry at your wife because you neurotically misinterpret her motives, and quite another to believe that *all* women are in a conspiracy to demean you. It is one thing to be angry at your children because of your own past Pain (they don't show "respect" and you have to feel the old worthlessness), and quite another to walk into a strange building and shoot people indiscriminately. Both the psychotic's behavior and his ideas generalize away from reality commensurate with his level of Pain. Conversely, with each felt Pain he becomes closer to what is real (in himself). Being real means to be relatively out of Pain. Each diminution of Pain, then, reduces the generalization process and thereby diminishes the psychosis. Degrees of psychosis really indicate degrees of Pain. When Pain is at its zenith, all reality is blotted out.

There are many ways to go crazy, and not all of them include hallucinations and delusions. We can simply become more and more detached (from ourselves) so that we are completely split, and one part of us watches the other part go through the motions of life.

I have thought about a rather whimsical, yet not so bizarre notion of how to prevent mental illness. We know that psychosis comes when feelings build and build with no social outlets. There is a movie house in almost every city and town in the world. If we could only gear our movie houses to be feeling centers, where it is all right to show great feeling at appropriate moments during a movie, I have a feeling that a great deal of tension could be drained away. Certainly, if movies could be shown to mental patients, with feeling encouraged the way we do at the Primal Institute, the result could be beneficial. Of course, I am speaking of palliation, alone. But palliation is a help when it involves feeling, rather than the usual suppression of feeling.

There are other things that could be done in mental hospitals. Thus far, there is widespread use of tranquilizers to make patients manageable. And tranquilizers accomplish that. They are like a controlling parent keeping a child in line, only it is all done chemically. I consider the widespread use of these chemical agents the single most important reason for why patients do *not* get well. As soon as a patient gets "hysterical," that is, as soon as he is on the verge of a Primal, instead of helping him into that feeling, a chemical (or electrical-shock therapy) lid is clamped on it and the tension builds again. A hospital therapist need not be an expert in Primal techniques for him to let the patient experience his feelings. They are the antidote for psychosis. All the craziness is due to the fact that the feelings *cannot* be felt. I think we have been too interested in "managing" people—too much "social engineering" and not enough letting them be. In a way, parents continuously try to "manage" their children, and that helps get them crazy. They then become unmanageable, and as the years go on find themselves in a hospital so they can be managed by experts.

Can psychosis be cured? Yes, but there are qualifications. One qualification is the degree of psychosis. Psychosis is not a monolithic entity. It has gradations of severity, just as has neurosis. If the person is "delapidated," to use a psychiatric phrase, talks only in "word salad," and cannot make any contact with another person, then I seriously doubt a cure can be accomplished by Primal Therapy. On the other hand, if the person can make contact, has a well-organized delusional system that can be communicated to another person, there is a chance for a cure. Ted's story is one of psychosis. Just before therapy he was found locked in his upstairs room, butcher knife in hand and tinfoil on his head to keep the enemy from shooting penetrating rays into his head. That's pretty crazy. I'm not sure it would help any to "diagnose" him as a "paranoid schizophrenic." It certainly wouldn't change his treatment any. "Crazy" is as good a diagnosis as any, just as "neurosis" covers a wide range of lesser aberrant behaviors.

Ted was pushed into the bizarre symbolism of psychosis by his great load of Pain and fear. His delusions took shape in terms of his life experience.

The first few days of his therapy were rather hectic because he was actively delusional. He would come into treatment saying that someone just honked their horn outside my office, signaling that the "Creolins" were after him. He was convinced that the enemy was sending warning signals to him. This leads me to the second qualification in regard to treating psychotics.

When a neurotic returns to his symptoms in the first weeks of therapy, he may have his old headaches again, but an actively delusional psychotic roaming the streets can be a danger. If Ted were just a bit more crazy (if he weren't suspicious that his delusions were crazy, that is, if there weren't a fraction of consciousness left to "know" that other aspects of consciousness were not real), he might have attacked a car containing those Creolins.* Serious psychotics need a great deal of care and should really have in-patient therapy. However, ambulatory psychotics make very good Primal patients.

There is a very good reason for this. The more you "fit in" with a sick society, the more sick you are. The well-adjusted attorney may be totally shut off. His therapy may take a very long time. The psychotic, however, is a mass of feelings. He has a better chance than the well-controlled person in our therapy because our therapy works in reverse from the conventional therapy, where defenses are built up. Our aim is to produce defenselessness, and the psychotic is close to that.

* Please see the chapter called "The Nature of Consciousness" for discussion of the split in consciousness of cerebral hemispheres.

Ted's therapy was much the same as for any neurotic. He needed no "busts" against his defense system. His Primals were earthshaking in intensity. For the first weeks of his treatment he was curled up in a ball, wailing like an infant. One major reason why he was psychotic was the earliness of his traumas. He never had enough time in life without assaults of one kind or another to develop a stable neurotic life-style. There was little love even from the very beginning, and that means there was little self from the start of his life to cope with Pain.

PSYCHOSIS—TED

My first acid trip was a super-bummer. I had promised myself that I would never take acid, ever. But someone said that if you take acid with another person, then afterwards you and that other person are like one. There was this girl. If I could only be one with her. She had some acid. We went to a light show together. Everyone kept looking at me, everyone knew that I had taken acid. I could see it in their eyes, I hated the crowds of people! I wanted to be alone. I was afraid . . . terrified. I don't know how I did it but I held all of my shit in. All my fear just made me quiver a little. All those people frightened me so. It was very difficult for me to say anything at all. I just sort of froze, and shook.

It became of supreme importance to be able to take acid, and to be able to control it. And so acid became my companion. One time Steve and I took a jeep and drove into an amazingly beautiful valley, far back into the mountains, where only miners and deer hunters had ever been. We were up early in the morning and dropped acid. I went off alone to be with nature. It was summertime, and it was the best acid trip so far. I was a few blocks from the campsite, in the midst of the forest, very high, having a fantastic time, when from out of nowhere a thought came which completely engulfed my body. *What if there's a bear around?* I had never been so completely seized with fear. Just like that, from a beautiful feeling of oneness with everything, to one of horrible shaking fear. I had no gun, no means of protection, no one to help me. Immediately I panicked, and started running. I was shaking all over. Then I was afraid that I was lost, and started shouting for Steve. He had a gun, and I had to be near him. I ran and ran but couldn't find the campsite. It seemed like forever, but somehow, some way, I found the campsite. He wasn't there, but I felt a bit safer. Finally I found him down by the stream, fishing, having a wonderful time, and the fear immediately vanished. I sort of told him what had happened, but not about the complete enrapture of fear and the panic. Within the next month I had purchased a .45 pistol. Every full moon, I would drop some acid and walk around in the mountains, alone, late at night, always carrying my .45. My friend knew it, and "understood."

It rarely occurred to me that my drug-taking was really very heavy. I kept telling myself that it wasn't any more than many of the people I knew about. Hell, some of them had dropped acid two hundred or more times. Shit, my dropping was small-time. Hell, I was okay, there was nothing wrong with me. During this time I was employed, and was even a manager, and had recently graduated from college. The pay was $425 a month plus commissions of $58 a month, and I could steal another $150 a month, so things were nice. The best part was that I didn't have to go to work because the owner lived in another town and I had the helpers under me to do the bookkeeping. Everyone liked working for me, because we would always get stoned at work. I had plenty of money to buy drugs, and lots of free time, so I continued to stay stoned. But this only lasted a few months until they found out and fired me. Shit, I didn't care. Steve and I split for Mexico, with lots of THC, and grass.

When we came back from Mexico, we each got our own cabin in the mountains again. Once again I was alone. I didn't have a job, but the state paid me $55 a week for four months for unemployment. That bought lots of dope. It became important to meet somebody else, besides Steve, and so I started to visit this other guy. No one ever came to visit me. One evening this guy was with two of his friends and they asked me if I wanted to drop acid with them. "Oh, yes, of course." I was so glad, someone wanted me to be with them. We all went to Steve's cabin and he dropped too. After an hour or so Steve went and hid in the bedroom of his cabin, and I just sat there with those people, absolutely petrified! I couldn't move, look at them, or say a word. I didn't know what to say. I just wanted them to leave but couldn't say anything. I was too afraid. I thought Steve would do the talking for me, but he was hiding in the bedroom. Finally they left. I just lay down and listened to the stereo for about five hours. I was just numb all over. It occurred to me to just leave the whole town, and start anew someplace else, where no one knew who I was. No one could know about what had happened to me that night. I'll never take acid again, I promised. I can't stand to be afraid.

I moved out of the cabin down into the town. I just couldn't stand the loneliness any more. It was a good feeling. And then it happened. *I found a fuck!* She said she loved me, and I her. It was springtime. I took a chance, and we took acid together. I started to cry over my mother's death; she said she loved me even more. *I was okay after all.* We stayed glued together for four months. She left me to marry her old boyfriend. Then another girl came along who was divorced and had a two-year-old boy. Right away she asked me to marry her and I wanted to. So I wouldn't be alone any more. My friend made a sarcastic remark about my relationship with her. Immediately after that I stopped seeing her.

My good friend, Steve, had gone to Mexico for a second time, and I was living with another friend, Bill, but the three of us were splitting the rent. Steve returned after a few months with his girlfriend, Susan, and a guy he brought back from Mexico, Chico. So all of a sudden there were five of us living together, and we were all friends. Chico was an "expert" on drugs, and he and Steve were going to start a marijuana farm, indoors. Chico would drop acid about twice a week and would stay stoned on grass the rest of the time. Before they arrived, I had stopped taking all dope for the most part, but got right back into the everyday stuff when they returned. I couldn't be apart from them, they were my family, the people I had always wanted to have around me. They made me feel so good. And I usually had someone to go to bed with. We all got stoned every day. I loved it.

One night, Bill came back with acid for everyone, and so we all dropped. It was the heaviest acid ever for me. All I could do was lie down and listen to the stereo. We played the same record all night. It seemed as if only the last part of the last song was playing, for that was all I could remember hearing. In my mind was an artificial sunset. It was like we were floating through space. No one ever said anything, but we would sometimes simultaneously start laughing. We were together, united, but said nothing, didn't look at each other. Bill seemed to be the leader, he seemed to know what was happening. Nothing like this had happened to me before. I opened my eyes, and the sun was rising. I was floating about three feet above my body, and was not conscious of my body. Steve was sitting near me, and seemed to be floating also, as far as I could see. My first conclusion was that I had died, and that what I was now experiencing was "heaven." So I asked Steve how I had died, for I couldn't remember the accident, if there was one, or any process of dying. All I knew was that I was no longer in my body, but floating, yet still conscious. Steve didn't seem to understand what I was talking about, so I dropped the subject.

I closed my eyes and stayed with the artificial sunset. Later, I opened my eyes again, and realized that my body was still alive too, and so the two of us, my body and my consciousness, rose and walked outside to see the real sunset. It was fantastic. Then as I looked over the town, it was no longer that town, but the small town that my father grew up in, and it seemed to me that I was my father. It was an incredible experience. Everything that my eyes could behold was part of that little town; the actual town that I was living in was not there. And I was a little boy, five years old. The experience made me laugh at the other people in the houses, they were so dead, so ignorant. Chico came outside and said if I looked at the sunset right, I would be able to see diagonal spaces in the sky, and there were. The sky was like a veil, with diagonal lines cut through it, and through the holes I could see trees, and another sort of world, on the other side. It was amazing, like Columbus discovering America. Chico then started to tell me about some kind of wave, and that it was a simple matter of tuning into the wave. He seemed to know a good deal about it all. It all impressed me heavily. Chico said he felt he was from another planet, but didn't know which one. He told me about an author named Rampa, and some things about astral projection.

From then on Chico wanted to be with me on my acid trips, and sort of set himself up as some kind of trip leader. I grew suspicious of him. He had such greedy-looking black eyes. I didn't trust him. Nonetheless, we took a lot of acid. I started trying to see other people's auras. Chico's was brown, which meant he was a bad person. On another acid trip, I started to feel a very strong sort of pull or energy at the point between my eyebrows, and at the same time heard a deep, heavy, rumbling sound. Well, these were all new to me, and I related them to Chico and his wave, and I grew suspicious of the sounds. Maybe there was something outside that Chico knew about and wasn't going to tell me about. Maybe something like a flying saucer, and maybe they wanted something from me, like my energy to run their ships, or something. That's why he wouldn't say anything about it. Of course, I was afraid to ask, and grew more and more afraid.

Later I decided to drop acid when Chico wasn't around, and so I got in my car and drove a few hundred miles to another town where I knew a girl. She let me stay at her brother's vacant apartment. I didn't really like her, because she wouldn't let me go to bed with her, but now I didn't care about that. We went to a bar, and then I took her home, went to her brother's and dropped acid. If those freaky sounds and things didn't happen this time, then I'd know that Chico was up to something, because they had only happened when he was around. I got high and closed my eyes to listen. *The sounds were here, too. They were here, too!* I could hear the flying-saucer people outside my door. I was totally panic-stricken. *And my gun was in my car!* I didn't know whether to chance it or not, but I ran to my car, got my gun, and made it back. But now that didn't even do me any good, *they could still kill me,* and were going to, because I wouldn't join them. I ran outside so I could flee on foot to my girlfriend's house. I could hear them closing in on me. I flagged down a police car and jumped in the car. I told the cop that someone was trying to kill me. I told him that I couldn't explain it. Oh, how beautiful the flying-saucer people's work was. I couldn't tell him about people from outer space, because he would think I was crazy for sure. They could kill me, and no one would ever suspect flying-saucer people. I was trapped. I told him to take me to jail, for that was the only place that I was safe. They couldn't kill me there. So he did.

I called my girlfriend the next morning, and she bailed me out. I had her drop me off at a shopping center. I knew they were following me, using their agents on earth to do their dirty work. Chico must be one of them, so must Bill. I would hide in the stores, for on one could kill me there. I tried to phone Steve, and finally reached him, and told him all about it. He said he would meet me anywhere, but that he wasn't sure that I had come to the right conclusion. Of course he couldn't know, they weren't after him, they hadn't revealed themselves to him as they did me. How could he know? I called a cab, then decided to take a chance and go to my car. I hurried and packed, thinking maybe I could give them the slip. I jumped in my car and headed in the opposite direction of my destination, hoping to fool them.

That night I slept in my car in the downtown area. No one would kill me in front of the main street area. I knew they could run me off the road as I drove back, so I would only drive during the daytime, when there were other travelers on the road. The next night I stayed in a hotel with my gun under my pillow. It would be hard for them to try to kill me in a hotel. At this point, I felt if I could escape from them somehow, I would move to another town, change my name, and start all over again. Steve met me the next night, in the town where our apartment was. He sort of convinced me that I had come to the wrong conclusion, and so I went back to the apartment where Chico was. I said nothing to him. I had to take acid again, to see if I was really crazy or what. I had to!

Chico wasn't there the day I dropped—it was in the afternoon. I got high and lay down on my bed. My head began to fill with energy. Suddenly I heard a snap and everything was okay. I instantly realized my craziness. I felt all-knowing. It was a beautiful experience. All my fear left me. I rose with smiles on. I told Steve that I was okay now. I felt so good, I smoked some grass and went "flying." I could see the stars, yet I was inside, it seemed as if I was floating in space. It was great. And Chico or Bill were not around. This was great. *I was okay after all!*

One day Bill arrived with some books; they were all on UFO phenomena. *The fear again!* It came just like that. But I tried to fake like it didn't bother me. I asked if these books had any fact to them, and Bill gave an emphatic affirmative. The fear grew larger. But I held onto it and it didn't get out of hand. That night I dropped acid again. As I got high, I left the house to see a girlfriend. We went to a coffee shop together. I heard myself saying to her the same sort of things that the Mexican, Chico, was saying to me, like about a wave and tuning into it. Now I felt I was working for the UFO people. Telepathically I felt them tell me to go back to where Bill, the leader, was. It frightened me to death. I was shaking. She came with me. I had to go to Bill or they would kill me. I didn't want to bother him. All of a sudden I saw a flash of light, and I was outside again. The image of the apartment remained with me as a wall of light, but my consciousness was totally outside in space. I could see the entire universe, and I was traveling rapidly. Then I started to hear voices, someone was telling me to come over to their side. I was frightened stiff. What did they want from me? Then Bill asked me, "How about it?" He wanted me for them. I asked him what he wanted from me, but he just grinned, and discontinued the conversation as another person entered the room. I was frozen in fear. I asked him if my girlfriend could be part of whatever he wanted, but he said no. What was going on? It all escaped me, but it was obvious that the flying-saucer people had finally exposed themselves, and wanted something from me, namely my will. Bill just sort of stared at me, and then all of a sudden my forehead seemed to open up and I could see about the room with another pair of eyes. I could close my eyes, and could still see about the room. When Bill saw this happening to me, he closed his eyes to prove that he, too, could see about the room with his eyes closed. Then there were screams, horrible screams, and I felt myself immediately enter my body. The screams scared me back into my body. Bill seemed to know this too, for he could no longer get what he wanted, and made a very sarcastic hurting remark to me. He then left the room. I tried to "make out" with my girlfriend, but as I held her, all I could see was a grotesque, horribly animalistic creature. That too frightened me. And then Steve came in, and kept asking what I saw as I stared outside. They couldn't know what I was seeing. Then they'd know that I knew about them. And above all, my best friend, Steve, was part of them, trying to win me over to their side for them. He made a sarcastic remark to me and left also. I was doomed. The rest of the night I spent shaking. The next morning, Bill wanted to know what my experiences were, but I wouldn't tell him. I was too afraid. They couldn't know that I knew about them.

I felt that they could kill me anytime now. It was just a matter of my slipping into the opportune time for them. They made me aware of their persistent presence by honking their horns at me. That's how they kept me afraid. They were everywhere and I had to escape from them. I was afraid to stay in the apartment any longer because they'd get me for sure there. The next night I spent with my girlfriend, but they had instructed me not to tell anyone about them, and so I was too afraid to tell her what was happening. But by the next day, I felt that they would eventually kill me, and I had to tell someone before I died.

I told her that we were being invaded from outer space and that they made their contacts to gain earth helpers by getting them high on acid. I told her to never take acid. She said she believed me. That next day I spent running, trying to get away from them, but had no luck. I took a taxicab to the next town. There I rode the buses all over in an attempt to escape. But all to no avail. They could follow me anywhere. They could probably tune in to my brain waves and follow me that way. I was never sure if I had escaped, so I jumped off the bus and quickly ran into a hotel. There I hid for several hours under a table in a banquet room. Then I decided to get a room, but as I was checking in, two high school kids walked through the door and walked up to either side of me. They stood there for a while, and then asked for some matches. *I hadn't escaped them!* I decided to go back and stay with some other friends. We smoked some grass, and I knew I was safe there for the night at least. I knew they knew where I was, but they wouldn't kill me here with these people. I figured they'd try to make the murder look as if I had had an accident or had killed myself, and so this wasn't the right time or place. Besides, they had a lot of time. My friends decided to watch TV, but the thing didn't work. It just gave a blur, and a low, resonating tone. They must be using a lot of energy in tracking me, this beam was phasing out the TV. It all was quite clear. The next morning I decided to go back to the apartment, collect my things, and go home with them. I changed my mind about them killing me at the apartment. It wouldn't look right, and it would bring too much attention to that place of operation. I wasn't sure what would happen that night—I just took a chance.

The morning after I left for home, with all my things. I told Bill and Steve good-bye, and that was it. I called my father, thinking that if someone was expecting me that they wouldn't try to kill me. I made it home safely. He knew there was something wrong with me, but declined to ask much about it. If I could have gone anyplace but home, I would have, but it was the only place where I could leave my things behind. He went to work in the morning, and so I stayed around the house waiting for "them" to make the next move. I kept feeling a strange tingling feeling all the time where my medulla oblongata is located, and it dawned on me what they were doing. They were slowly burning my mind away with a low-energy beam, and it would just be a matter of time before they had me, and no one would be able to detect the cause of death. I had two friends in distant towns, and decided to tell them what was happening, so that someone else would know that I was going to be killed, how, and why. I was afraid to write the letters, because they had told me not to tell anyone. I knew that they could tune into my mind and know my thoughts, they probably were recording them in their saucer, so they knew always what I was going to do. So when I wrote and addressed the letters, I tried to think of something different than the actual words and addresses to confuse them. Apparently they didn't have any of their earth members in my hometown, not yet anyway. There were no horn honks. Every day I wrote letters telling my friends, trying to explain the invasions, and trying to tell them what was happening to me. As many people as possible had to find out before I was killed. I begged them to believe me, and not to think that I was crazy. I waited for the flying-saucer people to make their next move.

When my father was at work I would wear a helmet made of tinfoil to try to deflect the damaging beams from the saucer. They couldn't get me until I had told my story to as many friends as possible. My death would prove that what I was saying was true. They wouldn't kill me at home, not in the house, anyway. I stayed inside and felt safe, waiting for their next move. God and the Bible were my only hope. I had to keep the faith. Just about anything I read was comforting. Oh, if I could only be free from them! If only I hadn't taken that acid that night, then everything would be okay now. Why did I do it?

And then they came. One night I lay down and fell asleep. While sleeping, I became aware that I was floating about the house from room to room. I flew into the kitchen, and there they were, two lads from the spaceship, dressed in uniform. Each one lightly grabbed one of my arms and escorted me through the window into our backyard, and we started ascending. I was afraid to say anything to them, but then I heard that rumbling sound again, sort of like a huge diesel engine. It was the sound of the saucer. I struggled to be free of them, and the next thing I knew was that I was awake, shaking in fear. They had made their move. Never had I had a dream so vivid; never had I been so aware. That was no ordinary dream—they had made actual contact with me. They had complete control of the astral plane.

Well, I had to leave my home. The next day I decided to write my brother and tell him what was happening. I knew he wouldn't understand, and that he would think that I was crazy, but someone in my family had to know before they got me, and my death would prove my sanity. I hesitated in sending it to him, but the barrier had to be broken. I sent it. Maybe they had contacts in the post office and could stop my letters. All I could do was try. That night my father took me out to dinner. As we left the house, I remember the outside light being off and the door being locked. When we returned the light was on. They could materialize themselves easily to turn the physical light switch. It was a warning sign from them. The next morning I announced to my father that I was leaving, and gave a destination from the top of my head. This was to be my big escape from them, and no one could know where I was going. I was afraid to think where I was going so that they couldn't read it from my mind. So in reality I didn't know where I was headed. I took no luggage. All my father could say was, "I know you're not telling me everything." I had bought some books on UFO phenomena and told him that he would find out what was happening by reading the books. In the books I wrote notes to him explaining it in more detail. One of the books related how a woman had a series of vivid dreams after her encounter with people from outer space, and that section was where I placed the note.

I went downtown, and slipped into an office building. From there I called a cab. All this time I wore a stocking cap, under which I wore my tinfoil brain-wave reflector. It had to work. It would distort my waves enough so that they couldn't trace me, or pick up my thoughts. It was my best try so far. The cab came and I had him take me to the next town. From there I started hitchhiking. I felt that I had lost them, but wasn't sure. I rode for several hundred miles until nighttime. The wondering of whether or not I had escaped from them kept battering my mind. Maybe they could no longer trace me? Maybe I'm free? But the uncertainty remained. It was just like being an escaped convict, only I hadn't done anything wrong. I got in the car, and went to the grocery store to buy a roll of tinfoil. I was going to make a super-brain-wave reflector so that I would lose them for sure. But as I returned to the car with the foil, and sat, I started to hear a buzz in the back of my head and knew that all my attempts to escape were totally useless. They had been following me every second of the way. So all attempts to escape from now on became ridiculous, and I checked into a hotel. I was too tired of running. They could have me.

From that point on I tried to relax. There was nothing else to do. Running was futile. My plan was to take the bus to my brother, and try to explain to him that I really wasn't crazy, and that this was all really happening. It was good to get to my brother's house. Here was another place where they couldn't kill me, and now that my brother knew what was going on, anything that happened to me would make it obvious. Before leaving home I had taken out a Blue Cross, Blue Shield policy in case their attempt failed a bit, and I was hospitalized. This was a comforting feeling also. But their honking never stopped. And my brother didn't really believe me. He thought it was possible, but I knew that he thought I was crazy. That was impossible. No one had experienced what I had, no one knew but me, and *I was all alone, always alone.*

My sister was living in the area too, and one day I went over to see her. I told her that I was afraid to go to sleep because I was afraid to dream. She said that if I did a lot of physical exercise, that I would be too tired to dream. Wow, that was it, that was the answer. Each day I would expend all my energy, before

I went to sleep, and then there would be no energy for them. It dawned on me that the entire hippie movement was instigated by them, and that one thing prominent among the hippies was their extreme lack of physical exercise. Plus I knew that drugs cause one to release his stored bodily energies, and so the puzzle was fitting together beautifully. And I had a way out. So that day I started all kinds of exercising, and really wearing myself out. Toward late afternoon I was in my brother's backyard running in place, and doing pushups. I happened to glance up into the sky and couldn't believe my eyes. Hovering high above me was a silver flying saucer. I looked at it, and then looked away, and thought that it must be Venus or something. It couldn't be them. But it was too big to be Venus. I gazed up at it again. It wasn't moving like an airplane. It hung motionless! Then from the side of it shot something that looked like a bursting sky-rocket. I looked away from it, shuddering in fear. I looked up at it again, and it was gone. I ran indoors, thinking that they might have shot something at me. That was their warning, not to do any exercise. That night I hesitated for some time, but then asked God to protect me, and started my exercises. It would be any time now, and they would get me, for now I was totally useless to them. My only hope was God. I was alone except for God.

My brother suggested that I see a psychologist. I didn't feel that a psychologist would understand any more than anybody else, but I figured that he might be able to give me some insight; at any rate I was interested in what he would have to say. The really good thing about it was that I would be able to tell someone else about the invasion, hopefully before they got me. I figured that my protection was the people who knew about them, and that the more people knew about what they were doing to me, the safer I was.

My brother had a friend who was associated with Primal Therapy. His friend worked with people who had freaked out on acid and said that Primal Therapy was the only thing that worked. Maybe I had freaked out, but it seemed quite obvious to me that I hadn't. It occurred to me that maybe the therapy was one of their cover-up schemes, and it was perhaps another trap, and that maybe they had won my brother over during the night in one of his dreams. But that didn't seem likely, because I didn't feel that he was evolved enough for them to bother with, and that he was much too set in his ways to be tempted by the wonders of the astral world. So I decided to give the therapy a try. But I knew that if the therapist had long hair he was one of them for sure, and that the trap was on.

Fortunately his hair was short and he seemed like a rather regular guy. He got me to cry about my father and asked me how I felt. I said, "pretty good," but kept wondering when it was going to happen, when he would prove my UFO story false. Well, he never did, nor did he even try, he just kept telling me that I knew myself, and had to feel it for myself. And that after several months of therapy I would begin to feel myself, and that everything that was apart from the real me would slowly be forgotten. And that's just about what happened.

I began to sort of feel the horn honks and could tell that they weren't directed toward me. I could feel a sharp pain that had always been with me. That got to be more bothersome than the UFO people. I couldn't really feel it, because every time I did I would pass out, or hurt very severely. I really didn't want to feel it, it was way more than I could handle. Within three to five weeks of this therapy, I had lost ninety percent of my fear of the UFO people. I didn't know for sure whether it was true or not, but I was very glad not to be afraid. Slowly the rest of the fear diminished. I flew back home and drove my car back to Los Angeles. I left my .45 behind. I slept outside, in the middle of nowhere, and nothing happened. It was so great to be free of that fear. It was so great! But my struggle with fear was just beginning. *It's always Daddy!* He always frightened me. *I'm not gonna be afraid of you anymore, Dad! I'm not gonna be afraid!* Slowly the fear recedes, the fear of everything—girls, men, parties, people, doing what I want to do, being as I feel, *my father.* It hurts, it always just hurts. I don't want to hurt. *I want my Mommy!* I don't want to be alone. Love me, Mommy, please love me.

Now they've gone and have left me alone. When I think of them, I see my father. He is my real fear. Primal Therapy has returned my feelings to me. Before, when I was afraid to talk to a girl, I would never admit my fear; now I feel the fear. I used to try to figure out solutions, ways to get around feeling the fear, like eating or finding something else to do, but the only solution that is real to me is to be afraid and feel the fear. I am afraid. That's me. To be with my feelings is really a nice feeling—to let them flow, no matter what they may be. My old crap has been with me so long that it's hard to replace it with the real me. I'll go for a few days and not have a Primal, and then a day comes and I have Primals all day long. Sooner or later the real me, the shitty me that I'm always trying not to look at, ignore, cover, do anything with but feel, comes through. And that is a good feeling. It's as if you like most of all that part of you which you don't like at all because it doesn't change and you can always rely on it. Primal Therapy simply showed me what it was. But even though I know it and know what it feels like, it also hurts to feel it, so much of the time I try to cover it up—and that's a shitty feeling.

One of the reasons I left therapy was because I felt I was relying too much upon the therapy sessions to get to my feelings. Feeling to me became feeling my pain, and to get there hurt. I wanted to get away from the hurting. I wanted to see what I was like without going to the group sessions. Right after leaving I would have two- to three-hour Primals every morning. There was so much shit to get out and I wanted to get it out as soon as possible. There seemed to be no end to it for me, so I just quit one day and didn't have a Primal for several weeks.

It always seemed to me that there was something to understand about the therapy, that there was a certain amount of knowledge that had to be had before one could become "straight." The therapists seemed to me to be teachers of a sort, and that the more times I went to the groups, and the more I talked with the therapists, the more I was supposed to get of this knowledge that they supposedly had. I wanted them to teach me. I wanted to be "straight," but felt I couldn't be until I had their knowledge. I kept trying and trying, and feeling that I was understanding more and more, but was never quite sure of what I was supposed to understand. I left the therapy thinking I didn't really have the "understanding" of the therapy that I wanted, but if I kept on having Primals, and making sure that I had Primals, that I could sort of teach myself, which wasn't quite as good as having someone telling me, because they knew better than I, but it was the next best thing. Not until I stopped my every morning Primal session by myself, where I forced the Primals whether I was feeling anything or not, did I understand and begin to feel that there was never anything to understand or to be taught to me. Not until I stopped forcing Primals instead of letting them build up inside until I exploded perhaps days later did it occur to me what Primal Therapy was really about. And that these explosions of mine, totally natural, and unaided by any therapist, were what Primal Therapy was all about. I saw that my trying to understand the therapy was my way of copping-out on my feelings. I wanted to *think* my feelings out of me, rather than *feel* them out, which was the more painful. By avoiding the pain with my mind, I also avoided the pleasant side of my feelings. I could never really feel good as long as I hid in my head. It's been hard for me to get out of my head into my body, and even now my mind covers many of my feelings, but my Primals are more frequent now. I don't hold back as much or as long. I used to feel that I was supposed to have Primals, like I was supposed to study when I was going to school. It wasn't really to please the therapists that I thought I "should" have Primals. It was to please Daddy, disguised as the therapists. For me to try to please the therapists was obviously crazy to me, but to try to please Daddy didn't seem crazy at all. But I knew I couldn't please Daddy. I quit having Primals because I wanted to. I was doing it to please someone, and that was both crazy and impossible. Then they just started happening. Me hurt. Me wanted to cry. Me. Me. Me. Me to be Me, and not me to please someone else. I never did this, or felt this, before Primal Therapy, yet it was me, all me doing and feeling this now, for no one else but me. There was nothing to understand; they weren't trying to teach me anything. It was just me, feeling me, for me. I would have thought it crazy before Primal Therapy. I would have been afraid. Now I want to be more me, be me, but I've got a long ways to go. I don't know that there is an end to it. It's just feeling, but each day that "just feeling" involves more and more. The more I feel, the more I find there is to feel. The one thing that holds me back is fear, fear of feeling. *Daddy, don't make me afraid! I'm not going to be afraid of you any more! Never!!*

I live alone now, and have a job. I don't have any friends nearby and I feel lonely a lot. I want to meet people, but I am afraid a lot. But not always. I no longer think that I'm crazy in the back of my head or that there's something wrong with me. I'm afraid, that's it. I want everyone to like me. That's it. All I can really say is that sometimes I'm not afraid, and that's really nice. Also bit by bit, and very slowly, I'm becoming less and less afraid. My shell is opening slowly, and more and more frequently, for short periods of time, it doesn't exist at all. There are no differences among my feelings—each one is as important as the next. The intensity differs, but that's my own choosing. It's all just feeling, every second of the day. Some days, and some times, I don't like my feelings, and begin to think that there's something wrong with me, or that I'm really crazy, but it turns out that it's just me, not liking me, not wanting me. So it's really no hassle. When I'm feeling shitty, I can either not like me and try to figure out what's wrong with me, and all the shit I should go through to get me to like, or I can just *feel* the pain. Many times I choose the mind trip, and cover up the pain. It hurts, dammit! I don't want to feel it all the time. But always, sooner or later, the "thinking it out" trip becomes ridiculous, and my Primals begin.

14 *On Paranoia*

I had an insight into paranoia the other day while driving. A man in another car suddenly pulled out of a side street and cut in front of me. I honked, and he began yelling at me. His yelling and his accusations were his way of covering the feeling of doing something wrong. In the instant between my honk and his retort, the paranoid process took place: namely, "I've done something wrong. Therefore I'm bad; therefore I'm unloved." To stop feeling unloved, he blamed me. He could not be objective about his driving error because my honk had aroused a whole history of being wrong and feeling unloved for it. So paranoia, "It's you, not me," is a way of shifting the center of gravity from inside to outside.

Sometimes, nothing externally dramatic has to happen. All that is required is that some inner feeling be aroused that cannot be tolerated—say, of homosexual leanings—and it is immediately and automatically projected outside of oneself. If a person can stand the feeling, if my driver had been able to accept the impulsiveness of his driving and admit his mistake, there is no need for paranoia.

Paranoia is different from a schizoid process, in which the person simply withdraws totally. Paranoia is a later development which occurs when a child can first verbalize, and therefore distort, his feelings. Let us say that at the age of three a child first feels that his mother really dislikes him, and that he will never in his life be loved by her. He begins to feel that total and devastating feeling of rejection. That feeling may become translated into "she doesn't like me *because*" . . . "I'm bad, I'm dumb, I'm ugly," etcetera. The child needs that *"because"* in order to rationalize the rejection and at the same time permit some hope that if he can change what is wrong with him he will be liked again. Later on, the child may feel in social situations, "They *won't* like me because . . ." He projects his early rejection onto new situations. Still later, the feeling may become, "They *don't* like me. They are ridiculing me behind my back." What was previously an anticipation has now become a reality. The essence of the paranoia is to block the early feeling of rejection that could not be felt and accepted.

In Primal Therapy, when many of the defenses have been stripped away, we see the development of paranoia ideation for the first time. A brilliant scientist who has covered his real feeling of being stupid (no matter what the reality of his accomplishments) may, when he comes close to that early memory of feeling rejected for doing something dumb, decide that I am trying "to make him feel stupid, but it won't work." Before the development of an ideational defense such as paranoia, an infant can only withdraw in the face of overwhelming Pain. He can't act-out, make deals, accomplish, etcetera. He cannot figure out that it "really is them, not me." In Primal Therapy, when we strip a patient of his acting-out, his making deals, his conning, etcetera, the Pain goes to his head, so to speak, and paranoia is the result. In this sense, acting-out often acts as a defense against paranoia. To feel totally stupid, for example, and not be permitted to act smart, means to be faced with great Pain. All that is left is for the mind to project that feeling elsewhere.

We may say, then, that paranoia begins at the very first time the child "knows" something is radically wrong and must "not know" in order to preserve his psychologic integrity. With the development of verbal skills, all the previous psychological and physical Pains can finally be handled ideationally. For example, birth trauma is a shattering experience. It leaves residual tension of a high order. As the child begins to think, he can use his thought processes as a defense to "think away" that feeling. He would become paranoid in order to establish a focus and locus for the inexplicable birth tension he suffers. He would blame the teacher or his peers whenever anything went wrong that made him tense—that rearoused the early birth tension. He would not need to blame them if he could feel his stupidity or his being wrong in school. But the combination of birth trauma plus early rejection produces an overload that cannot be integrated and so must be projected.

Paranoia must be dismantled in a slow and orderly fashion, by helping a person feel each of his Pains that contributes to the overload-projection, so that he can live in the now instead of projecting an inexplicable and unacceptable past onto the present. In order to solve the paranoia, we must help the person feel the history he has blocked so that the history no longer blankets the present.

Let us take an example, one I see often. A psychologist in training is not doing well. He makes continual mistakes week after week and he is faced with being dismissed from the training program. He begins to tell others that I'm really crazy and that I really don't know as much about Primal Therapy as I make out. With each week of failure, I become more inept in his mind, until the point is reached where in order to block the feeling of being a total failure, the trainee decides that I'm totally crazy and that I criticize him because I really don't like him. Or he begins to think that he's got a new way of doing the therapy that is better than mine, and that really I'm a poor trainer, undiscerning as to people's progress. As the Pain grows, the paranoid ideation becomes commensurately more bizarre and distant from the true feeling—"I'm stupid and I'm not going to make it; therefore no one will love me."

We see here that paranoid ideation proceeds along a continuum; the more Pain, the more strained the ideation. It can begin with simple phobias—a projection of an early fear onto the present. But the phobia is an *acknowledgment* of fear! In paranoia, that is lost; there is the fear of fear, hence the denial of any fear. As the paranoia continues, the person begins to act on his ideation. This is the dangerous stage.

What starts out as a simple fear of communism becomes the need to kill Communists before "they kill us." What starts out as an acknowledged fear of failure in training becomes an idea that Janov is insane, and, finally, the development of a special theory that moves way beyond Primal theory as it is known.

We must consider paranoia as the final defense. After the body has done whatever it could to contain a Primal feeling, the head takes over and twists it. Then the body accommodates itself to that idea and the person acts on it. One cannot talk someone out of his ideation because it was necessary to block Pain. The only answer is to help someone feel it.

15 *On Happiness, Depression and the Nature of Experience*

The search for happiness is not the sole prerogative of mentally ill people. It is, in a sense, a national pastime.

In order to understand happiness and depression, I want to start with a simple proposition: Experience is of the body as well as the mind. What happens to us in life affects us totally, and doesn't simply affect the mind. It is no revelation to say that the mind is connected to and part of the physical system, but failure to understand this has led to a misunderstanding of what happiness and depression are about.

I have pointed out elsewhere (*The Primal Scream*) that early events register in our systems even when there has been no consciousness of them. Thus, our systems register "trauma" while the mind—our consciousness—may be registering "happiness." In neurosis, where there is a body-mind split, one's conscious experience may be quite divergent from one's systemic experience. We can "lie" to our*selves* when we are neurotic. We can believe we are happy while pain rages quietly within.

Perhaps we can understand this more clearly by examining hypnotic states. A hypnotist on stage can take a dour, frozen neurotic out of his audience and "produce" a bubbling, "happy" person within a few seconds or minutes. Is that person really happy? If you asked him, he would say, "Yes, I am happy." He seems as happy as any neurotic might *seem* happy. He is merry, smiling, and seemingly untroubled. The objective criteria are there, but we know it is a false state. With the aid of hypnosis, the person has been able to lie to himself. Relieved of his hypnotic state, he might well revert immediately to his natural depression. This is no different than in neurosis, where parents "produce" pseudo-happy children who are not allowed to be grumpy or sad. They are usually not even allowed to be sullen, because this reminds the parents of their failure. One could ask these children if they were happy and get the same kind of affirmative answer that hypnotized subjects would give. Though both the neurotic child and the hypnotic subject could consciously report "happiness," their bodies would still show great tension. So their "happiness" would be cerebral, and not organismic. "Happiness," in the neurotic sense, then, would be an effective flight from the body. To halt the flight—to release the neurotic from his "hypnosis"—is to produce Primals and Primal misery—a true organismic state.

Why is the neurotic miserable? Because he has been robbed of himself. How it is done is of little consequence. The point is that when needs are not fulfilled, when one is not allowed to express himself easily and honestly, there must be sadness. Primal patients cry over not being held, not being listened to, not being allowed privacy in their bedrooms. As children they were being drowned with neglect and they were unaware of the subtle tragedy that was taking place. But piece by piece the tragedy was growing, only there was nothing in particular that could be pointed out, nothing that could be cried over that would let the child know he was drowning. His body was accumulating sadness. Later on, he will devise a panoply of devices to protect himself against the crushing weight of his deprivations. He will drink, work hard, go on shopping sprees, or whatever. As soon as he is bereft of an outlet, however, he is vulnerable to the sadness. Every neurotic is sad whether he knows it or not. Often he does not know it, because the purpose of neurosis is to hide the tragedy of one's early life. Meanwhile, the whole system is involved in those early feelings—becomes part of them—either to feel them or to escape. A good escape is called "happiness"; an ineffective one is "depression."

The neurotic is stuck in time. He is stuck back in his past whether he is conscious of it or not, so that everything he does is a symbolic portrayal of that past. All the intervening years between his original split and adulthood have meaning only in terms of the Primal feelings. They are never eradicated (except through Primal Therapy), and the best that someone can do is defend against them. This means that we are all open to sadness when our defenses give way. To suddenly be out of work, left alone, or isolated by one's friends—all constitute the soil of sadness. These are the times when the neurotic becomes depressed. He feels depressed because his body is depressing the Primal sadness—the accumulated sadness resulting from numberless early experiences where there was neglect, deprivation, humiliation, and robbery of the self. What the neurotic feels when he is temporarily out of defenses is the depression, not the feelings being depressed. He feels the pressure against those feelings pushing down into his system. That pressure produces labored speech and movement and total exhaustion, so that the depressive has little energy and moves about in slow motion.

Give a depressive a new outlet, a new job, a party, or a chance to go shopping, and all of the inner-directed pressure now pours out in manic activity. He will literally "throw himself" into his work. He will be "happy" for those moments when his work will make him happy. What has really happened is that he has found an outlet for tension—an outlet that continues to hide the Primal sadness. But great release of tension feels like happiness for the neurotic, and the relief feels better than that inner-pressured feeling that accompanies depression. So we can see that some of us shut down early in life and, sans outlets, become "dead" and depressed. Others shut down and "act" alive. If being the "happy clown" pleases one's parents, then the act will continue. The child will still be sad because he could not be himself. If there was no way to please, if one was disliked, suppressed, and rejected at every turn, then deadness and depression will result. Take away the "happy clown's" chances to perform, and the lurking sadness will begin to ascend.

Depression is not a feeling. It is what one does with feelings. It is the nonconceptualized accumulation of (and defense against) sadness. For a neurotic to feel anything totally would be to feel some of that sadness. A normal person is *never* depressed; he has no backlog of sadnesses lying unresolved inside. He is open to feel and does not repress unpleasantness. He will be sad when it is appropriate. But sadness is a "now" event, a real feeling related to real situations. Depression is a "then" event, unrelated to now except insofar as a current situation triggers something from the past. If the young child could feel each and every sadness, he would not be depressed in his life.

In order to eradicate depression, a person must relive and resolve all of the buried experiences of sadness inside. The dialectic of depression is that the more of one's early misery one feels, the less miserable he becomes. He will not become happy, because happiness is a neurotic concept, but he will become content . . . an organismic state wherein a peaceful mind is in accord with a peaceful body. Misery is the key to contentment. To avoid it is to keep it there forever. There can be no true contentment until the Primal misery is out of the way. Otherwise, the mind is lying and is out of harmony with the truth of the body. One does not simply drop one's misery. One does not "decide" to get over it any more than one would drop any other aspect of his physiology. The misery has become an integrated physiological phenomenon. Anything that drives the mind away from it is only an ephemeral diversion. That is why neurotics have that apprehensive feeling when they are momentarily happy; they feel it isn't going to last, something will happen to ruin it, and they are right. Their happiness is such a flimsy state that almost anything can spoil it. The latent misery is so large in comparison to any transient enjoyment that the neurotic has good reason to be wary and apprehensive.

Contentment is the obverse of depression. It is a harmonious state wherein the mind is consonant with the body. The pursuit of happiness is a neurotic endeavor of a body in Pain and a mind in flight. Normals enjoy events in the now, but they are not seeking after happiness. They know that there is only a state of full Being, no more than that. There can be no more than feeling each experience, enjoying what there is to enjoy. Anything more than Being is unreal. There is no super-ecstasy or "peak" experience; these are neurotic notions. However, there are states of intense feeling that are related to authentically stimulating events.

Experience, in the real sense, means to be a conscious human being—conscious of what is going on inside and outside. Depression is an unconscious state—unconscious of one's true, systemic feelings. The neurotic cannot be truly content so long as he has Pain. Nevertheless, there are some deluded states that many neurotics have come to associate with happiness and contentment. The most obvious is Zen meditation.

Zen would seem to be a sophisticated way of achieving "bliss," but when examined carefully it turns out to be nothing more than self-hypnosis, a super-repressed state. What is blissful is the efficacy of the repression. The person's mind-trip is so efficient that he effectively has left his body. In the literature, this state is often called a transcendental experience. The entire notion of bliss and transcendence appears to be both specious and spurious. One must ask, "Is there really a nonphysical self that can be transcended, a self that hangs in space unattached to the rest of us?" "Is there a nonphysical self that does the transcending?" If so, which self is that?

For the normal there is only one self—the real self. It is organismic and nondivisible. For the split neurotic there are two selves —the real and the unreal. The unreal has indeed "transcended" the real one in a mental way. In fits of self-delusion, that unreal self can even imagine a state of bliss. That is why meditation and other peak experiences are so transient. The truth rises constantly to negate the lie of the mind. The neurotic who transacts big business deals is in the same position as the Zen devotee, only his mantrum is expressed in dollars and cents on which he concentrates, and repeats *ad nauseam*. Is he happy? It would be accurate to say that his consciousness, narrowed and focused on money, takes his mind away from his unhappiness. That is why he requires more and more, and why mantrums have to be repeated year after year.

The notion of experience as a total event has other implications. To experience all of oneself means to be automatically masculine or feminine. A whole woman is one who speaks and moves as a female. A neurotic woman may "act" like a woman, but her body and her voice may betray her. She may speak baby-talk or not be fully developed physically because she still is a baby.

Perhaps we can understand the notion of "deep Being" better in physiologic terms. Within our bodies are millions of sensors that feed information to the brain. They tell us, *inter alia*, if we are in pain, where the pain is, and other specifics. When we block pain from consciousness, we are blocking sensation. We are reducing, in short, the sense of ourselves. That is why there is no way to "be," no mental gymnastics that deepen experience when there is this continuous blunting. We experience *ourselves* experiencing the world around us. Experience can be only of that self.

What is clear for the neurotic, then, is that there is no way to *make* himself happy. There are roles he can play that will transform him. An actor can play a liberated Zorba on the stage for years and still be depressed each night when he leaves the theater. Neurotics are very much like the actor playing Zorba. For the time they are in the struggle, working for a high grade or to make big sales, their "role" keeps them happy. It's when the role stops that the real self takes over, and the real self is sad. That is why a depressive is closer to himself (in depression) than at any other time. He would be a better Primal patient then, than if his role were working. The role, in short, takes each of us further away from ourselves, but the real self doggedly trails that unreal self around, waiting for its chance.

Now we can understand why success doesn't make people happy. Why it is that a singer who finally achieves stardom wants to be an actor. It is because success doesn't produce the magic happiness. These people need another struggle. They can never be free not to struggle, because they have learned in their culture that struggle and hard work are the way to happiness and success. Success is evidently an illusion. Like prestige and status, it is no more than someone else's idea about us. As an "outside" event it cannot affect real, internal changes . . . it cannot make us feel loved when we are not. When one has lost with his parents, later success won't change it.

This also helps to explain something about conventional psychotherapy. Why is it that people will stay in therapy for years and never get out even when very little is happening? They stay precisely *because* little is happening and they need hope. After two or three years of therapy they still feel miserable and have to believe that just a little more of it will make a difference. The fact that the therapist suggests that this may be the case helps reinforce remaining in the therapeutic struggle, hoping for the elusive happiness or contentment. The reason that the contentment or happiness is elusive is because the patient has been eluding the one thing that could really bring him contentment—Primal Pain. There is no painless road to contentment for the neurotic. Pain is the *cause*—and the resolution—of his misery.

One major problem with conventional psychotherapy is that it often tries to help patients toward a new style of living (a new role), instead of helping them *feel* the life they are living. This is an important distinction, for the neurotic is trying to get something *out* of life instead of experiencing real life—those living processes inside his body.

To become well, the neurotic must reach into his past to retrieve the present. The job of therapy is not to produce happiness. We need to help patients feel that past as something separate from the present. To engage the patient in now confrontations, to discuss his current relationships, is to neglect the past and thereby keep it raging inside the patient. To be a warm and attentive and understanding listener can temporarily help a patient feel relief, but it cannot make him content. Because he has retranslated everything in his current life in terms of the past, he will still act out with people, trying to get them to be the good daddy or mommy. Once he really feels that he never had a good parent and never will, he can be relieved of the struggle. To do anything else with a patient is to keep him stuck in one-dimensional time where everything he does is a symbolic portrayal of his past. He will discuss how this woman made him miserable, how so-and-so is castrating, and he knows that he should leave her if he is ever to be happy, etcetera. But we know that he would not be content if he left her. We understand that wives and husbands do not make us unhappy. They only aggravate unhappiness and provide us with a focus for the source of it. When a man manipulates his life so that he can be the little boy, he will have to marry a dominating, "castrating Mama." He wouldn't be able to have it any other way. He marries her because he is a little boy, not a man. He is not castrated—he simply never grew up. It is not her fault—she can't take away a manhood that doesn't exist. She simply unconsciously fell into the role of "Mama." Need keeps them both in a miserably unbalanced situation.

Sometimes neurotic needs mesh very well, and a wife plays Mama—keeping her little boy happy. They have a "happy" marriage. When the little boy loses his "mama," he begins to hurt— to hurt from the early feeling of never having had a real mama. He will be depressed—depressing that feeling and many more— until he finds someone else to mother him. His depression will be a vague, unconceptualized state. His misery results from not being able to manipulate his present in terms of the past. That is depression . . . the loss of hope and struggle. As long as this person can act out unconsciously having a mama (having a motherly wife) then he does not have to feel his misery. His happiness is a delusion . . . a delusion that will send him to an early grave, but he will die "happy."

I believe that we have not clearly understood the nature of true happiness because we have dealt with the overt behavior and conscious reports of neurotics—where happiness means making their unreal front work. The whole idea of a happy state is a fantasy thought up by depressives. What they really want is relief from their depressions.

The job of Primal Therapy is to retranslate a person's moods, such as depression, into those specifics that go to make them up. No one session can do that, but many Primals can. Primals, then, are the specifics of depression; conversely, depression is the repression of Primals. Once Primals begin and the defense system (of which happiness and depression are results) is cracked, then the person will feel mostly sadness. He will feel event-related feelings and not be torn apart by moods.

No one leaves his childhood behind until he has fully experienced it. Neurotics keep trying to make their (little) selves happy. They try in various ways to fulfill childhood needs symbolically. They buy themselves presents on shopping sprees and feel exhilarated for the moment. But all the presents in the world won't make up for parents who were not glad that their children were alive. Normals do not need things to live for. They are not waiting for that party or dinner to start living. They are already alive.

16 Manic-Depression

One of the more unfathomable diagnostic syndromes is manic-depression—that seemingly inexplicable state wherein the person swings from great bursts of activity to total depression and inability to do anything. It is not uncommon for prospective patients to call and ask if we have had experience with "manic-depressives," having been given that label by their previous therapist. We have had some experience with this kind of person, and our experience indicates that it might not be the mystery we thought it was.

The mystery seems to be that without warning some endogenous demon arises to engulf the person in depression and may leave again without any obvious external changes. The avenues of investigation of late have been both genetic and biochemical. There is the thought that perhaps some biochemical factor is released at critical times producing these alternating states, and somehow, if we can factor out that chemical, we can intercede and prevent its release or mute its effects. Others think that it all may be genetic—some hereditary factor transmitted in the genes.

I believe that manic-depression is a spurious diagnostic category that really does not explain very much. Mania and depression are unconscious and automatic defensive maneuvers—methods of handling Primal feelings. It is those feelings that lie at the bottom of the mania and depression, and it is those feelings that make manic-depression understandable. Most often, those feelings are of being worthless, unimportant, and unloved. Being manic means to be in flight from those feelings. Being depressed means to have them all bottled up and compressed inside. The energy source is the same; it takes great energy to keep those feelings down. Once there is an external outlet, that same energy is poured into it. Both are defenses—not special diagnostic pathologic states. Both deal with the identical underlying feelings; and those feelings are not pathological, they are real. What is pathologic is what blocking those feelings makes us do. Let us take an example.

A young boy is largely rejected. He grows up sullen and "down." He feels "worthless," because anyone who is not truly loved feels he is not worthwhile, not deserving—not "worth loving." But he is given an outlet. The family is very oriented toward academic achievement. And so he tries. He enters school and does well. He goes to medical school and then on to psychiatry. This takes care of about thirty years in which he can continually struggle and look forward to a love he is never going to get. He has children and is able to keep very occupied. Everything is in front of him. So long as he doesn't slow down, he can avoid depression. He is young and has the energy to keep up his manic life. Only he doesn't know it is a manic life. He is just a "busy" practitioner. He makes money, lectures, and is generally an "important man."

One day he is forty-five. His children do not meet his expectations. He cannot live through their achievements. He has to push them to achieve because they were foils for him so that he could keep the worthless feelings away. They won't do anything for him any more. Meanwhile, his practice has diminished and he can't keep up his ten-hour day. He begins to look around him; there isn't much to look forward to. He is not terribly happy with his dependent wife. He has been sick and doesn't have the energy he used to have, and his doctor tells him he must only work a half day. All the elements are there for the depression . . . all the external circumstances are driving him into his worthless feelings;

but because he doesn't even know they are there and cannot connect with them even if he did, he becomes depressed—he depresses the feelings.

If suddenly this man were offered a lectureship at an important university, or if he were made consultant to a major hospital, he might become manic again. His flight is to try to feel worthwhile. He is not fleeing the depression in any direct sense. Depression is what happens when he can't be manic. Swings in his mood are alterations in defense. When he is "up," he is gay in spirits, bubbly, and active. He's got hope—unconscious hope for love, for being smart and successful. He seems like his old self. His therapist is satisfied, because a productive defense seems better than an unproductive one, and there is hardly anyone more productive (at least in volume or quantity) than a manic. The manic feels better, because he isn't feeling; he is doing. His defense is working better. Since many therapies judge wellness by productivity and functioning, it seems logical that once a person is out of his depression he seems to be getting better. Indeed, the therapist will often encourage manic-ness—"Get out and do. See friends, take a trip, etcetera." Actually, he is closer to health in his depression—closer to his feelings.

One of the reasons conventional psychotherapy has been so unsuccessful with the manic-depressive is that there has been an attempt to build a defense rather than take it apart. Since the defense constantly sits on top of the Primal feelings, the so-called wellness of the person has been spurious.

Every depressive is also a potential manic, and vice versa. Sometimes the causes for the changes in mood are not apparent in terms of what is going on around the person. But we have to understand that it takes effort to be depressed, so much effort that the person acts "labored." One day that energy to repress gives out and the person becomes agitated. He may need drugs to stop his agitation (they also keep him depressed). Or he may take drugs to stop his depression. Those drugs, by and large, are stimulants. They produce an agitation. Then the person simply has to direct that agitation into social channels. What those drugs do is handle the defenses by either souping up the person or quieting him down. They either put the lid on the feelings or take it off. They certainly do not change the underlying source.

There are biochemical changes that take place with alterations in defense modes. Key agents are serotonin, epinephrin, and norepinephrin. To concentrate on these biochemical factors is to avoid looking at the whole man. If we look at chemical mediating agents alone, I do not think we will ever understand the whole phenomenon. Not that it is not important to know what happens to our brains and bodies under certain states. It is. But chemistry begs the question, "cause or effect."

Depression is the beginning of feelings. The person afflicted is down inside them, although in a nonconnected way. The manic is galvanized by the fear of feeling. Often there is no consciousness of the fear. Rather, it mobilizes and merges into the activity engaged in, so that it is not felt. If the person were forced to stand still and be alone, then he would feel that panic for what it is. Because the manic is still a step removed from the depression, he is further from health. This is the opposite from the conventional point of view, which sees keeping busy as a psychological virtue.

We often delude ourselves about the "sudden" onset of depression. Sometimes just meeting an old successful friend can make one begin to feel like a failure and produce it. Or, just reading about someone of equal age who has made it can do it. It doesn't have to be a catastrophic *external* event; it only has to be something minor which evokes the catastrophic *internal* event. Primal feelings are always there so that slight alterations in one's social milieu can trigger them and make them appear as some endogenous apparition.

What all this means is that there is no deep manic-depressive syndrome. These are different aspects of an identical problem, and simply to look at the ramifications of these states is to be left in a quandary as to its real nature.

17 *The Meaning of Meaning*

The search for the meaning of life has not only occupied the thoughts of philosophers for centuries but seems to be an increasing preoccupation of neurotics as well. Each new Primal patient is asked to write a letter about himself before treatment. Many of these letters indicate no specific problem; rather, the general tenor is one of not getting much out of life—a "what's it all for?" attitude. The existentialists, in particular, have noticed the increasing complaints of meaninglessness suffered by psychiatric patients. Indeed, the existential theme of Victor Frankl, for example, is that the search for meaning is the prepotent drive of humans.* He says, "Man's search for meaning is a primary force in his life and not a secondary rationalization of instinctual drives." He goes on to say that the meaning of existence is not invented by ourselves but rather something that is detected. Frankl points out that a poll conducted in France showed that eighty-nine percent of the population polled admitted that they needed something "for the sake of which to live."

The Primal assumption regarding meaning is as follows: *There is no meaning to life, only meaning to experience, which is life in process.* I think that the search for a meaning to life is only a neurotic prerogative, which began when the young child was

* Victor Frankl, *Man's Search For Meaning*, Beacon Press, Boston, 1963, p. 99.

forced to change the meaning of what he saw and felt in order to survive.

The Primal definition of neurosis connotes that the child suppresses the meaning of his life with the unconscious hope that through his struggle he will find a more palatable meaning. His search will be endless, because he has not felt the true meaning of his early existence. As he grows older, the *search* often *becomes* the meaning of his life and, frequently, there is scarcely any hope by the person of finding a definitive answer. The *answer*, in fact, is something to be avoided, because it tends to eliminate the struggle to find it. The real answer must also be avoided because, in the end, that answer means Pain. To feel Pain, then, is to rediscover meaning.

Meaning, in the Primal view, is *articulated feeling*. Life is its own meaning. The more deeply one feels, the deeper the meaning of his life. To be unfeeling is to be meaningless. Robots may be able to think better than men, but they are forever doomed to meaninglessness because they do not feel. Unfortunately, too many neurotics have been robotized by parents who would not let them feel.

I would disagree with Frankl's "will to meaning," because I believe that only those who have lost personal meaning are the ones who search for it. Post-Primal patients, for example, rarely are concerned about meaning, and even less so about philosophic concepts. The philosophic question that the neurotic often puts to himself about the meaning of life is but the sophisticated transmogrification of the more personal *psychologic* question, "What is the meaning of my life?" The normal person, in my opinion, feels the meaning in each of his experiences and is not trying to derive from them a special meaning that doesn't exist. The paradox of the neurotic is that when he lifts the question of meaning to a philosophic level, when he makes it a cerebral, intellectual pursuit, he insures not finding an answer—the answer which I believe lies only in being able to feel.

The neurotic tends to ward off real meaning in preference to an assigned, unreal meaning, because each real meaning is connected to his Pain and is automatically deflected. It is spontaneously supplanted by pseudo-meaning. When someone says to the neurotic, "You look nice today," it is instantly rejected, because it may be linked to, "No one ever thought I looked nice enough to be loved or thought I was totally presentable." Instead of accepting the compliment and saying, "Thank you," it is rejected with, "Oh, I really don't look so nice today." The real meaning is not felt. Another example: a conventional therapist, during one of his sessions, may make a meaningful and accurate interpretation of his patient's behavior. The patient takes up the insight with alacrity and explores all the possibilities of it; that is, he "works it through." If, as a child, this patient had to be smart to be loved, for instance, he might be using all of his intellectual faculties in order to be smart for the doctor and feel loved. In this way, he may convert a potentially meaningful insight into a meaningless ploy. He may do this to keep from feeling the self that could not be loved without a show of brilliance. Meaning, in this case, is warded off by the Pain. Meaninglessness, then, becomes the defense against meaning. Psychotics are often obsessed with meaning, preoccupied with the meaning of someone's facial expression or the specific words he used—looking for meanings in them that he cannot feel. Or, better, making those contrived meanings work for him to cover what he cannot feel.

The person who does not feel lacks a meaningful existence, even if he has been to India and conversed with gurus, found God, or has a Ph.D in philosophy. Meaning is *not* something to be detected, *not* something to be discovered by wise men, *not* something that overrides life, but, instead, is something embedded in the life processes of each of us. I do not believe that any ritual, cant, chant, or litany can enhance a meaningless life. Nor would I say that conventional psychotherapy, even a therapy that discusses meaning as its central technique, can make the neurotic feel any more meaningful. I would suggest, moreover, that the neurotic tends to get involved in more and more activities in order to feel a meaningfulness. And if each new activity still does not produce meaning, he may be forced to attend more functions, make more plans, set more courses, join more organizations, or go to more parties.

In a society that stresses production of goods and not feelings, getting the job done regardless of how one feels about it has become our *summum bonum,* and thus many people can get the job done yet feel that what they do has no meaning to them. One patient, at the beginning of his therapy, told me, "I have a fascinating job. It's too bad it doesn't interest me."

Some intellectual neurotics tend to be drawn to philosophy *because* it contains no definitive answers. They don't seem to want anything to be real and final. They prefer seeing all sides to everything, to hedge and equivocate so that they can go on searching forever. It is unfortunate that most extant forms of psychotherapy have tended to keep patients in this search. Some forms of therapy have been mildly veiled philosophic-theologic systems in which the therapist becomes the expert on how to lead a meaningful life. Because these therapies offer no final solutions and tend to equivocate, some neurotics feel comfortable in them. They never have to forgo hope of a salvation that is always just around the corner. The nature of psychotherapy itself tends to prevent the very feeling of hopelessness and finality, which could, in my opinion, produce a meaningful life.

Many forms of existential therapy concentrate specifically around the question of meaning. Frankl states that neuroses "do not emerge from conflicts between drives and instincts but rather from conflicts between various values . . . from moral conflicts . . . in a more general way, from spiritual problems." Frankl, therefore, deals with his patients in spiritual terms. He says that spiritual issues are taken seriously instead of being traced back to unconscious roots and sources. Part of the here-and-now approach of the existential therapies is to deal with the meaninglessness in present terms—in the context of present situations. As Frankl puts it, "to pilot the patient through his existential crises." The therapy, then, "regards its assignment as that of assisting the patient to find meaning in his life . . . to make him *aware* of the hidden *logos* [meaning] of his existence." Being intellectually *aware* of one's existential void does not, in my opinion, help someone feel. On the contrary, being aware helps to cover the void.

Frankl has much more to say about meaning. For example, he believes that the search for meaning arouses tension, and that this tension is an "indispensable requisite for mental health." This, essentially, coincides with the predominant existential thinking, namely, that tension is the result of the gap between what one is and what one should accomplish in order to become. The existentialists believe, in general, that struggle for meaning is of the essence. To quote Frankl again: "What man needs is not a tension-less state, but rather the striving and struggling for some goal worthy of him." Again, my view is that this struggle for meaning is by definition neurotic. That tension is what *blocks* the attainment of meaning [feeling]. I do not believe that meaning can be given to anyone, not by a parent, a child, or a therapist. I would suggest that the attempt to derive meaning through others—of a parent trying to find the meaning of his life through his children, for example—is a vain exercise. It is my clinical experience that those who lost some of the meaning of their lives by deferring constantly to the desires of parents unconsciously expect again to recapture that meaning by having someone, a therapist in this case, tell them how to live and what to do. Sometimes therapists get caught up in this expectation and exhort the patient to try this or that, go here or there.

Because I do not think that meaning can be dealt out by wise men, Primal Therapy does not deal with meaning, as such. It neither exhorts nor suggests what should be done. In this sense, it is nihilistic. Its sole reference point is what the patient is feeling inside, not what he should be doing tomorrow.

It is a lonely discovery to find that there is no meaning to life, and I suspect that the post-Primal "blues," which set in occasionally, have to do with this discovery. Some patients want redemption for their lives of misery. Their neuroses were in most cases an attempt to make a senseless life meaningful. They have spent decades, lifetimes, inventing meanings so they would have a reason to go on struggling. Thus, Christmas and Thanksgiving take on special significance by offering supposed occasions of deep meaning—"We're a real family," "I belong somewhere." Depression often results when the neurotic tries to extract meaning from an event that is essentially meaningless. In most cases, there is no real family.

Neurotics need to believe that there must be some metaphysical reason why they are on earth, some end or order that will transcend the purposelessness and chaos they feel all the time. They are willing to believe in almost anything to avoid the knowledge that the only reason we live is because we are alive—no more, no less.

I think the neurotic is particularly desperate and clings to religion, philosophy, or psychotherapy because he feels that life is short and death lurks; he senses that he has never lived and doesn't know how to live. He must believe that there is a greater reason for his lifeless, dull existence beyond working and sleeping every day. He must believe that there is a better life somewhere else, even if it is in the hereafter. He is willing to trust others to lead the way because he gave up the only real answer years before—himself. Primal Therapy restores that self to him.

18 On the Difference Between Intellect and Intelligence

In Primal terms, neurosis means that aspects of consciousness are blunted, that consciousness is diminished because of Primal Pain. Intelligence, in the Primal sense, is to have an open consciousness —to be totally free to see what is; to feel what you think and think what you feel. It means having full use of one's thinking faculties. Neurotics can be intellectual, but not intelligent. They can accumulate facts and figures, or even knowledge of the world, but they cannot use what they know to live an *intelligent* life, which, in Primal terms makes them stupid. What does *"intelligent"* life mean? If we think of it in terms of animal life, the answer would be apparent: intelligence means the ability to survive—to stalk prey for food, to hide from predators. The answer should be little different with humans. What good is it to "know" a great deal when that knowledge does not help in survival? To be intelligent means to know one's needs and to know how to fulfill them. To be neurotic, however, means not to know one's needs or how to fulfill them. What good is it to be a professor with wide-ranging knowledge of the universe when one cannot maintain a steady relationship with other human beings, when one ruins one's children and finds himself divorced time after time? How intelligent is a person who travels around lecturing on children while neglecting his own children? What is intelligence if it cannot help one to feel content?

Several forces conspire to make the neurotic stupid. First, there are the infantile Primal Pains, which blot out major areas of consciousness—traumatic birth, traumas in the crib, and other pre-verbal painful experiences. These repressions affect later thinking even though they occurred before a child could conceptualize; they affect the ability to conceptualize freely. Anything that reawakens an early hurt or the fear—having to read before a class, for example—will scramble thinking, because the Pain will be overwhelming. Second, there are crucial scenes early in a child's life when the *meaning* of incidents and experiences begins to become clear to him. These are times when many previous disparate experiences crystallize and begin to take on specific meaning—"I'll never be good enough." These realizations are so catastrophic that they are shunted away from full consciousness before they can be recognized. To be fully aware, then, would mean to have felt devastating realities. So again, aspects of consciousness are denied. The experiences of the child are fragmentized, and though he may learn a great deal about isolated events, about rocks or the moon or about trees, his consciousness is nevertheless selective, specialized, and compartmentalized.

The third force conspiring to make the neurotic stupid derives from his inability to trust his own ideas when he knows them. Even though he is unwilling to accept certain religious ideas when young, he may later have to, in order to keep the love of his parents. If he thinks out loud, "I hate my teacher," he may again have to substitute different thoughts if his parents admonish him not to say anything if he can't say something good about people. In this way, he will have to deny reality to feel loved, and sooner or later this denial, his "selling out" of his intelligence, will become automatic. He will have to think unreal thoughts to keep from feeling his Pain.

As the child becomes split by his Pain, he will develop philosophies and attitudes commensurate with his denials. He will have a warped view of the world. Having a scatter-brained mother may lead him to the idea that women are not to be trusted, or to a philosophy based on the subjugation of women. Thus, intellect becomes the mental process of repression in the same way that the body constitutes the physical armor against feelings. To feel the truth, "My *mother* is a hateful, unloving person," is to stop the neurotic generalization process to all women. To feel the truth is to liberate intelligent thought about women in one's present.

So one's early awareness is shaped by Pain. Repressing Pain limits awareness, and feeling Pain liberates and expands it. A person can be erudite in terms of understanding philosophical writings, but he will be stupid in the Primal sense until his own philosophy grows out of his body. We understand now why it is so difficult to change a neurotic's ideas with facts, reasoning, or even counseling. He needs his ideological padding, and he will incorporate into it whatever he needs to strengthen it. He will study, refine, and select his information so that his views and his intellect *do not change.* He will not learn by experience until he is free to experience what is real—himself.

A philosophy doesn't have to be formalized. It can lie in how one *feels* about war, militants, sex, or national goals. To deny one's own weakness because there was never anyone strong enough to offer protection may require developing a philosophy about the necessity for strength and power. To deny the need for help may lead to derogatory ideas about those who ask for it. What all this means is that ideas flow from feelings. Straight ideas flow from a straight system, just as warped ideas flow from blocked inner reality. To block a need for fatherly warmth may lead someone to believe in genetic bisexuality or homosexuality. But feeling the early fatherly deprivation will lead to radical changes in one's ideas about this subject.

The more reality a person is forced to hide in his youth, the more likely it will be that certain areas of thinking will be unreal. That is, it is more likely that thought process will be constricted so that generalized extrapolations cannot be made about the nature of life and the world. Conversely, to be free to articulate one's feelings while growing up will lead to becoming an articulate, free-thinking person, unhampered by fear, which paralyzes thought.

What are ideas, after all, but symbols of reality. The truly "bright" individual can see the truth in symbols, but the "stupid" person (who can even be an erudite intellectual) can only manipulate these empty symbols and will be forever plagued by an inability to "understand" anything. Of course, it is possible to *learn* a correct idea from a book—sex is not dirty—but an idea will not help one to function in a real way until it grows out of inner experience. Ideas in the neurotic are something apart. They are unanchored, floating in the mind, unattached to the system in any real way. That is why one can have perfect ideas about child-rearing and still be a poor parent. Or one can know how smoking causes cancer, but still continue smoking a pack a day. The smoker is stupid, because though he knows facts, he lives an unintelligent life.

A young child can split from his feelings and learn every aspect of engineering. He can be a "smart" engineer or scientist even while what he is developing can be used to wipe out civilization. His brains can be corrupted in the same way that his brains were corrupted in order to make him neurotic. His intellect is something apart from his feelings, so that it can be used in a most anti-feeling, anti-human way.

Intellect, then, is an abstraction produced out of fear, while intelligence is a unified body-mind experience. To be unneurotic is to let go of the unreal world of the mind.

We can see how anxiety affects intelligence in terms of the difficulty some neurotics have in concentrating. One patient expressed it this way: "I could never be smart because I could not concentrate. I couldn't study a road map without becoming flustered. Everything was too much. I felt so agitated that my mind seemed to be flying around all the time. Half the time I was so busy daydreaming to make myself happy that I couldn't think about anything else." Pain is distracting. It keeps one's mind from being totally on any one thing for any length of time. That is why one can read the same paragraph five times over and each time discover that the mind has floated away in a fantasy. Similarly one may need to have instructions repeated over and over.

Neurotic intellect is an order superimposed on reality, which is why neurotics continually have come up with neurotic psychotherapies. Neurotic intellect is subject to indoctrination and brainwashing—because neurosis *is* brainwashing. So long as the neurotic has lost his full internal frame of reference, his mind can be swayed by false ideas and inaccurate systems. So long as he is neurotic, his judgment will be poor; he will not be able to use his intelligence to know how to act in any given situation. He will be seduced by his needs so that those needs supersede judgment. He will be cheated and fooled, because he is not free to see objectively the kinds of people with whom he is dealing. He will become overly hasty when someone dangles fulfillment of need in front of him. Or he will be overly fearful when he should be taking certain decisive steps. He is truly a specialized man, living in his head because his body is out of touch and reach. He will deal with each piece of news he hears as an isolated event, unable to assemble what he sees and hears into an integrated view. Life for him is a series of discrete events, unconnected, without rhyme or true meaning.

Often, when the neurotic is split, he does not flee to his head. Instead, he may become "dumb" so as to not know what is going on in his life. The defense he chooses will depend in some measure on what the parental needs are. If they need someone naïve and weak who can be controlled, then the child may become unthinking. He may flee to his body if they need an athlete. If they place high value on intellect, he may take to his mind and become a mathematician and become lost in abstractions. This does not mean that intelligent people cannot be mathematicians. Rather, it means that math may become the defense of the neurotic; the more abstract it is the better. The super-intellectual is acting-out being smart, while the benighted person acts-out being stupid. It is analogous to the turned-off person who acts-out being lively (demonstrating evidence that he is still alive), versus the turned-off person acting-out being "dead."

One sees dramatic changes in the uses of a person's intellect after Primals. One research worker during a Primal finally confronted his therapist in group (and then his father in his mind) and begged for love. His connections were, "I could never ask my father for love directly. I thought I had to *earn* it. So I got smart. It was my way of asking." Afterwards, he was no longer the eager worker, anxious to publish and "show the world." Another person who was an intellect had a similar Primal: "Explain it to me, Daddy, so I won't have to figure everything out for myself." Whenever he asked his father a question, the father answered, "Figure it out for yourself. It'll build your character." So he stopped asking, got smart, and compulsively tried to figure everything out for himself. He wouldn't think of asking directions to a place while driving. He'd roam around acting smart, seeing if he could get somewhere without help.

Another patient had a Primal in which he was in the crib and being jostled and picked up and then put down time after time. He didn't know what was happening to him, and a later Primal was, "I've got to figure out what's happening to me or I'll get hurt." So he, too, filled his head full of irrelevant facts, became a psychologist to figure out why people do what they do to others. He developed a set of ideas in his psychotherapy (called a "theory") which did not change in over a decade of doing his work. He learned in Primal Therapy that his ideas could not change until the feelings that drive those ideas changed. He could never, for example, get past the notion that psychotherapy is a process of "figuring out" things for the patient, until he felt why he had to "figure out" everything in life—instead of letting it be.

This same person had another interesting Primal after he started doing Primal Therapy. He was having trouble with a patient who could not get to his feelings for several days. The therapist began to feel "dumb." The worse the patient did, the more stupid the therapist felt. He made mistakes by intellectualizing and acting smart with his patient. Then the therapist had his Primal. He felt that there was no way to be smart in this therapy as he had been most of his life. He could not "figure his way out" of the problem as he usually did. He had had to be smart for his mother most of his life, and being himself meant being dumb. He finally felt that to be himself was all he could be . . . *that* was being smart. Before, he denied himself and *acted* smart—which was stupid, in the Primal sense.

Neurotic societies further the dichotomy between the mental and the physical. There are physical workers and mental ones (white-collar and blue-collar workers). In the popular mythology, laborers aren't supposed to think or use big words, and intellectuals do not perform physical labor. Both, being split, may be exploited so that their brains and brawn are used and corrupted in the service of the system. The division between mental and physical workers means that an intellectual can study and work at something, coming up with solutions that have no relevance to real people. The worker can remain at a mindless job, never using his brain at all. In a real society there would be no dichotomy, no split between the body and mind worker. Intelligent people would not tolerate a neurotic, split society. They would not be content to work at unthinking jobs. I believe that the neurotic split has been the reason that a truly psychobiologic psychotherapy has not been discovered heretofore. Mental workers (psychologists) have tried to find "mental" solutions to problems that were psychobiologic.

Why is it that post-Primal patients become intelligent as a result of their therapy? One key reason is that they can see the *connections* between events. What they see fits into a frame of reference. A good deal of their previous thoughts and attitudes had been built on blocked feelings. To remove the blocks is to pull away the foundation for those ideas. Thus, the way is paved for the quick formation of new kinds of thinking based on reality. One patient, who previously saw Peace Corps service as a "humanitarian" enterprise, clearly saw it for what it was for him—an effort to get others to love him. After several Primals dealing with this theme of "service to others," he came to understand the dynamics of his job as a social worker in a black ghetto, as well as understanding the reality of what such jobs mean to neurotic individuals. Writers with new insight into human behavior write with a fresh depth that did not exist previously. History students suddenly understand the reasons for wars and poverty because they have dared feel the "why" of things. Before, they may have been content to memorize dates of wars and economic depressions, believing they understood history when all they really understood were isolated facts. Probing below their own surface permitted them to probe the depths of other things. Feeling a new calm has allowed some of them not to be overwhelmed by problems of mathematics and logic. Anxiety doesn't immediately intercede when they have to think about something. They can absorb new data because their minds are not cluttered by the past. There is a new kind of creativity to their thinking because they are free to think in new combinations instead of the same old rigid patterns. They become "smart" because they have no stake in maintaining certain sets of ideas, which were really only defenses disguised as logic.

19 *Reflections on the Implications of Primal Therapy*

ON THE IMPORTANCE OF CONTEXT

I was talking to a patient recently who had just finished a Primal in which he had been thrashing about his playpen, kicking and screaming. He came out of it saying, "I feel so loose. Now I can really move my body." I remarked that certainly he had always known he could move his body freely. He had been a member of a growth center where body exercises were engaged in continually. What was so different? He said, "Sure, I knew I could move freely as an adult, but I never knew it as a baby." Until he felt what had constricted him in his past, until he felt those scenes where he was constantly being told to sit still, and could finally move around *as that baby,* his body was bound.

One other example: A homosexual patient had had hundreds of transient sexual experiences as an adult. What turned him on was to have his chest rubbed. He believed that his chest was his key erogenous zone. During a Primal, when he was deep into an early need for his mother, I put my hand on his chest. His body plunged into spasms of Pain as he experienced that great early need to be soothed by his mother. His insight was, "I've been touched on my chest by lovers a thousand times. I always thought it was a sexual feeling. After I felt that surge of Pain during my Primal when you touched me, I realized that all that previous sexual feeling was just Pain traveling to my cock." Until he felt the touch *in context,* any touch he received as an adult produced *blocked* feelings. That is, his sexual arousal upon being touched by a lover wasn't feeling; it was a diverted sensation. Early feelings were blocked and rechanneled to the genitalia *just so* that Pain, hence feeling, could be avoided.

Until Primal contexts are experienced, almost everything is a substitute for the real thing. Food, sex, money—all are used to quell feelings and are therefore ultimately unfulfilling. That is why homosexual relationships are often so transitory, why someone needs more and more money, power and prestige. That is why we need more and more compliments or attention. Someone can say one negative word after offering a host of compliments, and what will stick in the mind is that criticism. That is because the criticism set off the Primal context—that is, the real feeling of the person—and compliments are only transient tranquilizers keeping the feeling at bay.

What this means is that Primal memories preserve the body in its rigidity, ramrod posture, frigidity, etcetera, until they are brought to consciousness; not adult, intellectual consciousness, not the analytic insight consciousness, but one that grows out of liberated Primal memories . . . a consciousness that arises out of feelings. Adult neuroses are embedded in those encapsulated memories, and *they* are the context for neurotic behavior. Getting one's "head straight" is only partially helpful, because it is the "adult head" that is getting straight. So even when one adopts new and healthy sexual attitudes, the Primal memories keep the body frigid. The old unhealthy attitudes don't leave when we adopt new ones in adulthood. They are just covered over. The old attitudes remain inaccesible to consciousness because they are shrouded by Pain.

We can see how useless the confrontation and encounter therapies are. While the therapist is operating in the present, the patient is living out of his past. Though the patient is expressing anger at his peers in group therapy, his real anger is toward his parents. Expression of current anger, then, is unresolving, because it is out of context. Until the therapist understands and deals with the context, he is entangled in the symbolic, derivative labyrinth of the patient's neurosis. He is helping the patient stay sick while going through the motions of getting him well.

The context is what is real in us. No radical change is possible without dealing with it. Liberating the blockage of feeling produces non-neurotic, feeling adults. The dialectic is that the more we feel of our childhood, the more adult we become, and the more we can enjoy things as adults. The less we feel of it, the more it is preserved, the more force it has in our adult actions, and the more it must be tranquilized in some way. Being the baby frees the adult.

ON REGRESSION

The notion of regression has been used in psychology since the time of Freud. Generally, it means a return to earlier, less mature behavior. A regressed person is infantile, dependent, and often unable to take care of himself. In psychoanalysis, it is considered a sign of mental illness. So, let me state my thesis: there is no such thing as regression as psychologists have known it.

I became interested in the concept of regression after lecturing to professionals and running into a recurrent theme that they brought up, namely, "Isn't it possible to regress someone back to infancy in Primal Therapy and have them never come out of it?" These professionals point out that psychotics are usually infantile and unable to take care of themselves, and isn't that what we are bringing about?

I believe that neurotics are regressed all of the time. That is, they have never *progressed*. They act-out their little selves only they aren't conscious of it. The defense is grownup behavior. We are *symbolically* mature, while in reality immature or childish. Our early feelings are with us each minute, stored as memories exerting their force, and ready to emerge as soon as the unreal, symbolic, grownup self is removed. It isn't as though we go back in time and become children. We go to what is real *now* in our systems—those little-child feelings. We do not regress people; they are already there.

The best evidence I know for this assertion is found in dreams. As soon as our conscious defense is weakened in sleep, we become the children—we are back in our childhoods, in the old neighborhoods, old schools, etcetera. Do we regress in our sleep? That would not be an accurate way of putting it. We go to what is real. The same procedure occurs in hypnosis. We can do age regression and take someone back to the age of five, let us say. He will feel five because what happened to him then is in the memory bank. I recall that years ago I used hypnosis to take deep slivers out of my children's hands. Once, when my son was eight, I hypnotized him and brought him to memories at the age of five. I brought him out of it and told him to go to bed, since it was late. I inadvertently forgot to tell him that he was eight. He couldn't find the bedroom; when he was five we lived in a different house. This is no doubt the kind of thing that professionals wonder about when Primal patients go back in time.

But there is a very important difference between hypnotic regression and Primals. In hypnosis, consciousness is narrowed so that the person is disconnected from his later experience. That is, he *is* five years old. In Primals, consciousness is expanded so that the early memories are finally *connected.* The reason that a psychotic has been considered regressed is just because of that kind of hypnotic disconnection. The psychotic has not been able to create a mature, socially approved defense. He is totally the child. Consciousness is the key factor that allows people to mature. Disconnection keeps us in the past.

The dialectic of growing up is feeling little. The person really stuck in his past (regressed) is the well-functioning, encased neurotic who has no access to his childhood. The problem thus far has been that professionals have seen patients act immature and childlike and have concentrated on building up defenses against it. They helped cover the one thing that would have insured maturity—feeling. Neurotics appear mature because their symbolic self acts that way.

In Primal therapy, we take away the beard, cigar, and the sophisticated front, and help a person feel small, unimportant and helpless. Anything that removes conscious defenses elicits the child. Hypnosis and sleep do it. And psychosis is no more than a state that happens when someone cannot create the symbolic behavior appropriate to a culture. The only way someone can get stuck in his childhood is when he doesn't feel it. In short, there is no such thing as regression in mental illness. Regression really means "Primal State." When it is felt, it is gone. When it is not felt, it is symbolized and remains.

SYMPTOM FORMATION

A tensionless body will last a lot longer. We may have to re-think man's life-cycle and add decades to it if my assumptions are correct. I had an insight into this the other night during a nightmare, a recurrent one I've had for thirty years. The content is not relevant here. What happened was that during the nightmare I was open enough to make the correct connection of the terror, had a Primal in my sleep, screamed and thrashed about, had dozens of insights, and then woke up. My heart was still palpitating from the Primal. What happened before, perhaps once or twice a month, was that I would have the nightmare with palpitations that would wake me up; I would feel terrified, wait a while, and fall back to sleep. I knew that my system couldn't take those kind of trip-hammer palpitations for too many years before they turned into a coronary. As I had more Primals and my system opened up, I could finally make the connection to the source of the terror. I had resolved my recurrent nightmare. If I had remained blocked, then one day that assault on my system would have finished me off, and nothing I could have done (except having Primals) would have prevented it.

I want to discuss this same night from another aspect. For the week prior to the nightmare I had been having root-canal work on my teeth, and I had to take Demerol for pain. I went off

Demerol the day before the nightmare. I know now that going off
the drug produced the nightmare. This leads me to think that
painkillers and tranquilizers are the most dangerous of drugs. By
suppressing the Pain all during the week, I had built up a pressure. When I went off the drug, a rebound effect occurred in
which all the pressure-pain was released at once in my sleep. My
system could not integrate all the Pain, and so symptoms, palpitations, were produced. Fortunately, I was open enough so that I
could connect the Pain to consciousness, and experience a Primal.
The nightmare resulted because all the Pain released at once
could not be immediately connected, and so I had to symbolize a
portion of it. That is, the body was processing the pain; the mind,
unable to properly connect, rationalized the dream story into
something symbolic. So long as the experience remained unconnected, and therefore symbolic, it could never be resolved and
would occur again and again until I would have had my coronary.

The reason for the buildup of pressure was in part due to the
fact that during an ordinary non-drug week I could have minor
dreams that would slough off some of the tension. These dreams
might be frightening, but they would not be nightmares. It is for
all of these reasons that I believe tranquilizers and painkillers
both hasten death and, in the meanwhile, exacerbate mental illness. Indeed, they do calm the person, make him feel better, and
often reduce his hallucinations and delusions (that is, reduce his
need to symbolize temporarily), but a rebound effect builds up
that makes the person, when off drugs, more symbolic than before. This is because one cannot eradicate truth; and the truth of
the neurotic and psychotic is his reverberating circuits of Pain in
the body. Death is the price we pay for holding down this Pain.

One other example comes to mind about this, which will, I
hope, help us understand symptom formation. During his last
month of therapy, a patient wanted to hurry his therapy along
and took a small amount of LSD without consulting his therapist.
He was flooded with Pain. His body, unable to absorb such an
inundation, produced a sharp pain in his stomach, which did not
go away until months later. He went to a physician and was diag-

nosed as "pre-ulcer." He took antacids, stomach relaxants, all to no avail. He also continued having minor Primals. Then one day, months later, something triggered him off and he was ready to have a crib Primal. It dealt with the excruciating fright of no one coming to feed him, accompanied by terrible stomach gnawings and baby wails. He came out of the Primal symptom-free and has had no trouble since. He made his connection when his body was ready. Until that time, his body was saying that it was being flooded with more Pain than it could handle, and thus the symptoms occurred. The symptoms were specific. They were focused in the original area of deprivation and trauma. The LSD had unleashed in random fashion too many Pains to be integrated. They were focused in his most early and vulnerable area.

Physical symptoms result from an overload of Pain in the same way that mental symptoms, such as hallucinations, delusions, or nightmares, result. Both are signs that the system cannot handle the Pain, disconnects from it, and then it is felt as pressure, which moves into the mind and down into the body. The symptoms are the natural way we try to absorb the Pain in some way. If it cannot be connected in a Primal, then the *feeling* of Pain becomes the sensation of Pain, a pure pain felt in the body as a stab here and there. In a general way (and with plenty of exceptions), the depth of the repression is related to how deep the symptom occurs in the body. We have seen deeply repressed patients with colitis improve and then develop skin trouble when their feelings got closer to the surface. We have found stomach pains to move up into the chest, while those with hemmorhoids improve and then develop stomach trouble. Of course, there are target organs that are areas of special vulnerability or weakness, which continuously reflect tension states, so that any tension produces a symptom in that area.

I want to say more about my nightmare. Sleep does not necessarily signify unconsciousness in the Primal sense. Many people are far more unconscious walking around than post-Primal patients are in their sleep. For people who have had Primals, it is possible to integrate early Primal Pain while asleep through the medium of the dream. After all, the fact that I could connect, have insights, and be totally conscious of what transpired in my sleep during the nightmare means that there was a consciousness of the experience. That is, there was consciousness during my sleep. This means that in Primal patients there is a confluence of consciousness-unconsciousness; it is a continuum that sometimes makes it difficult to distinguish between the two states. There is a kind of merging of conscious and unconscious, and this is as it should be. For after Primals, everything that was unconscious becomes conscious, day and night, awake and asleep. Everything, in short, is accessible to consciousness. No mysteries of the body, no dreams that cannot be fathomed, no symptoms that cannot be understood (unless they are the rare, purely physical ones). I have found from my own Primals that my dreams and nightmares foreshadow Primals to come. That is, they first enter my conscious life in my defenseless sleep state. I may symbolize them at first and only have a nightmare, but one or two days later I will have the Primal. That is what a nightmare is—a Primal symbolized.

When it becomes clear to the general populace that Primal Pains kill, far too early in life, then the necessity for Primal Therapy for that populace will become a matter of conscious urgency. Society will have to gear itself to a widespread treatment program for the *real* killer—Primal Pain. Heart disease, strokes, kidney failure, and similar catastrophes—these are the results. These are the areas that finally succumb to that fantastic pressure that is Primal Pain. One has but to witness, or better still, to experience, that pressure in a Primal to realize what thunderous energy we suppress all the time and what a miracle it is that the human system can walk around with this pressure and *never know it!*

ON REDUNDANCY, COMPULSION,
AND RECURRENT SYMPTOMS

My wife sometimes accuses me of being redundant. I come home at night and often say something like, "Gee, I like this house. Let's try to pay off the mortgage and really *own* it." It seems trivial enough. Recently a developer decided to put in a large tract near us, and this may force us to move. It made me anxious. From the Primal I had about this, I felt that, "I've never had a real home, and now that I finally have one, I am being forced to move." That feeling, "I need a real home," was made up of a myriad of experiences of living in a place that I never felt was mine—where the idea of having what I *wanted* to eat for dinner (instead of eating everything placed in front of me) never once crossed my mind. I lived in "their" house. I was redundant in my ideas about my present home (wanting to really have it) because I had never felt and resolved that old feeling. The ideas about the need to own my own home kept revisiting me as often as that old feeling would intrude.

I still like my home, still need a real home, but I am not so inordinately attached to it. This whole situation gave me an insight into other kinds of redundancy, such as compulsions and recurrent dreams and symptoms. *They are all the same.* A person will have a recurrent headache as often as his Primal feeling revisits him, just as for the same reason another person will feel compelled to exhibit himself. A recurrent dream is again another aspect of the same phenomenon. And, indeed, stable neurotic behavior of any kind is held in its continuity by underlying unresolved Primal feelings. It is no miracle, then, to expect a cure of compulsions or recurrent symptoms when the underlying feelings are gone.

The notion about redundancy as it is related to Primal feelings helps us understand something about creativity. There are artists who have been making the same statement (in artistic form) for decades. They do not grow and change. Dixieland jazz players may play in exactly the same way for fifty years, for example. Though the times change, styles and ideas change, these artists continue living in the past. Perhaps there are good artistic reasons for this need to preserve a heritage, but the point is that these artists are redundant, hence often boring. Just because that redundancy is couched in artistic form doesn't alter the fact. Within this framework, the truly creative artist, the one who grows, is the one who is free from his past.

The function of the compulsive symptom (or compulsive idea, such as the one about owning my own home) is to tranquilize the feeling. One patient began reading books the minute he became anxious. The compulsion, in fact, works in the brain very much like an actual tranquilizer; the cerebral cortex is activated to repress feeling. Whenever I would begin to feel that painful feeling, "I never had my own home," instead of feeling it, I would develop the idea of owning my home. That idea tranquilized and suppressed the real feeling.

Compulsions can take the place of pills if they work well enough. That is why a man driven in his business or profession seems to get along so well. It would do no good to tell him to take it easy; indeed, taking him away from his work, or retiring him, removes his natural tranquilizer and leaves him more vulnerable to boxed-in tension and the subsequent coronary. Needing to have a list of phone calls received quells the feeling that no one wants us. Putting over big deals suppresses the feeling of unimportance. In one fell swoop, resolving the underlying Primal feelings removes compulsive symptoms, ideas, and actions.

ON LOSING CONTROL

One of the most frequent questions asked by prospective Primal patients is, "Isn't it dangerous to be so out of control?" This question is based, no doubt, on the fact that in Primal Therapy patients "let go"; they let it happen and do not try to control themselves. In order to answer the question about what happens when a person loses control, we have to pose another question: "Control of what?" The answer to that latter question is, "Control of one's 'self.'"

For neurotics, the loss of control means that the repressed self, the years of hate, sadness, and fear, will suddenly be unleashed. For normals, there is no problem. There would be no underlying Primal force, hence no problem about loss of control. Control is only an issue because we have grown up with psychologic theories that posit a kind of Dante's Inferno running around the unconscious, waiting for its opening. These theories have developed out of observation of *neurotics;* when neurotics lose control, all of the repressed force does come up, and it arises with such regularity that it seems to be something genetic or constitutional. The dialectic in the loss of control during Primal Therapy is that the more loss of control there is, the more *in control* the person becomes. Another way of saying it is, that control is easier because there is less repressed feeling there.

How did all this control happen in the first place? Why did we make control such a virtue? And why did we internalize so much of it? I am going to give a simplified answer. It has to do with need. When a society becomes organized in such a way that there is an elite, exploitive class, which feeds on the labor of others, then certain groups are not having their needs met while others in the elite are oversupplied. In order to keep the exploited members from expressing and securing their needs, control is necessary.

Control takes place in several ways. First, there is brute force; the imposition of punishment against those who demand their needs be met. This is a gross and very unsubtle way of doing it. The more subtle method is to convince those who need: one, that they don't; or two, that their needs are for something else. It is a diversionary tactic that controls the minds of the needy so that eventually they forget that they need or what they need. When they catch on to this diversion, brute force is called in once again.

In personal terms, we see this so often in people who no longer even know that they need help, would never demand or ask for it, and cannot even believe they deserve it. They decide early in life that their lot is a poor one, adjust to it and make no demands. So a secretary never knows that she could be anything else. The workers never even think that the factory in which they work for twenty years ought to be partly theirs. A child never even knows he should be held and picked up and cared for. In subtle ways, need is denied, suppressed, and altered. Instead of wanting to be held by mother, a man becomes promiscuously sexual. Instead of expressing one's dislike of parents, the child beats up other children.

The main point is control. Parental need automatically becomes the child's control. If a parent "needs" to feel respected, then the child must be "respectful," with all that entails. If a mother needs to be thought of as attractive, then the child may not say anything to the contrary without fear of loss of love. Thus in subtle interplay between needing parent and needing child, the child will lose in order to keep up the hope of future fulfillment of his need. If all children were given into their needs, there would be no acting-out of those needs symbolically (beating up one's peers) and no need for control. But because needs are rarely met, what has become the greatest good of our society? Control. Control of one's needs and feelings. Thus, a former First Lady is thought of as elegant, dignified, and poised because she did not break down at her husband's funeral. Not only do we acquiesce to control and deny need, we demand that control. We are most willing to stay in line, not demand or ask too much, if that means approval and love. The loyal citizen is one who works hard and does not complain, the one who would never take "charity."

"Ask not what your country can do for you," has become our national watchword enshrined. Who is the most patriotic? The one who negates himself the most. What greater control over the self exists than in the military—and there is where the young patriot is expected to go to demonstrate his patriotism. That control began early in life, when the child was shushed when he spoke or laughed too loud, given the "eye" when he was too exuberant and joyous, quelled when he was too mobile. Slowly the life in him was being crushed, replaced by control. Is it any wonder that he can grow up and stamp the life out of others in a literal way without regret or remorse?

What is the principal problem in the schools today? What is discussed most often in staff meetings? Control. What is the most supported psychologic research today? Behavior modification (control). What is one of the key indices for maturity in psycho-analysis? The postponement (control) of gratification. What do we do when a child wets his bed? Buy a machine that shocks him when he wets his sheets. What does a local mental hospital do when alcoholics take to drink? Shock them. What do we do when an exhibitionist shows himself on the streets? Counsel and demand control. "Law and order." Everywhere, in every institution, we are concerned with control, because everywhere we are depriving people of their needs. Without control there is no exploitation.

This does not mean that control is always overt. Watch any neurotic parent for just a few minutes and you will see continuous control, shushing, reprimanding, and disapproval. Seldom will one see this parent pick up and hug an acting-out child. Yet that is why he is acting-out. We all seem to be off in the wrong direction, racing to head off the results of deprivation instead of insuring that the deprivations cease. We do not seem to understand that none of the myriad and ramified problems I have discussed would exist if we were psychologically and socially to concentrate on meeting need. Primal Therapy is the opposite of control. It directs and addresses itself to need. Because it advocates loss of control in its therapy, Primal theory becomes a threat to the entire institutionalization of control.

Neurotic children are wild and in need of control because neurotic parents only understand suppression—having been denied their needs, they had no choice but to suppress themselves or live in perpetual agony of unfulfillment. They act-out their denials against their children, who then grow up and ask the question, "What happens when you lose control?"

More

The neurotic always wants more. What he wants more of depends on his symbolic needs. If he is an intellectual who has fled to his head, he will want more facts. If eating is his defense, he will want more food. Others want more money or power. It is never enough because a real need is being fulfilled symbolically instead of being felt for what it is.

I have been acutely aware of this in trying to explain Primal Therapy to intellectuals. No matter how much data is presented, they always want to know a little more. When a person cannot feel what is right, he is unsure of himself, and there won't be enough facts in the world to help him feel sure. So the intellectual gathers facts to cover his insecurity in the same way that someone gathers food around him in order not to feel empty and hollow inside. If a person has a Primal helplessness, he may be driven toward more and more control of situations in order to avoid the painful feeling. If the Primal feeling is powerlessness, then he will be driven toward power needs. "More" is the byword.

Both the boss and worker want more. Neither could ever feel satisfied if the basic feeling is dissatisfaction—of never having been satisfied by one's parents. If there were no excess wants, there could scarcely be the worker-owner struggles that exist today (probably, there would scarcely be owners). For no one would want more than he needed. No one would be interested in exploiting someone else. "More" is what drives a sick society— more profits, more buildings, more cars, more branch offices. It is not a matter of educating society to want less. Education cannot do that. It is a matter of having people feel what they really need. Then they won't have derivative wants. They won't want every person they meet to go to bed with them—which ought to eliminate much infidelity and the marital problems that go with it.

Parents won't want more and more respect (meaning fear)

from their children in order to quell their own feelings of being worthless. Politicians won't want more and more power to use against the people. Intellectuals won't spend their lives in the useless pursuit of facts for their own sake so as not to feel stupid, unimportant, and unwanted. Feeling the Primal need radically reduces all of the derivative wants so that life becomes simpler, less acquisitive, and more relaxing.

ON THE NOTION OF ULTIMATE JUSTICE

In Los Angeles recently, a bizarre multiple slaying involving five people produced some typically neurotic reactions from the public and in the media. At first there were great efforts to prove some kind of drug involvement on the part of the victims, and others tried to show that they were addicted to the occult. The underlying reason for all this, I believe, is the notion that people just don't die for no reason. Those people, somehow, had to deserve it. This is the analogue to the widespread idea that we don't suffer needlessly, that there must be some reason for it. And, more importantly, there must be some final justice and reward for all we've been through, even if it is in the hereafter.

Neurotics cannot accept death, and much less stupid death. They cannot believe that a stranger can come up to an innocent person and in a flash end his life for no reason, forever. It is difficult to believe that there is no justice, no one watching over us to even the score, no one to make up for our past deprivations. It is intolerable to think that we were beaten, ignored, and humiliated for no reason, and that nothing will ever change it. Neurotics must feel that they were unlovable to be treated so badly and *that* is the reason; because to feel lovable and *then* to be unloved is to feel the full brunt of the Pain. "You get what you deserve in this life," is the neurotic's theme song; what it should be is, "You get what you don't deserve." Believing that someone died for a good but mysterious reason is the analogy of the belief that good happens to you when you suffer and struggle. "Nothing comes easy," is another neurotic theme that parallels this. It all means that nothing bad happens if you're good, because if it did, then there would be no reason for anyone to be good.

ON WHAT IS LATENT AND WHAT IS POTENTIAL

In the psychiatric literature one continually reads "latent homosexual," or "latent psychotic process." In school reports one often sees, "John has great potential, which he is not using." So I'd like to state my thoughts about latent and potential as they relate to psychological processes . . . they don't exist. Nothing is latent. It either is or isn't. Sometimes needs and drives are unconscious, but they are not latent. They exist in strength, only they are not recognized. A need for a father is a need; nothing will make it stronger or weaker. Latent is usually meant to connote some weak tendency that can be brought out, given the right circumstances. But tendencies are always as strong as they are whether or not the opportunities exist to act them out.

The same is true for potential. Everyone has potential—if they weren't sick, they'd be well and do well things. They aren't well, so what's the point of talking about potential? Someone either is or is not at any given time. Potential is a meaningless phrase, because it talks about a state of being that doesn't exist. "John could be good if he weren't bad. John could be smart if he weren't dumb. John could be studious if he'd study." John also could be a girl if he didn't have a penis. The point is that John is what he is. It makes as much sense to say that John should settle down and be studious as it does to say he should be taller.

NEUROSIS AS SOMETHING PHYSICAL

I saw a Primal in a male homosexual yesterday that reemphasized for me how truly physical neurosis is. He was a man fairly far along in Primal Therapy. Suddenly, during group, he had a terrible pain in his face. He began clawing at his face, yelling,

"It's disappearing, it's disappearing!" His face was contorted. This went on for about twenty minutes. Then in one large up-heaval his face relaxed and it seemed to all of us to be a different face. As he came out of the Primal, he said, "I just lost my unreal fag face. It hurt to have a face that wasn't natural, only I didn't know it because unnatural became natural to me." And indeed, he had lost his unreal face. But the face was only ready to change after many smaller Primals, which chipped away at the unreal front. The change of face was a concomitant of a total psycho-physiologic change.

Though I could most often spot a "fag face" in the pictures patients send to me before Primal Therapy (or in men on the street, for that matter), it never occurred to me that this kind of characteristic face (and posture, for that matter) would go away with all the rest of the unreality. But then again, this is more evidence of the total physiologic nature of neurosis. The unreal "fag voice" and "fag gait" change, so there is no reason to expect the "fag face" to remain the same. The unreal face literally dissolves in the face of reality. It was something superimposed on the real one. Here we see how parental values and demands become lit-erally superimposed on our real selves—how the external and so-cial become something internal and organic.

THE UNREAL FRONT

I have stated that in neurosis the unreal front covers the real self. Dramatic evidence of how this happens was illustrated in some recent cases. One woman of thirty-five was taken into ther-apy because of sexual frigidity. However, in her third month of treatment she began stuttering so badly that she could hardly speak. She neglected to tell us in her letter of application that as a child she had stuttered severely. Moreover, she had com-pletely forgotten it, since at the age of eleven she underwent the Van Riper method of stutter control. The Van Riper treatment was a complete success, so much so that her control became automatic and fairly unconscious. When we lifted her controls, the original speech problem came back with a vengeance. After getting to the feelings below the stuttering, it disappeared for good. In this sense she gained real control, although control would not be a proper term; she simply spoke naturally.

This case is instructive in several respects. Symptoms can be controlled, suppressed, and hidden, but that does not mean that they are eliminated. Control of behavior is spurious and ephemeral until the Primal force is eliminated, and it doesn't matter whether that behavior is stuttering, drinking, or violent outbursts. That is why we hear such canards as, "Once an alcoholic always an alcoholic." As long as someone is only suppressing his symptom, he will always suffer from the possibility of that symptom, just as that stutterer always had a latent speech problem.

Two other similar cases can be cited. A cultured English teacher came into therapy. She spoke in measured cadences, sophisticated and rather elegant. During her fourth week of treatment, I was doing her therapy in group one day when I noticed that she was talking in a deep Southern accent. This accent did not disappear in her therapy. She was reared in Oklahoma and always was ashamed of being an "Okie." She developed "cultured" speech to cover her real accent. When the unreal front slipped away, she became an Okie again.

Quite similar was a boy brought up in the New York slums who became an actor, also with cultured speech (or better, "cultivated" speech). During therapy, he often had trouble forming correct sentences. He felt more at home as that tough slum kid who spoke his feelings, instead of the actor who was putting up a sophisticated front.

Of course, it doesn't always work this way. I remember taking a German refugee into therapy. He had lived in this country for many years, yet had a thick accent. On the day he started treatment with one of the staff, I went on a one-month vacation. When I returned, I noticed that his accent wasn't nearly as deep. When I inquired about it, he remarked that he felt very alone in this country, and that one of the ways he had held on to his past was in his speech. As he eliminated the hold of his past and lived more in the present, his speech became more Americanized.

The unreal front is defensive behavior, which produces an alienation from ourselves. As I have noted elsewhere, it is a survival mechanism. But what is not usually understood is that the defense keeps the real self intact, thus aiding survival not only in its defensive aspects but in the way it preserves the self. For example, the real "Okie" self doesn't disappear because it is an embarrassment. It remains inside in pure form.

Getting straight, then, is not a matter of having straight ideas. Very sick people can have some very straight thoughts. Some psychiatric patients can say very straight things, yet what is lacking is the feeling that goes with those thoughts and utterances. Getting oneself together produces straight ideas, straight bodies, and natural speech. If we understand that the brain is connected, or misconnected, to the unreal front, then being well means proper neurological connections, which eliminates the necessity for that front.

ON PHOBIAS AND FEAR

There are tremendous fears early in our lives—being left in the crib unattended, being abandoned, being beaten severely. The most disastrous feeling as a little child is that there is no one who cares, no one who will be there; the total feeling of being alone and unprotected. The fear is catastrophic, becomes repressed and results in chronic anxiety. That is, it becomes a vague and diffuse apprehensive, tense state. This substrate of anxiety either remains vague and free-floating so that the person feels afraid much of the time with no tangible reason for it, or the fear is siphoned off into channels that are called phobias. Anxiety is the general pool which is fed by any number of repressed fears. The person then may develop an irrational fear, such as of elevators, and if it weren't elevators it would be something else. The phobia is being fed by the Primal pool. To deal with the phobia is just damming up the spillway. Until the basic fears are felt and removed, there will always be phobias or anxiety states. Anxiety *is* fear unrecognized, and phobias make the fear recognizable and, one hopes, manageable. It's fear translated into the present but in the wrong context.

One of the most common fears or anxieties is the fear of death. Perhaps there is a normal fear of death and perhaps there isn't. We shall have to poll more post-Primal patients to make sure. Thus far, I see little evidence of an abnormal fear of death in these patients. Many patients have come in with these fears, however, and I want to discuss their meaning. When a fear is triggered in the present, it is apt to set off an entire constellation of early terrors. One of the most significant early fears is engendered by the birth process (see Introduction to Birth Primals in *Anatomy of Mental Illness*). At birth many of us are literally in danger of dying—from strangulation by the cord, by a breech position, or by lack of oxygen. This sets off the most primordial terror of death, long before the infant can conceptualize it. Later on, the child and the adult may develop a horror of death that preoccupies his thoughts. His thoughts are being formed around an unconscious real memory, a real danger of death. When that real danger is felt in a Primal, much of the inordinate (the Primal *Anlage*) fear of death is lessened in the patient.

Of course, it is not just birth that endangers life. Not being fed on time, not being given adequate liquids, not being protected in the crib—all endanger life. These, too, form a residue of death-terror, buried memories which add to the later fears of death. Until the real threats to the child's life are felt, the person is filled with the imminence of death. So it is no wonder that he is preoccupied with it.

Politics in a sick society provides an illustration of how the Primal fear is manipulated. The politician tells the people they have good reason to be afraid; he focuses their fears on the "enemy," insists upon strengthening defenses, and promises to vanquish the enemy and allay fears if people vote for him. In other words, fear of blacks, militants, youth, communism, socialism, are socially institutionalized fears. Because the neurotic's fears never do go away, there is always a need for any enemy and a need to stay defended. If the neurotic can get a good, solid phobia going, such as of snakes or spiders, he may not need an enemy phobia.

Projecting fears, then, is the way neurotics can keep them ostensibly recognizable and manipulable. The person can avoid spiders, high places, and elevators. He can kill the enemy, but nothing the neurotic does will ever be enough; he will have to manufacture new enemies, whether they be spiders or Communists. The dialectic of fear is that the more one feels his fears, the more courageous he is—to be himself.

THE COLD WARRIOR

Ideas flow from feeling or their denial. This is another way of saying that the head is attached to the body and the notions in that head reflect in some way the state of that body. A simple idea such as, "I don't like to travel," may reflect deep fears of being away from home, fears of being in a world of strangers, and feelings of being a lost little boy, afraid of straying too far away. All of these feelings, derivative of thousands of early experiences, later help shape the notion the person has about the desirability of travel. Further, there is a consistency about ideas, a logical or illogical concatenation (an outlook or philosophy) bound by Primal feelings. I was aware of this when examining the various ideas held by the superpatriot or Cold Warrior. There is a remarkable consistency in his views. He wants immediate and single solutions. He does not see the value in cooperation; rather, he sees relationships in terms of power—dominance or submission, not equality. He is suspicious and cynical, and interprets moves by others as belligerent. He is hostile and rationalizes this hostility as necessary to meet the ubiquitous enemy against whom one must constantly be on the defense. He is unwilling to take a critical examination of anything, and rationalizes that those who do are "eggheads," soft-hearted intellectuals. He is against mental health programs for obvious reasons, and decries introspection as weakness, for the "bleeding hearts." He does not believe in complaining; he is tied to the virtues of loyalty and obedience— "Love it or leave it" is an apt slogan. He has few ideals and even less hope. He sees only the daily practicalities and dismisses theoreticians as fuzzy idealists. He believes in the maxim of hard work and competition. He is so torn by conflict that he cannot tolerate peace and harmony. He must believe in constant threat so as to justify constant defense. He suffers from socially institutionalized paranoia. He is a product of a sick society that does not meet his needs and convinces him that it is not government's job to do so. Nobody should have it soft. No one should have things just given to him without working for it. He believes in the struggle.

His destructive society provides him with an enemy whom he must fight, and he can be absolved of blame because he kills for it (society); he kills for abstractions such as patriotism. He sees violence and power as manly virtues, part of being a good citizen. All those not for him are against him; and those not over him are under him. Conciliation is traitorous. He is gullible while pointing the finger at others as "dupes." Those who need and demand are "agitators." Because he has no lever on himself and is removed from his feelings, he tends to be taken in by the appearance of things rather than drawing from depth analysis. He doesn't believe in giving in to feelings, and he praises institutions such as the military, where individuality and feelings are methodically stamped out.

He is terribly fearful and is reassured when his leaders tell him he should be; they direct his fear toward outsiders instead of helping him see it is inside. There really is an enemy; he is here, and if we stamp him out we won't have to be afraid any more. No matter how much protection he has, it will never be enough to quell his insecurity.

He is the reciprocal of the Cold War society. He is manufactured by it and in turn helps to maintain it. He is a danger because he has been powerless, often growing up feeling dominated and placing his reliance on the ultimate in power—the Bomb. Fear freezes his stance so that facts cannot change him, and even the threatened annihilation of humanity will not divert his monomaniacal tenacity to his ideas.

Denial is the key dynamic of the Cold Warrior. When he starts out being forced to deny all inner reality early in life, he must become unreal and adopt unreal ideas. No one gave him anything. He was made to work constantly while being told that it builds character. Having bought those irrational ideas to make his deprivation tolerable, he comes to believe in them. He is consistent in his denial of reality, because even one thread, one real belief might lead him eventually to what is real in him—his Pain.

What neurotic parents have done to the inchoate Cold Warrior is make him repress almost anything he feels. Repression becomes his modus operandi, and it is a small step from repression of what is inside to the reflexive repression of events outside. So, repress the agitators, militants, strikers, etcetera. A University of California study did, indeed, find that right-wing students were more sexually repressed and inhibited. This automatic repression makes the Cold Warrior deride permissiveness, whether in school systems or in family discipline. Things have to be tough to be good. We can see that it is no accident that for almost every problem, the Cold Warrior comes out with the most unreal solution.

A survey at Cornell asked students the following questions: "Which do you personally count on as the more effective deterrent against war, the atom bomb or the United Nations?" In addition, each polled person was given tests to measure his faith in others. Two of the items were: "Human nature is fundamentally cooperative"; "No one really cares what happens to you when you get right down to it." Those with little faith in others were called misanthropes. Seventy-seven percent of them placed their faith in the Bomb. These students were asked what the U.S. should rely on to prevent war. Sixty-two percent of these misanthropes said,

"Military power." They were three times more likely to expect constant war as in the order of things; twice as likely to doubt that war could be eliminated. Another study at MIT found that those who believe war more likely are more apt to use corporal punishment on their children. When one believes in and uses violence, cessation of even a Cold War makes him a warrior bereft.

Though the Cold Warrior feels weak he must never show it and must never allow others to. He believes in the front. He has bought all of the unreality because somehow he was convinced that he was loved. The ultimate denial is that there was no love. He rarely sees himself as unloved, yet eschews affection, particularly among males. "Little boys don't kiss their fathers. They shake hands." "Little boys don't cry and act like sissies." He often has displaced his needs into religion and onto God. He says, "Trust only God. He won't let you down." "He watches over you. He cares and protects." He does, in short, all the things the parents should have done but didn't. That's where the needs go— to a place where they can be safely expressed but can never be fulfilled, except in fantasy. A place that exhorts members to deny earthly pleasures, and themselves.

When the Cold Warrior finally feels his unlove, then all the philosophy based on its denial tends to crumble. No one has to talk him out of his ideas. They were held together by and evaporate with the Pain.

ON SPEECH

We all have characteristic speech patterns. For the neurotic, it is a good example of how he lives out the past each day of his life, how he unconsciously brings the past into the present. One homosexual spoke sibilantly until he had the Primal of trying to be "mother's little angel." He never felt that past as something separate before the Primal. His speech pattern was part of his neurosis of trying to be loved. He also walked like a little (fag) angel—buttocks welded together with hoops of steel while tread-ing on eggshells so as not to intrude too strongly into the world.

Each word of the neurotic recreates the struggle for love—trying to be a man with a low voice for Mommy, for example. If speech patterns are an integral part of the neurosis, then many speech problems are going to be solved automatically when the neurosis is dismantled.

Even how we form words betrays the neurosis. Some neurot-ics don't talk straight—they talk out of one side of the mouth, as though they cannot be direct in their speech. This is part of the split, where one side of the face is different from the other and one part of the mouth is dominant and takes on more of the burden of speech. Speech is an excellent index of what we are trying to be in order to be loved. Some of us are subdued in our speech; we were, indeed, subdued. Neurosis cannot be solved apart from speech. The post-Primal patient should not have the high, squeaky voice or the dead one, unless by some rare chance something is wrong with his vocal cords or he is in some way physically limited.

The voices of Primal patients drop dramatically. This is ac-counted for by two factors. The first, and most important, seems to be the sheer quantity of Pain inside. The voice drops as more Pains are resolved. We can understand this better if we visualize parallel lines drawn across the chest and abdomen. Each major Primal seems to drop the voice to a new level, as if the defense system worked in layers. The second factor is the quality of the Primal. One man had a dramatic voice drop after a Primal in which he felt himself shriek and scream as an infant when he was hungry in the crib. He knew at that instant that he had main-tained a high voice in the unconscious hope that somehow he would eventually be heard. His voice became fixated in infancy due to an unresolved trauma. The high, shrieky voice became an integral part of his developing defense system, a system designed to help him survive.

There are other dimensions to neurotic speech. One patient always ended his sentences on a higher pitch, as if each sentence were a question. He was terrified of being wrong, and his speech became a habitual way of avoiding declarative statements. He never took a position, even in the form of his speech. Halting speech is a variation of this fear of being wrong . . . checking out each word as it leaves the mouth, making sure it doesn't offend.

Babyish speech (lisps, etcetera) are clear indications that one has not left one's childhood behind. The past intrudes with every word spoken. Babyish talk is really an indication of how we act out our childhood unconsciously later in life. A well person has a natural, rhythmical speech. It is neither too fast nor too slow. It is like his gait or his physical gestures—an index of integration of body and mind.

AMBIVALENCE
Vivian Janov

There is a line in a recent movie where the adult son of an aging man says, "I hate my father and I hate hating him." The movie tells of a true generation gap. The father, suffering from the hardships of his own childhood, becomes an obnoxious parent who cannot be reached. Although the son understands his father, he can only feel his *own* feelings. This is the seed of *ambivalence* in all of us. It is the conflict between needing the love of parents and their inability to give that love fully. It is the conflict of *understanding* their pain but *feeling* your own. It is saying, "I know you had a rough childhood, but what about my needs?"

Ambivalence occurs when we begin to have one feeling about someone only to be bombarded by conflicting ones. For example, many of us agonize over what our parents have done to us, how cruel and thoughtless they were. And then immediately we understand them and their deprivations. The agony and the need is the child in us feeling; the understanding is the "guilty" adult who sees the reason for their behavior and sympathizes. Thus ambivalence is the conflict of feelings between the child in us who needs and the adult part of us who understands. However, the "adult" understanding *never* affects the needy child. That is why ambivalence goes on and on, so that a mature, gray-haired person is still in conflict over his parents.

The young child accedes to his parents' needs automatically, and as long as he does, he will not feel unloved or in conflict. As he grows older, he will become ambivalent when he understands that he cannot be what they want and still be himself. Someone is going to have to be hurt. The decision about who that will be is the source of ambivalence. The child, being himself, automatically means that a neurotic parent is going to hurt because he made this child into what he needed just so he would *not* hurt. The child had to be talented, polite, clever, or whatever so that the parent could feel loved. When the child is himself, the parent feels unloved. When the child must be unreal, his true self is unloved. That is the choice. Between the real and unreal self; between your need or your parents' need. The price of making a parent feel loved is neurosis!

In Primal Therapy, there is a "seesaw" of feeling toward your parents. At a crucial point, the seesaw comes to rest at, "I'm sorry you hurt, but I cannot change your life. I have found my real self and my real feelings, and nothing and no one will ever come before them."

ON CRYING
Vivian Janov

As I was driving home alone after group one Saturday, I began to think about all the crying the patients and I had done that day. My mind started a kind of free association and I thought of the reactions of outsiders to Primal Therapy: "How do you get people so broken down?" "Do they always *cry* so much?" "Is that *good* for them?"

Of course, anyone involved in Primal Therapy understands that crying is a by-product of feeling and reliving early childhood scenes. As these thoughts came to me, I focused on the act of crying in itself. To me, the body has always been a fascinating organization of perfect machinery. Every organ has its function and every act of the body is aimed at its homeostasis. We eat when hunger pangs come, drink when thirsty, and sleep when tired. Crying then, must also be a natural function of the body in its efforts to maintain. We cry in response to Pain, and thereby relieve tension. At that moment I felt completely tensionless . . . all cried out.

Then, I wondered why most human beings leave crying behind in their early childhood. They don't stop laughing, sleeping, or getting thirsty. Society cuts off the natural outlet of Pain: crying. Children are told they are too big to cry. They are never told that they are too big to laugh or smile. Parents shush our tears quickly, and we all grow up swallowing tears, having a lump in the throat, brushing a tear away—but rarely crying. Primal Therapy restores this ability and this function, and I realized that this *in itself* is therapeutic. Of course there are amazing insights, body and personality changes as a result of the therapy, but somehow the process of crying that is restored in the therapy seems to have been overlooked as a marvelous concomitant.

Conversations with Primal patients are just as likely to have crying as laughing in them. They will cry openly while attending a movie. Reading a letter, hearing music, or seeing Santa Claus may suddenly bring a flood of tears with no warning. There is something healthy about responding to the moment. There is something beautiful about it, too!

I couldn't help thinking that the population, in years of choking back tears, has created a bank of tension that has contributed to the mental and physical illnesses with which it is plagued.

ON WANTING AND CARING

If you don't get what you need when you're young, you will always want. If you get what you want when you're neurotic, you will always need. The only thing you can get out of Primal Therapy is feeling your needs, say, for caring. If you get caring in conventional psychotherapy without feeling the *catastrophic* need, then that need is frozen, buried, and becomes an encapsulated force driving wants thereafter.

The only thing that is real in neurotic adults is their needs. It is what is inside. Neurotics are never going to get their parental needs fulfilled. But if they feel their *wants* for them, they then can become feeling human beings who can get true love in the present from others. Until that blocked early need is felt, all current "love" and caring simply covers over feeling.

Neurotics struggle mightily to extract love in the present from those around them, and the reason that it is never enough is that the old unloved feeling remains to be fulfilled. The only gift a therapist can offer his patient is to help him feel that pain of unmet need. To fail to do that only leaves a therapist one prerogative: to redirect the symbolic effort—from stealing cars to studying law, from sexual drive to academic drive. Success in conventional therapy is usually adjudged in terms of how well that real drive has been socially channeled. Success in Primal Therapy relies on how deeply that drive has been felt and resolved. Need-drive is the focus of Primal Therapy; how one directs the drive is usually the focus of other therapies. Thus, one measure of success in conventional therapy would be, "The ability to engage in constructive productivity." The measure of success in Primal Therapy would be to *feel* how one had to be productive in order to feel loved. In other words, encouraging productivity in some neurotics is using the sickness for treatment.

Caring is not something transmitted through the airwaves from one person to another. Caring is seeing to it that the one you love has his needs attended to, whatever those needs may be. When a person becomes neurotic, his needs become transmuted and bottomless, and then caring becomes another matter. For caring, to neurotics, means endless attentiveness to sick wants—prestige, honor, respect, loyalty, etcetera. Because a person was not respected for his thoughts and feelings very early in life, the minute someone in adult life fails to show him respect, he is left to feel the early, unfelt disrespect. Thus, he must be in a constant struggle to get respect. So, his children may *never* be disrespectful without incurring his wrath. There can never be enough respect for this person. To feel that early humiliation and lack of regard for him on the part of his parents is to take all his drive for the (symbolic) respect away. Thus, he can be an easier parent, allowing his children to say their feelings to him without fear. He can be truly a caring person.

ON MARRIAGE

Marriage is just another relationship, formalized though it be, between neurotics. Neurotics will continue to act-out in their marriage, and it does not take a marriage counselor to help a faltering marriage; it takes a therapist. There is no such thing as having to "work at" a marriage. Normal people just are, and they let others be, which includes the spouse. Why should one have to work at any relationship? "Working at" means trying to be something you're not; when you "are," there is no need to "work at."

People inside a marriage are driven by underlying needs. Just because they are married does not change that fact. It is needs and Pain that distort marital relationships. Someone can say to a husband, "Look at how miserable you are making your wife by your infidelity! Can't you act more responsibly?" But what is often the case is that the infidelity has nothing to do with the wife. The neurotic may have married his "mother" and now is the little boy "playing around." He does not intentionally want to hurt his wife; he just wants to have fun or feel loved.

Why can't the love of a wife be enough? Because neurotics feel unloved, and no amount of current affection and appreciation is going to change that. A person may be unfaithful because of the unconscious hope of finally feeling loved. Or, growing older and seeing his lost youth ebb away, he may want to recapture an adolescence that never was. There are hundreds of reasons for just the problem of infidelity, and these are not "marital" problems, though they do cause problems in a marriage.

When problems arise, the partners often seek counseling. Counseling attempts to deal with the presenting difficulties or symptoms. It would seem that counseling is often one more evidence of the split—of the way we split up human beings. The marital counselor deals with the more superficial aspects of his clients, as though they were entities apart from the deep-lying feelings that drive behavior. I don't think that whole people can be divided up into specialties with efficacious results.

I can't think of a serious problem in marriage that isn't really a problem of individual neurosis. Counselors do not have the training to handle serious psychological difficulties. The rationale is that such training is not needed because the counselor "doesn't go deep." Every product of behavior in humans is tied to something deep. To deal with human problems is to deal with deep feelings. We may pretend to abstract surface behaviors to deal with, but this only helps the patient keep himself abstracted from those inner processes that are the core of his problems. Feeling people do not need to learn "how to" in marriage, as a rule, because marriage means two people living their own lives fully, making no inordinate demands on one another, not possessing each other and not depriving one another. Overpossession, inordinate demands, deprivation of sex and warmth are all signs of neurosis.

ON DEATH AND MOURNING

My father died recently. I took to bed and had Primals for four days straight. I want to discuss my Primals because it offers an insight into mourning. What I cried about was the father I never had. I was crying for me. That's all any neurotic can do when he is filled with Pain. Each day I felt an entire strip of feeling that was apart from any other feeling. One day it was,

"Say I'm good before you die." Another day it was, "Be my good daddy." Still another Primal was, "Don't go now. I still need you," and so on. Each feeling consumed hours of memories and new feelings and then insights.

When I finished with the four days, which left me so weak I couldn't get out of bed, I could cry *for him* for the first time—for the tragedy that was his life. Until my need was out of the way, no feeling of mine could be objective and external. After that cry for him, I have never cried since, nor have I mourned. It feels like it's over. Not that I don't remember it all with sadness.

Had I not had Primals to fall back on, I would have had a general depression and mourning that might have gone on for weeks and months. It never would have been resolved because I would have had no idea why I was really crying and mourning. I still needed a good daddy. I have described my Primals as "strips of feelings" because they came out so discrete and insular, like each feeling was a thread that one draws out of one's insides which brings with it all of the past that is relevant to that particular feeling. It may seem heartless and cruel to say that my first act after his death was to cry for me, but had no choice. I didn't will it that way. It happened that way because my needs took precedence over any other thing as they always do.

Later, I wondered how it felt for my father to know he was fatally ill, surrounded by all those doctors, being alone and frightened. I started to console myself that it wasn't so bad. After all, he was old. But I knew that this was rationalization. He was a scared little boy, bewildered by what life had come to for him, and he died in his childhood.

YOU CAN'T GO HOME AGAIN

In the morning paper was a story about the trams in Venice being retired after forty years of service. I grew up in Venice (California), and at first I had a "funny" feeling about the news.

Then I felt the feeling—one more piece of my past has been removed, insuring that I'll never have that past, no matter what. This led me to think about change, in general, both environmental and personal. It seems that for many neurotics there is an upset about changing the landscape because it unconsciously reminds us that we'll never get a crack at our missed childhood again. It must be similar to when we see those gray hairs, wrinkles, and bald spots.

I speak about a "missed" childhood in a dual way. First, many of us were so out of it, so unconscious and not there because of our anxiety, that we never truly experienced our youth. Secondly, youth for many of us was pure Pain, the helpless victims of parental whims and cruelties. It was too often filled with chores and duties and rigidified schooling, so that there was no happy, buoyant childhood to look back on. This is the essence of reminiscing. We can't let go of our past because we never had it. Someone who had a long and good childhood isn't concerned with reminiscences and longings. He isn't overwhelmed by change. He has had his childhood and has no need to recapture it.

VIOLENCE IN THE MEDIA

The prevalence of violence in our society, I attribute to neurosis. So many of us cannot be what we need to be and cannot get what we need from our parents that hostility and violence seem to be ubiquitous and universal human properties. When society witnesses a violent outbreak, such as assassinations of political figures, there often is a renewed interest in finding reasons. Instead of examining the interaction of human beings, however, we tend to look toward some current and tangible event upon which to focus, such as television or the movies. But the mayhem on television and in the movies is one more example of an outbreak of violence; both film and street violence are considered manifestations, not causations. Thus, reducing the *manifestation* of violence on television can have little effect on the acting-out of street violence. Altering television fare seems to be only manipulating the symptoms. Suppressing the symptoms may help us pretend that we are getting well, but the disease will remain with all of its original puissance. Though I am on record with a Senate subcommittee on television violence (more than a decade ago) as being against the showing of so much of it on television, I am now wondering whether it might not be a temporary expedient needed to drain off the hostility of a neurotic society. Certainly, it is less harmful than war. Perhaps through this vicarious draining process it actually helps reduce the possibilities of street violence. In any case, it would seem that violence in the media cannot instill hostility in viewers; the most it could be expected to do is channel already existing inner rage. One might quarrel, then, with the kinds of methodology of mayhem shown, but not with the fact of violence itself. I want to stress the point that hate cannot be instilled by preachings, exhortations, or by drama on the screen. Hate is a reaction to hurt. Without hurt I cannot see how someone could make anybody else feel continually angry at another person, race, or country.

As possible evidence for the Primal view of television violence as ameliorative, I cite the recent results of the legalization of pornography in Denmark.* It was found that after legalization, the quantity of pornographic material purchased and the number of sex crimes both dropped. I take this to mean that the greater exposure to something that is repressed in society lessened the need to act-out previously hidden feelings. This is to say, the more out in the open things become, the less the internal sickness.

I believe that the violence seen through our media is a reflection of the neurotic rage residing in a great number of people. How else can we explain the movie advertisements, which invariably show men fighting and killing? It would seem doubtful that multimillion-dollar movie corporations would gear their advertising toward violence unless they somehow understood the Primal principle that neurotics relate to and are interested in fulfilling their needs. These corporations invest huge sums in ad-

* *Los Angeles Times,* December 14, 1968.

vertising the violent aspects of what may be an otherwise innocuous film, because they understand that violence sells tickets. What these ads seem to do is offer the public *hope* of discharging what lies seething inside of many of them. The mechanism by which this is accomplished is "identification." The viewer "identifies" with the screen character, and thereby couples his internal feeling with the action of the characters on the screen. The drama (and dreams) becomes the rationale for the already existing, latent feeling. This is the feeling that drew the person into the theater in the first place.

The popularity of cartoons shown to *adult* audiences at the movies seems related to one monotonous theme: the big guy finally gets smashed, bashed, and outwitted by the little guy (the little guy being inside the viewer). It doesn't matter whether the little guy is a chipmunk or a rabbit. Anything that will allow the person to externalize his hostility seems welcome. Perhaps it is more suitable that the characters are animals. This means that there is nothing to figure out or wade through; there is no complicated plot. It is straight, unadulterated violence.

The fact that people continue to patronize violent movies and television shows seems to be an indication that they are hooked onto a feeling they cannot resolve. I don't think that what they see will harden them. In a strange kind of way, they may possibly become "softened." That is, they may rid themselves of some of their overarching and burdensome rage . . . in a sense, reduce their need to view and act-out violence. When someone has hardened himself against feeling because of unmerciful attacks by parents when honest feelings were shown, I don't think that all of the Disney shows ever made will alter that state.

I believe that sadistic movies act as a magnet for the hostile neurotic, drawing him back year after year, plugging him into one unreal connection after another, offering release for as long as he stays plugged in. The person may attend such movies for thirty or forty years and not alter his need in the slightest. In a sense, this is like most compulsive behavior, which is a search for just the right connection.

The moviemaker must take care, however, not to make his situations too ambivalent for the viewer, thereby confusing him. So far as I can see, the straight "motorcycle gang" fighting and brawling through ninety minutes of mindless violence seems to do well at the box office. The dramatic plot must be similar, in my opinion, to the neurotic's dreams, which are really personalized and tailored by the neurotic to suit his own denied feelings. Hopefully, the dramatic plot must be a carefully constructed, tension-building rationale for final release of hidden feeling. The plot must justify the anger in some way, to allow the viewer to obtain relief without guilt. One must keep in mind that Primal anger often exists because the person was *not* allowed untrammeled expression of feeling in his youth. Thus, in the movie he must feel "right" about the release. I have wondered whether it were possible to do a random sample of the dreams of a cross-section of people, factor-analyze them to extract commonalities of plot form and substance, and make a movie following those lines. It seems to me it would be a sure-fire hit. It would, in my opinion, take the guesswork out of moviemaking and help reduce the need for opinion surveys about what shows people would like to see. The best reference, it seems to me, is the type of show that people put on for themselves every night in their sleep. Would people put on the same show for themselves each night if they weren't interested?

There is a possible danger in violent movies for unfeeling children: the suggestibility of what they see. If a child is not permitted to feel at home, he may, in some instances, try to copy the kind of romanticized and idealized behavior he sees on the screen. If a child is allowed to act on his feelings, I do not see this as a danger. Suggestibility, in my opinion, occurs when a child grows up being forced to accede to his parents' will, so that he comes not to rely on his own feelings. And here, again, I want to reiterate my position that violent movies do not produce unfeeling, hard people. Only neurotic parents seem to do that.

There may be a high correlation of crimes of violence with watching television violence, and it might be tempting to suppose that watching television or movie violence somehow causes street violence. I think, on the contrary, that they are highly correlated because angry people turn to these programs and angry people commit crimes. I seriously doubt that if all violence on television, for example, were to be curtailed at once, that such a measure would make a dent in the angry feelings of neurotics, who would soon enough find substitutes.

To digress from the general topic for a moment: movies and television, too, are systems; or better, manifestations of an economic system. They produce what sells. Evidently, violence sells because it fulfills an apparent need of many viewers. One may plead, placate, educate, and show facts, but it is doubtful that in the long run a significant reduction in violence will be obtained. When neurotic needs change, I think violence will no longer be profitable and that, in my opinion, will dictate what is shown to audiences.

THE MYTHS OF THE GROWTH CENTER

Sweeping the nation is a phenomenon called the growth center—a place where people go for a weekend or a week for lectures, encounter groups, nude bathing, massage therapy, and general release. The growth center, by and large, is heavily oriented toward the bioenergetics approach (see discussion of this in *The Anatomy of Mental Illness*) and manipulation of the body. The mainstay of the weekend experience is the encounter group, a group experience that may last for twenty-four hours. Here individuals are encouraged to encounter one another both physically and verbally. The encounter is based upon several myths— honesty, disclosure of the self, freedom, and the abandonment of inner constraint. The idea is that through honest self-disclosure there is liberation and a growth of the self. So we need to know what honesty and freedom mean, and exactly what the self that everyone is improving really is.

THE NATURE OF THE SELF

A great deal is made in encounter groups of the "self"—self-awareness, improving self-confidence, enhancing a self-concept, building self-esteem. We ought to know what the self is before we go about being aware, improving and building it. Is the self just thoughts? Do we change it by changing thoughts about it? Can we change it by having more confidence in it? And, what is *it*?

The self, in my opinion, is our totality: our total psychobiologic being, including the liver, brains, eyes, tongue, ideas, feelings, muscles, blood system, and so on. Does self-confidence mean to have more faith in the liver? If not, what, then? I believe the whole concept of the self as used in encounter cultures is erroneous. The self is not something divulged to others; it is experienced. The self is not something we try to be aware of; self-awareness and self-consciousness are neurotic states. As Ray Bradbury says, "Reality never sums itself up."[*] The well person just is himself. Indeed, the times we are most aware of ourselves, like giving a speech before a large group, is when we are most not ourselves; when we are most split and uncomfortable. Is a coyote aware of himself? Does he have self-confidence? Obviously, these are meaningless terms when applied to him. The coyote is not split into a side that feels and another side that thinks about his feelings.

How does a therapist build confidence in someone? Does he tell him lies and make him believe them? Does he encourage the person to think differently than he really feels? If a person acts as though he is unimportant because he believes no one cares about him, he does so because that was no doubt true earlier in his life. Do we convince him to adopt a new image, or is it better to help him feel how no one cared about him?

It may be that a neurotic has ideas about himself quite different from the truth. He may act unafraid and superior and really

[*] *Los Angeles Times,* October 24, 1971.

feel terrified and inferior. His actions and thoughts are the way he acts out a necessary defense in terms of his life history. A few words of discouragement or encouragement in his adult life won't change those thousands of times he was derided, ignored, and humiliated by his parents.

The self responds as a totality—ideas and bodily processes—to events in life. If one has new ideas about himself but still suffers from constricted blood vessels, tight muscles, pallid complexion, lack of beard growth, etcetera, we can hardly say that the self has changed.

The self begins in the womb, with events that occur during that time. It is built upon a genetic legacy. It is produced each minute by life-events. It is warped and shaped by an interaction multiplied thousands-fold. Can there be a breakthrough into that self in a group encounter? No. Because there is no core to break into—no single entity or moment called the "self." All we can ever do is open up our systems to *feel* our selves as much as possible, so that whatever happens in life we can fully experience as a self. The real self is no more than an open psychophysiologic system, undivided, and functioning wholly.

ON THE NATURE OF FREEDOM

A new patient had recently had what she described as a "liberating experience" at a well-known growth center. Several of the people there were having dinner when they asked this woman what she would like to do or have at that moment. She said she would like to hold two penises and be spoon-fed. Whereupon the growth leaders unzipped their flies and accommodated her while their wives fed her. They did this under the aegis of freedom. This episode raised the question for me about the nature of freedom. Is it really doing what you want? No constraints or rules? Total abandon?

It is easy to confuse abandon with freedom, since the common notion of being free is being unconstrained, to have a wide variety of choices. The dialectic of personal freedom is that the only way to be free is to feel what constrains us. One doesn't become free by total abandon (since this patient was still tight, taut, and tense afterwards), nor does one become free through symbolic games such as breaking through groups of people who encircle someone, nor does it have any meaning when one is incapable of knowing what choices will really serve his needs. The deeper one sinks into those old historic feelings that constricted him, the more free he becomes.

What is the point of doing anything you want if you don't know what you need? In the aforementioned growth-center experience, symbolic-neurotic acting-out was encouraged as if that would make someone be free. All it does is reinforce neurosis. What this woman later learned in Primal Therapy was how much she needed a father. In the growth center she settled for tangible symbols of a father.

So freedom is not a matter of endless choices; choice is meaningless when nothing satisfies. Freedom may mean the absence of choice—simply knowing the one thing one needs for satisfaction and choosing it.

Above all, freedom implies the recognition of choice—that there is a choice, an alternative to what one is doing. So many neurotics never have any notion that there is another way to be. For them it is not a matter of choosing between alternatives; it is in the recognition that a choice can be made.

We have become accustomed to externalizing the notion of freedom without understanding that freedom is a psychological state; one can feel personally free in jail or tightly bound in a forest. One can roam the world for a lifetime and never have a free feeling. One can rail about freedom for women and never be satisfied with societal concessions because that plea is simply a transmogrified externalized personal projection.

Is freedom a moment-to-moment event? Or is it a life-style? A number of people seem willing to settle for the momentary freedom that drugs bring, only to settle back to their personal prisons when the drugs wear off. Others think it is going somewhere like a growth center for a weekend and "letting go." They have never discovered that you can't "let go" of your history.

There are some who spend a lifetime acting out a freedom they can't feel. They wear funky, wild clothes, have all kinds of sex, take whatever drug is available, take off for somewhere whenever the urge hits them, and the appearance is one of freedom. We have treated people like this, and some of them find out that their acting-out is trying to shake off a religious past. It doesn't matter what form the constriction took. There are many ways to foul up one's thinking so that it won't permit the feelings of the body. And having that body *act* free never changes those early, internalized prohibitions. This is just another way of saying that the only freedom lies in being a feeling person unhampered by his past.

ON BEING HONEST

One of the aims of the confrontation-encounter group is to help people become honest; to aid them in expressing themselves openly and honestly. They do this by saying what is truly on their minds to their group peers, being able in the encounter situation to attack someone else verbally, to criticize, or to express tenderness. The question is, "Is that honesty?" And will that make a person more honest? Honesty means saying the truth. When one says how much he loves another group member, is that true? When one openly expresses hostility to someone who bugs him, is that true? Rarely. More often it is displaced, symbolic feeling. How can a person be honest when he can only *think* about his feelings and not truly feel them? Neurotics are in a constant state of self-deception; otherwise they would be well. One does not *disclose* oneself to others. One feels it, and that makes any disclosure unnecessary—particularly in reference to a contrived caring situation, like marathons and group psychotherapy. Feelings are not "revealed"; they are experienced! Is it honest to say "I care about you" in group? Does a neurotic really know what that means? Are those words a truth? Or is the hidden feeling behind it—if I'm nice to you, will you like me?—what is real?

The answer is already apparent. Honesty means the ability to feel one's motives so that what one says stems from one's total state. Honesty lies much more than in just what one verbalizes.

What the neurotic usually does in encounter groups is verbalize in the present out of his Primal Pool of the past. His statements are disconnected events unrelated to their historic roots. Someone is mad at someone because they talk too much, instead of feeling what Mother's constant rapping did to them as a child. Once that old feeling is felt, there is no reason to encounter anyone who talks too much. One can do that forever and never get honest—never resolve what is true.

When one is totally connected, one is honest with himself. When one is disconnected, there is no way to be honest because motives are hidden, rationalized, explained away. One says "I love you," when he means "I need you." One says "I hate you," when he means "you make me afraid," and so on. Even to say "one is honest with himself" is misleading. Being oneself *is* honesty.

How many of us were told by our parents how much they loved us? How many of us felt loved? Their intent was not our reality. Were those parents honest? They thought they were, but the truth was somewhere else.

All of this simply means that if one cannot feel the truth, one cannot be honest, no matter how well-intentioned.

20 Changes That Occur in
Primal Therapy

People usually come to Primal Therapy because they are tense and/or depressed. In the course of their therapy, a lot more changes than their tension and depression. We usually have no way of predicting what these changes will be. We could not know, for example, that a singer would increase his range by an octave or that someone would grow in height. We could not know that someone would hear bass tones for the first time in his life, or that someone else would begin perspiring for the first time. We had no way of knowing that someone would relive his surgery, either, but all these things, and many more, have come to pass. They are really what makes this therapy exciting, for the range and variety of change continually surprise us.

Some things are far more crucial than others. Continuous relief from severe arthritis has implications for many others with this affliction. Many months have passed since the letter was written by the woman who had arthritis, and she still has had no recurrence of her problem. There was no way for us to know in advance how the arthritis would turn out, or even if it were psychosomatic. We knew afterwards that it was, and the way we knew was by listening to and observing the patient, *who told us*. I have no idea how many diseases are in reality psychologically induced. But I am sure that much of the physical disease we see is Primally derived. As the years pass, we will have a more extensive literature on the kinds of disease that are amenable to treatment by Primal Therapy. We will have time to follow up the cases, such as the woman with arthritis, and we will have a lot more to say then about disease in general.

MARTIN

"I'm sinking, I can't breathe. There's Daddy, can't he see me? Can't he hear me? *Please see me, Daddy.*" These were my feelings as a boy of four and a half in a swimming pool as I began to drown. This scene had a most important effect on me, for it was from this point on that I began to act-out in every possible way, "Daddy, see me."

Before this experience I had led a relatively satisfied childhood. As an only child I was given a great deal of attention from the entire family. Everyone always commented on what a good little boy I was, and therefore, my parents took me along with them wherever they went. Since I was around adults, I learned very early how to win favor in their eyes, especially by never crying.

It was during summer vacation that my parents and I went on the trip to Palm Springs where the pool incident occurred. My father and I walked to the pool and sat at the shallow end by the steps and began to play. Suddenly, I fell into what seemed to be clear blue water; it was so beautiful. Then I felt that I could no longer breathe and I could see my father's legs in front of me. There was no air down there but I thought surely my father would rescue me before I would feel any pain. I tried to scream under the water, but nobody could hear me. My daddy didn't help me soon enough to prevent my feeling the fear that I was dying.

During my first three weeks of therapy, my therapist asked me to bring in photographs of myself as a baby and as I grew up. It was then, after studying those pictures, that I could see the physical changes that took place after the pool scene. It was then I began to act-out more, being what my father and mother wanted me to be, "a little grown-up," since they were both two very immature adults. I rarely if ever cried, especially in front of my father, even if he had hurt me. I acted out my role as "big man" in every conceivable way in school, at play, and even physically I became very stocky and fat.

At the age of eight and a half I began Hebrew school, as many Jewish children do. It was there I met the man who became the most important influence on my life; the man who became my father, the cantor. It was then that I began my training as a junior cantor, and a long relationship with this man who accepted me no matter what I did. I did not realize then how much pleasure I derived from singing loud, as loud as I could. However, there was one problem that I had to overcome, and that was I was tone-deaf (could not carry a tune), and I had a bad voice.

Over the next few years I was able to overcome these problems and eventually became the best junior cantor. Along with this I became the best junior adult. This resulted in my receiving the respect of the entire congregation, my relatives, and friends. Only once did my father come to see me—on the day of my bar mitzvah. Nevertheless, I kept on singing, and as I reached adolescence I began to participate in musical performances in the public school as well. Since my father never looked at me (going back to the pool incident), I then wanted the entire world to see and hear me, but it never really satisfied me.

Along with most thirteen- and fourteen-year-old males, my voice changed. An interesting thing happened to my voice; I became a bass at a very early age. This simply meant that the quality in my voice was dark and heavy. It was a very mature voice for a boy my age (I have recordings and tapes); however, I can explain the method by which I was able to make this deep sound. I will later explain in more detail.

As I went on to college it was my intention to become a lawyer, and I gave up the thought of pursuing a musical career. However, I did support myself by being a part-time cantor, and

I maintained my contact with singing in that way. There is one interesting characteristic about my voice; even after the training I had received, I was unable to sing softly. This was directly related to the pool incident, because if I were to sing softly, I would have to feel the feelings related to no one seeing me, meaning that I would have to feel that my father and mother did not love me. No matter how much training I had, this one unfelt feeling did not permit me to sing artistically. During therapy I felt those unfelt feelings of fear and death that I did not feel in the pool, along with many other feelings, which helped to release me from the vocal straitjacket that my neurosis put me in.

After having been in Primal Therapy, many things began to happen to me. I will only speak about those changes I feel to be the most significant. In terms of my physical condition, I lost weight and began to take on a more slender shape, as well as other phenomena, such as a temperature drop and lower blood pressure, which had always been on the high side. Other symptoms such as smoking were no longer needed once I felt the feelings that compelled me to smoke. The greatest change occurred in my vocal ability and my ability to sing artistically. After having been in therapy for two months I was able to sing softly and enjoy doing it. I no longer felt that need to always be the center of attraction. The quality of my voice changed from a dark one to a much sweeter one, since I no longer had to sing *at* my father symbolically.

Many insights into vocal production and singing followed in the next few months, and my voice developed rapidly. Almost a year later I was introduced to a voice teacher who had been recommended to me by a friend. I had heard that this voice teacher had a technique that developed the voice naturally and that his students all sang very correctly. I then went to his studio and sang for him. Much to his amazement I sang very correctly, and all he said he could do for me was help me to understand what was going on in my throat and help develop my natural voice.

It was during the first few weeks of voice lessons that I was thoroughly amazed at the exercises and techniques that this teacher used. Many of the thoughts and ideas that he used were Primal in their nature, as well as many of the terms that he used. One important concept that he has is that all voices are to be treated the same, and that the only difference between the voices is the thickness of the vocal cords, which gives each respective voice its timbre and quality. In my case, I was able to respond quickly to his technique, since there was nothing in it that I felt would be unnatural, as well as the freedom that I feel as a complete human being.

To explain the complete vocal apparatus in detail and the technique used to develop it would take a very long, scholarly approach. I will instead define a few of the terms used in the correct usage of the voice and their relationship to Primal Therapy in my case alone. As we know, vocal production is made by air passing through the larynx, which houses the vocal chords. The vocal chords then vibrate, and the sound is heard as it comes out of the mouth. There are resonance cavities in the head that give brightness and quality to vocal production. Therefore, there are two places from which the voice quality or tone can be made; one, the chest voice, which is the speaking-level voice and the heavier-sounding part of the voice; and two, the head voice, which is the high-sounding part of the voice and where the resonance shifts from the chest to head. The chest voice is actually the voice that is produced by the lower half of the vocal chords, which produces a lower pitch. As the pitch gets higher the chords begin to tighten, and one sings on less of the chords as the resonance shifts behind the soft palate into the head. The natural voice has an even balance throughout the entire range and is able to keep the higher tones connected (instead of sounding like falsetto, it is connected to the chest voice), thereby giving it a fuller sound, which most singers are unable to do. If an individual is able to do this, then his range will increase to possibly three octaves. Most men sing in the chest, women in the head; but the two sounds are disconnected or split from one another.

In my case I never developed the head tones and sang only with my chest voice, and by imposing my larynx down I was able to make what sounded like a very mature and dark sound. This, of course, is not correct vocal production, for no matter what the pitch, the larynx should stay in the same position and only the resonance should shift. Since I always wanted to be "big" and never cried, I was never able to release the pressure and allow myself to get into my head voice, or as my voice teacher said, the "little or small" voice. It was during therapy that my crying went from a deep chesty sound to the crying that was like the baby that I never had the chance to be. My teacher also said to put a little cry or grunt behind the sound so it would help to keep the sound connected (without cracking in falsetto). It was then that many of my insights into voice became much clearer to me. If we recall the cry of a baby wanting something, there is a total connection there of sound production that the entire human being is involved in. This is the baby's only form of communication, and the tone in the "wah" has the grunt in it as well as the connected sound in the head tones which gives it its shrill quality. This I believe is the shrill of the Primal Scream or cry, the totally connected sound which is the same sound that a baby makes instinctively.

It is each individual's neurosis that causes one to act-out in a certain way, and may also cause the voice to function in a way that best fits one's neurosis. For example, some girls talk in a very babylike manner, in a very high pitch or disconnected head voice. Usually this is accomplished in much the same way as my deep sound was made, except the larynx is high. Many times women with low voices also have other characteristics and symptoms of their neurosis, as would male homosexuals.

To me it is quite obvious that if a child were healthy and not turned off from himself, that the development of the natural voice would be easily accomplished. The healthy person would be able to create beauty with his voice and sing to make music and not to act-out. As he would be a connected person, so also would be the sounds that he made vocally. The more one sings like the baby cries, the more natural the sound and beautiful. If for a moment we recall the great cantors who sang the soul music of the Jew, their basic appeal was that they could pour their souls out and had a cry in the voice. As in their case, I too cried my Primals out through song, for I know that singing is to me the closest thing to a Primal.

I am now studying music and singing, which for me is the most natural thing in my life. I am doing the thing that pleases me the most in life; and no longer must I sing to not feel, but sing and cry if I must.

GLORIA

"I've been in therapy only two months and it feels like two years. At first I thought my defenses were too many and too strong ever to be able to break through them. I also thought that at any time, if it got too rough I could just leave and everything would remain the same. I soon learned that it could never be the same again. I found out too many terrible things about myself, mainly that I don't love my son, and with this knowledge I then realized there was no turning back. I wasn't at all sure I could go forward, but I knew I could never go back to being what I was. The realization was that whatever I do or say now, my child has already suffered at my hands. I didn't want it to be so irrevocable, but it is, and now only Primal Therapy can help him. As horrible as it is knowing this, I also feel it has saved my sanity. I went insane once, and I always thought that if the stress were great enough, it could happen again. It was just too hard looking and acting like what I was supposed to be.

There are also other changes in me. My hearing is different. I found this out while driving. Before, I could never get the bass on the radio low enough, and now I turn the treble up. I perspire, something I haven't done in many years. I was trying to dehumanize myself. It wasn't voluntary, it just happened. Also, I was an aspirin addict—six or eight every day for all the headaches

and body pains I had. I now get pains only when there is a repressed feeling, and when I feel the feeling, the pains go. My
breasts have grown, and while they are still small, they are much
more than they were. I am less tired, not as angry, more spontaneous, open and unafraid to speak up. My breathing used to
be labored—I couldn't seem to get a deep enough breath. This
is no longer a problem. And things are better with my son. I
don't exactly know how better, but I don't seem to not love him
as much. My anxiety is much less, and when I do get an attack
I am able to trace it back to its source.

I am beginning to be what I never could be. I am thirty-seven
years old, walking around, thinking and feeling like I am still a
little girl. That little girl is slowly leaving me. I am both glad and
sad to see her go. It is very painful to let go of my me's. I was so
split it feels strange to be *almost* one person. (I was four people:
a crying baby, a little girl, the functioning me, and a me watching
the other three.) I am or was carrying around all my unfulfilled
me's, and as I slowly feel them and what they needed and never
got and know they never will get, I become one. It is also nearing
the end of my wanting from other people what my parents never
gave me.

I am not what I was when I began this therapy, but I am also
not yet what I am—just someplace in the middle, working my
way back to the me that was, a long time ago.

KAY

When I was eighteen I still had both "baby" cuspids. A dentist
pulled them and performed surgery so that my impacted permanent cuspids would grow into place. Only one of them, however,
grew at all. It grew very slowly, and after about seven years had
only grown halfway down. Since it didn't grow any more during
the following year and a half, I had it capped. I was then twenty-
seven, and the dentist told me that the probability of any further
growth was practically nil at my age.

Two years later I started having my Primals, and my impacted permanent teeth began to grow. The one that had been capped grew all the way down, making the tooth appear too long with the cap on it. The other one, which was imbedded so high that it had never been visible, has grown one quarter of the way down and is still growing. It is as though feeling those once-blocked baby feelings unblocked the natural growth of those teeth. I wouldn't be at all surprised if that still-growing cuspid completes its growth, since my once underdeveloped breasts grew to a natural size after my Primals.

ALICE

Dear Art,

I had a dream the night of my final day of individual therapy that draws a vivid picture of what changes have occurred in my life since undergoing Primal Therapy.

The dream, simply stated, was this: I was a stiff baby-doll-like figure. And I was pregnant. The fetus inside of me grew vigorously. It suddenly burst inside of me, full of energy, full of life. The baby killed the body that encased it. The baby was *alive.* The baby was me.

And that is what happened to me. I feel as though that baby, the pure *me,* was released for the first time. I am alive at last.

Before therapy I was a "baby." But being that baby was my way of not being me. An excuse for not making decisions, an excuse for being opinionless, an excuse for not living like a real human being. I was a baby for Daddy so he would love me. I was a baby for my boyfriends so they would take care of me, make decisions (if not for me, then with me) so I wouldn't be responsible for anything.

I have come a long way from being Daddy's baby doll. My father used to have a way of manipulating me into being that baby that he wanted. I stayed that way for him. For twenty-two years I had such a driving need for his love that I never allowed my real self to live.

Shortly after individual therapy I had lunch with my father. I had just found an apartment and was telling him how excited I was to move in. He, in his mild, subtle (and *deadly*) way told me that he would love to give me some money to find a "nicer" apartment. I told him that the money had nothing to do with it—that this was the place that I *wanted* to live in. (God, just to feel right saying I *want* still blows my mind.) Then he made his move that kept me dead for so many years. He dropped his chin to his chest, looked up at me with his sad blue eyes, and said, "But you're still my little girl." A wave of heat shot through my body. I said, "I am not *your* little girl any more." I made him cry. I still have Primals over this scene. I had to hurt him (my warm, soft daddy who always loved his little girl) in order for me to live. It was either me or him—and I chose *me*.

Choosing myself over my father and confronting him with it was the one step I had to take in order to really live. Somehow finally being straight with my father opened me up. I can now be real (really me) with people. I used to be "good" or "nice" or "sweet." Those were the killer adjectives. Now I am just me, and it feels good.

Sincerely,
Alice

P.S.   I applied for a new job last month with the Board of Education and was required to have a complete medical examination before I was granted acceptance. I was astounded to learn that I had grown half an inch. I was so amazed that I ordered the doctor to recheck, just to verify. It was true. Six months ago I was 5'½" and now I am 5'1".

MARA

My teeth came in crooked. My overbite was so extreme that I could stick my little finger in between. Also, my teeth had lots of spaces, one especially large one in the middle. At the age of thirteen, my teeth and my jaw position were so bad that I had ulcers on the side of my mouth. When I swallowed, my back teeth chewed on the inside soft flesh.

At thirteen I got braces and also had to wear a jaw strap fourteen hours a day to change my whole jaw structure. They told me I would only have to wear braces for one and a half years, but it came out to almost three and a half years and about $3000 of work. When I was sixteen, the braces came off and my teeth were absolutely perfect. The doctor said that he had never seen such perfect bottom teeth. After the braces came off, I wore a retainer until I was eighteen, and my teeth no longer moved. They were perfect at this time.

When I started therapy, my jaws started to ache on the fourth day. It felt just like when I had the braces on and the teeth were moving. This ache continued until about the middle of my second week, before I realized my teeth were moving back to exactly the same way they were before the braces. When I woke up in the morning I became aware that my jaws hurt especially so. Also, I noticed that when I woke up my mouth hurt especially so. Also, I noticed that when I woke up my mouth was always closed really tight, and sideways.

At the end of my three weeks I went home and got my retainer. My teeth by this time had moved so much that the retainer wouldn't even fit in my mouth. It hung there, hooked on only one tooth, and finally I was able to get it over both back teeth but it still was too tight to cling to the roof of my mouth. I kept wearing it, all the time, not just at night as I had done when I first got my braces off. At first it seemed like they weren't going to move back. I wore my retainer twenty-four hours a day for over a week before the retainer finally fit into place at the roof of my mouth. The movement of the teeth was so strong at this time that when I took my retainer off just to eat, it was difficult to get it back in. Sometimes I take it off for a while now, when I go to group, and it seems that it's getting a little less difficult to put in after I haven't worn it for a while. It seems to me that the reason my teeth and jaw moved out of place is because when I was little I was always grinding down so hard with tension. When I have Primals of wanting my mom, I also get the ache in my jaw, and it is definitely associated with sucking. It seems I'll have to wear my retainer until I have felt the need to suck and the night tension bite goes away.

RITA

Dear Art:

The more I think about what happened to me right after I returned from having an abortion in Mexico, the more I am convinced that there is no such thing as NO PAIN. Let me explain.

The entire trip, even the fact that we had to take one, was a super-struggle. We should have been careful. And because the baby had been conceived under such sick circumstances, it would have been even sicker, if not criminal, to have had it. It had to go. How? Of course I didn't find out until the tenth week that I was pregnant—this may seem inconceivable to anyone outside of Primal Therapy, but to me every little symptom or bodily behavior is symptomatic of a Primal Pain. The swelling in my breasts was not unusual—ever since the first months of therapy their size has varied. The nausea, too, could have been indicative of a psychic pain, especially since every time I had a Primal (and I was having some big ones then) it left me. I had always been irregular in my menstrual cycles. It came then as a surprise when the doctor confirmed my fears of the previous week. Of course the abortion could have been done right here, legally. But that meant waiting a few weeks, and meanwhile the fetus would be growing rapidly. Most likely the abortion would have had to be performed by the induced-labor (or simulated-labor) method. And that meant physical *pain!* So off to Mexico we went to have it done immediately, and thus rid ourselves of the worrisome anticipations.

Everything was perfect. When I was told I would be given sodium pentothal (or a similar drug), I requested that someone take down any remarks I might make while under its influence—

I remembered the only other time I had taken the drug, before therapy came into my life, I awakened bathed in tears, with the nurses staring at me and saying "poor girl." I wasn't taking any chances now that I knew what the body was capable of under-going without the mind's knowledge—if I was going to do any crying, I hoped to be able to make some connections later. But I didn't cry. I remember feeling the pain of the needle in my but-tocks and in my arm. I remember counting and then nothing. The nurses said I didn't utter a sound. I know now that I must have been in a kind of suspended-pain state. When I awakened back in my room, I screamed at what seemed to be a severe menstrual cramp. I was given a painkiller, and everything was fine until I returned to L.A. and allowed myself to have a Primal in your office.

I was back on that operating table with my legs strapped onto that inverted, saddle-like metal chair. The doctors were staring. I felt and cried the humiliation of being thus exposed, helpless, the most private *me* lying there. Men. The whole thing with my father came to mind, especially since those too were Latin men. I cried and cried and screamed at my helplessness, hating them less and less as I loved myself a little more each time. How I had been humiliated—how a woman is humiliated in a Latin country —how I have been humiliated!

As intense as that feeling was, it gave way to a more precise, less vague or diffused pain, a real physical pain. It felt sharp, by strokes. It wasn't clear at first exactly what it was, but then I saw the doctor with a razorlike instrument in his hand and I knew that I was feeling then the pain I had not felt on the operating table. My body was making the connection with the head at a moment when it was safe to feel, a *later* moment. But the pain is the same. There is no difference. Afterwards I remembered a line from your book that had somehow engraved itself in my mind. It talks of the pain of a five-year-old in a grown man, and you say something about the pain remaining as "pristine pure" as the day it was first felt. For the body there is no time. The body feels all the time. And the times we don't feel what goes on in our bodies is because we do not allow ourselves to make the connection with the head. When and if we do make the connection, we are right back there, a week ago or twenty years ago. It is all so clear now. That is why I had had so many nightmares after my baby was born two years ago. I made the connection "Pain" in my sleep while my defenses were down, the connection I hadn't made before because a drug kept me from feeling in my head what was going on in my body. Painkillers then don't kill the pain they are supposed to. *Nothing can kill pain!* Whether it is physical or emotional, it will stay there until some connection is made sometime or until it kills us (whichever comes first). I remembered too how Grace had gone through her entire tonsillectomy on the office floor! *It must be true!*

Rita

MARIAN

Dear Art,

Here is a report on how my arthritis is doing.

When I was in high school I began to be bothered by pains in my right arm, wrist, hand, and fingers when I had a lot of writing to do. Every so often I would have to stop writing, shake my arm and hand, and extend and flex my fingers to try to relieve the pain. This didn't help much, but at that time I didn't think about it being arthritis, so I didn't know anything to do to relieve the pain.

As I got older the pain became worse, and other parts of my body became involved. It was particularly noticeable if I drove for any length of time. I would notice that my knees and ankles would become stiff and sore and my shoulders, elbows, wrists, and hands would hurt quite a bit.

In 1965, when I was thirty-two years old, I was seeing a general practitioner about another medical problem and I mentioned that my hands hurt a lot. The doctor felt around the finger joints and manipulated my hands and fingers and said I had arthritis. I was quite surprised, because I always thought that arthritis was a disease of the aged, so I asked him for more information. He said the kind of arthritis I had was not rheumatoid and would not cripple me, except for the pain. He told me to keep my joints warm and dry and prescribed Aristogesic for the inflammation. He also suggested aspirin for the pain. Over the years the arthritis gradually got worse.

In September and October, 1969, I had an ear infection and saw an ear, nose, and throat specialist, and he told me part of my ear pain was coming from the arthritis in my jaw. He suggested that, for a week or two, I avoid food that required chewing. During the two months that he treated me, my jaw did not improve even though I ate only soups and soft foods. The doctor then suggested I get cortisone shots in the jaw joint to get rid of the pain, but I hate shots, so I did not comply with his suggestion.

On August 30, 1970, I started Primal Therapy, and my arthritis has already improved noticeably. At first the improvement came every three or four days and lasted an hour or so after therapy. Now, after each Primal my joints feel as if they had just been oiled, and the effect lasts for a day or two and I feel like a new person. I don't know just exactly how to describe the improvement, but I guess it is like my joints were rusty hinges but after a Primal they become well-oiled ball and socket joints.

It happens this way: as I am getting into feelings from my childhood, the arthritic pain increases until I think I just can't stand it. But I stick it out and go with the pain, and as I get through the feeling, the physical pain disappears immediately.

For instance, during one Primal I was experiencing an incident from childhood when I had done something wrong and my mother and dad were getting on me about it. What they were saying to me hurt badly, but I was bound and determined not to let them know how hurt I was. I was saying over and over, "I won't let them make me cry," and as I was feeling this my legs began to stiffen and ache. The more I felt the hurt, the more leg pain I had. Suddenly I realized that even if I cried my parents would not know they had hurt me. As soon as I felt this, the arthritic pain disappeared and my legs felt altogether different.

From my experience in Primal Therapy, I know that my arthritis comes from my childhood. I know I used my body to defend against feelings, and each time I felt hurt, or unloved, or alone, etcetera, I stiffened some part of my body to stop the feeling. Now all I have is the ache of arthritis. But since my arthritis lessens with each Primal I know that eventually I will be free of this pain.

Marian

KATHY

I've been in therapy three and a half months and the changes that have taken place in my body just amaze me. The changes are all happening on their own—I have no control over them. My biggest change is my thyroid problem. I have been taking thyroid pills for twelve years for hypothyroidism. It started out when I was fifteen, my periods were very irregular. The doctor gave me a blood test and discovered my thyroid was low. He gave me a small dosage and it didn't seem to help much. So he increased the dosage to about one and a half grains a day. My periods were still irregular, so he put me on birth control pills so my period would be "normal." Eventually, I was off the "pill" and my periods were "normal." But I was still on the thyroid. It was just an indefinite thing that I would be on it the rest of my life. As years passed, I had more tests, and I always needed a stronger dosage. Finally, for the last three to five years, I was up to four grains a day. Since I've been in therapy and my old feelings are coming out, my body is restoring itself back to a normal state. I was not aware of any change in my thyroid until after two months in therapy. My heart began to pound really hard all the time, even lying still in bed. Suddenly I thought, "My thyroid!" I have decreased my dosage gradually, on my doctor's advice, until now I'm not taking any at all. My heart began to slow down within one day after I cut the dosage. Amazing to me—my body. I'm getting it back! My other symptoms such as dry hair, splitting nails, and dry skin have hardly appeared. I have gained about five pounds. My body has been "spurred on in a dead heat" for such a long time, it deserves this rest at last. Sometimes I feel tired, but if "I" was my body, I'd be tired too. I'm just so happy to have myself back. And it's happened so fast—a twelve-year addiction down to nothing.

Kathy

21 *Primal Therapy–the Therapist's View*

A saying circulates in Primal Therapy, about the relationship of the patient to his therapist, which goes, "He who gets up off the floor first gets paid." What this means is that at times it is difficult to tell the therapist from a patient, because they may be on the floor together having Primals in group therapy. This kind of thing leads me to write about some of the unique aspects of Primal Therapy.

Even though a therapist works with a patient during his first three weeks, it is entirely possible that when Saturday group comes around, the therapist will come to group as a patient along with his patient. He simply announces in staff meeting the day before that he is going to be a patient and needs a replacement. Sometimes no such announcement is made, because something during group triggers the therapist into a Primal. It may be that his patient, who may have finished his Primal for the day, will help him. Even though everyone knows who the therapists and the patients are, there is no special magic about being a therapist —no elitist group knowing a special "scientific" language. It is the patient who makes all his own discoveries, so that there is no aura surrounding an omniscient therapist.

There is a feeling in Primal Therapy that we are all on a very special voyage; all sharing shattering experiences, and all "in the same boat." There is, therefore, a feeling among Primal patients that is very different from other patients in conventional group therapy. We have all seen each other feel in the deepest, most agonizing way, heard each other tell everything there is to be known about ourselves, wailed like infants, hugged our teddy bears—there is nothing left to hide. So the atmosphere of total honesty is refreshing. No one is trying to be the bright one, coming up with clever insights and analyses of someone else. Each person is there for himself, and that is what produces the closeness to others.

The therapists also have nothing to hide. There is no pretense of the "good doctor." They are not acting like the good daddies neurotic patients sometimes want their doctors to be. Because there are no prestige or power needs on the part of the therapist, there is no unconscious manipulation of the patient to serve those ends. Patients neither have to be obsequious, humble, deferent, or anything else. We are all just people helping each other, and some of us have the tools to do a good job of it. But the patient is not kept away from these tools. He is taught how to get into Primals, what techniques are valid, and he learns whatever there is to know about helping himself so that he does not have to helplessly give himself over forever to an expert. He is in a place where no one is telling him what his feelings mean; he can just have them. Primal patients have a Primal buddy—someone who helps them with their Primals. Offices are available at the Institute every day so that patients can drop in and use them for their buddy system. The atmosphere is one of the Institute being the patients' place, not the office of the doctor, and they use it however they wish.

The first contact we have with a patient is usually a letter—his autobiography—and that is where our trouble begins. Everyone who works at the Institute has had Primal Therapy, so that they are all relatively defense-free. When a letter comes in that is full of misery and suffering, few of the staff can get through it without crying. Considering the volume of requests for treatment we have, just reading the letters is no mean feat. Each application is carefully discussed, and many people have to be turned away because of the lack of staff. In many cases, it is a life-and-death matter. People turn to us after years of analysis or other kinds of therapy, believing that we are the last hope. So to turn them away, as we sometimes must, can be disastrous in a number of cases. People are not turned away easily. After an applicant receives a letter of rejection, there are often the pleading letters and phone calls, letters from their doctors or families or friends. It becomes a Herculean task to turn away anyone.

When a patient is accepted, a great deal of preparation goes on. Many patients are traced throughout their therapy in terms of physiologic changes, so we need to establish base lines in terms of brain waves, pulse, blood pressure, deep body temperature, and a host of other measurements. A staff meeting is held during which the applicant's letter and autobiography is read and discussed in terms of his defense system, techniques to be employed, and so on. Often, each hour of the therapy is videotaped and discussed by the staff daily to measure progress, correct possible errors, and plan for the following day's therapy. Each patient receives a great deal of attention. Our aim, of course, is to insure that each patient accepted gets well, and this is most always the case. When a videotape is shown, there is rarely a divergence in comments from the staff about the techniques employed—testimony to the precision of the therapy. When a mistake is made, it is spotted immediately by all. I can remember sitting in on staff meetings of clinics and psychiatric hospitals where no precision is required or expected, where each staff member simply does "what he feels comfortable with." The implicit assumption in those staff meetings was that psychotherapy was much more an art than a science. There was never a thought given to the possibility of *predictive* changes brought on by specific techniques. This was not due to indifference on the part of the staff members; it was simply that we had no systematic clinical procedure available to us.

Another novel feature of these Primal staff meetings is that the autobiography and clinical progress of every patient is discussed weekly, so that each therapist is familiar with every patient. This allows for interchangeability of therapists in group therapy, where any therapist can treat any patient with a full knowledge of where the patient is.

The intensity required of therapists is often exhausting. They therefore take a week's vacation after each three-week therapy period—and they need it. Though they only work a few hours a day, the work is emotionally trying, and I have the feeling that Primal Therapists "burn out" in a very few years. We do all we can to safeguard their health. Part of the reason that the therapy is tiring work is its precision. It isn't just a "rap" session or being a good listener. It requires complete concentration every minute so that each therapeutic move is accurate, timed right, and economical. Patients usually finish the three-week period feeling that it was the most important time of their lives and have a special feeling toward their therapist, who often literally has saved their life. That feeling is not "transference." It is a real feeling of gratitude.

No matter who the patient is, he usually comes out of a Primal saying, "It's amazing!" Even after years of doing Primal Therapy and after seeing thousands of Primals, I still come out of my own feeling how amazing it is to have a feeling transport you back in history in a most literal and thunderous way. Patients invariably state that there are really no words to describe Primals, and in particular, what goes on in Primal groups—each one of which is truly a "happening." It is most difficult to enjoy seeing a play these days, because make-believe drama pales before the drama of Primals. Make-believe feeling is just no substitute for the real thing.

While I'm on the subject of Primal groups, I should point out another hazard for therapists—some of us are in danger of losing part of our hearing. The decibel level during a group has been measured (when we were planning how much soundproofing we needed) and it must be close to jet noise.

In the group room, every conceivable item that might re-awaken an old circuit is utilized. Toys, teddy bears, real cribs and playpens, dildoes, punching bags, plastic nipples and bottles for nursing are just some. These "toys" seem bizarre in terms of ordinary therapy, but when someone is wide open to his past, they take on special meaning. Patients put in a crib (when the time is appropriate) will wail like an infant, try to roll over and be unable to (because the time they are reliving is before such activity was possible), begin sucking reflexively and often so rapidly as to indicate that it is an automatic and involuntary action.

Several therapists move around the room, helping patients who might be having trouble getting into a feeling, either because the feeling is so painful or because they need to talk their way into a feeling. Most patients whose defenses have been broken down in the first three-week period need little help. They are usually a mass of pain, and it just pours forth bits at a time—the body shutting down when it can tolerate no more for the day. It is later on that patients need help most. When they get down to feelings and scenes where they began their major split, they need to be reassured that someone is there to see to it that they don't go "crazy" in their flight from the feeling. The fear is justified. If they were not in Primal Therapy and were open to that feeling, it could well drive them into bizarre ideation.

When a patient leaves group for good, he simply stops coming —no explanations, phone calls, or elaborate preparations in conjunction with his therapist. He attends group on the same basis— when he feels like it. Groups meet almost every day in the week, so that patients know that if they have a Primal coming on, they can attend group within a few hours. Primal groups are different from conventional groups in other respects. I can't remember when a patient has ever come late for a group. Nearly all of them are there a half-hour before starting time, and literally start without us. They do not come to get the therapist's love or approval; they come to get themselves, so they work toward no goals and have no standards set for them by anyone. If a patient has latent transvestism, he may wear a dress to therapy and it is never commented upon. It is accepted as his way to get himself into a feeling. Patients who need to be nude take their clothes off, also without comment or notice by anyone. It seems to me that in nude therapy where nakedness is made such a "thing," there is the implicit assumption that the body *isn't really* accepted as just part of us.

Primal groups are unusual and almost ineffable. To the outsider it appears bizarre, because each person is there doing his own thing: one is playing guitar (because the guitar is his only friend, there when he needs it, it responds to him in a feeling way, etcetera); another is reading pornographic material ("I'm looking for an excitable Momma to take the place of the unresponsive 'dead' one I had"); another is playing with his teddy bear, the one he had at five; another is punching the bag and shouting at his tyrannical father, while still another is in the crib, feeling those early feelings of being abandoned for hours at a time in his crib or playpen. There is no group leader keeping everything under control, organizing the situation. In contradistinction to other forms of psychotherapy, patients are encouraged to be neurotic *in the group;* to act-out their fantasies or idiosyncracies in order to get to feelings. For example, if we know that people act-out *their feelings,* then acting-out in a special therapeutic situation will often awaken those feelings. Once that is done the person is directed by special techniques into them. So, a patient who spends hundreds of dollars on pornographic material stands up in post-group surrounded by dozens of books, holding his penis and finally feeling what it is he is after—in the case above—a feeling mother who will show emotion toward him. Another patient made a whip just like the one his father used on him. We held it over him and he was able to get into the early terror of his father. We will sometimes wrestle a patient if he needs to feel overpowered by his father.

The whole point is not to act well and then be sick outside. Better to be "crazy" with us and get through that act. The dialectic of all this is that the more one lets oneself "go to pieces," the more together he gets.

Acting-out is never encouraged for its own sake—that would simply be enhancing the neurosis. The aim is to get inside the compulsion and feel what is driving it. An exhibitionist will show himself and look for that excited or shocked expression from women in the group, and then fall on the floor screaming, "Momma, show some feeling, please!" A peeping Tom will take advantage of the fact that a female patient is nude and stare at her genitals—and then feel what it is he has been searching for in that act. It is all out in the open; nothing is held back.

As I have said, in Primal group therapy it is possible for a patient to oversee a Primal by his therapist. One day our secretary could receive a patient in the reception room, and the next day have a Primal in that room. After her Primal, she could go on with her receptionist duties. The atmosphere is one of feeling. I am certain that to an outsider, even to an outside psychiatrist seeing all this for the first time, this would be so bizarre that they would either be tempted to flee or send for the wagon.

There are entire families in Primal Therapy, and it sometimes happens that a son will come in and do his father, or a daughter will help her mother. No one lives the abstract role of "mother" or "son." Each is a person who can help another. In group, it is not unusual for a son and mother to be lying near each other, each calling for Mother . . . the "old" mother, in the case of the son, the mother he needed back then.

To make sure about the patient's progress, we continually measure his body state (for those under the research program). We match the physical measurements with the "blind" evaluation of the therapist as to the patient's progress. So, if the therapist indicates "full Primal" on his sheet, we will usually find significant drops in the physiologic measures. If the therapist notes "blocked" on his daily sheet, we will see a rise in those indices. What is odd, I believe, is how little we use "psychologic" measures. We take into account the patient's statements about his feeling states, but no psychologic tests are ever administered in this "psychotherapy." The reason is obvious. This "psychotherapy" is really psychobiologic therapy, and the mind isn't treated as though it were something isolated from the physical system. What could be accomplished by psychologic tests? Open patients have access to their unconscious, so there is no need for the so-called "projective" tests. No therapist need infer or interpret anything. The patient is not being diagnosed so, again, the need for diagnostic tests is obviated. Indeed, I can't think of a single valid reason to administer a psychologic test to a Primal patient. The only thing that could validate a projective test, for example, is the feelings of a patient. Since the patient is already feeling, the test becomes superfluous.

It doesn't matter what the "mind" projects, even when it projects "normalcy." Even when the signs on a Rorschach, for example, indicate a healthy individual, if that individual shows a high tension level, the psychologic test is useless. The lack of psychologic tests (which, incidentally, are interpreted in terms of the theoretical persuasion of the tester) makes secret, classified psychiatric reports done up in special patois unnecessary. Nothing is withheld from the Primal patient. The whole notion of emotional testing is to get signs from a patient in terms of his test responses and figure out what those cues mean. Since no one in Primal Therapy is telling anyone what his feelings mean, there is no need for tests.

Occasionally after a group, it is entirely likely that patients and therapists will go out together for something to eat. The feeling is that we are all here to help each other, and that doesn't set anyone apart from anyone else. Because there is no transference in our therapy (that is, we "bust" it so that it is taken back to where the feeling is being transferred from), there is no fear of special feelings on the part of the patient who is socializing with his therapist. We all know that the therapy has nothing to do with the relationship between the two, only the relationship to ourselves. When a patient has a Primal coming up that requires an individual session, one therapist may substitute for another without any problem.

After several months of therapy, we offer a "pick-up" week, in which the patient gets another week of individual therapy. This therapy will often be done with a different therapist than the original one. The aim here is to get into things that require more attention than can be given in group, and also to keep track of the patient and his progress.

There are many psychologists in this therapy who are waiting for their training to begin. They wouldn't think of taking a job doing conventional therapy, so our Ph.D.'s do other things—work in the post office, lay pipe, deliver telegrams, short-order cooking, etcetera. They do what is simple and real, by and large. They don't try to sell anyone anything, nor would they take a temporary job in a social agency where they could not offer people Primal help. No one suggests these jobs to the patients; no rules are made as to how or where one works. Patients come to their own conclusions about what they want to do in life, and very often it is not what they decided to do while they were neurotic. Many professionals do not leave their chosen fields, but they do approach their work quite differently from before. Actors select real parts for themselves when they can and take far less work than before.

Primal Therapy is unique in other respects. It is totally engulfing rather than just another thing one does in life. Thus, Primal patients can scarcely talk or think about anything else for the first several months of therapy. Therapists are also completely engaged with the patient's life and are not insular professionals. They often call up the patient to see how he is doing. The difference, I believe, is that the therapist is not there to be a reflector for the patient; he is there to get him well. During therapy, there is a great deal of physical contact between therapist and patient. Some of it is just affection, but most of it is designed to reawaken Pains dealing with lack of physical warmth in one's early life. There is no intellectual route that can accomplish this.

It should be clear from what I have said that Primal Therapy is truly an upheaval, and that no one enters it lightly. If the patient isn't really suffering and is not totally committed, the therapy will not be for him. Paradoxically, this therapy works fastest on the people that classical therapists believe are the sickest—the perverts, alcoholics, and drug-users. When impulses are bursting to the surface, it takes but a slight turn to alter the impulse from acting-out into a full Primal. So curing a serious alcoholic, even when he is in his forties or fifties, is not a difficult task. This therapy takes more time with those who have "made it," the intellectuals who have climbed the success ladder. Our most difficult patients, therefore, are psychologists. They have been so brainwashed into thinking that thinking is the way to solve problems that they need a completely new orientation to the significance of feeling.

Primal Therapists, having felt their needs, are "unneeding," so that the patient's needs always come first. If this means seeing patients late at night or on Sundays, then it will be done. If it means telling a patient that he made a mistake and wishes to apologize, that will be done. How refreshing for the patient not to have a perfect therapist, and how relaxing for the therapist not to have to be the expert.

PRIMAL NIGHT AT THE MOVIES

We have regular showings at the Institute of what we call "Primal Movies" (*The Yearling, La Strada, The Search,* etcetera). These movie nights are not quite what one sees in a regular movie theater. The purpose of an art form such as the movies is to elicit feelings. What happens in the usual movie house is that feelings are evoked but then must be squelched out of embarrassment, fear of disturbing others, or whatever. In this sense, a really emotional movie produces harm to the viewer, because he must again suppress himself.

At the Institute, the audience *reacts*. Scenes that are emotional trigger off Primals, and the patient simply rolls over and has his Primal. The noise is often deafening and the movie becomes difficult to hear, but by the time the movie is halfway over, most of the Primal audience is on the floor into their Primals. I'm sure this sounds bizarre, but it is *real*. The conventional movie house is set up in an unreal way. Where else can we ever have our feelings if we can't have them at a time when a movie scene evokes some deep feeling in us?

Movie houses are really the only places where children can have feelings, suppressed though they may be. Certainly, in neurotic households most of the child's feelings are repressed, particularly crying, and particularly when that crying is over something other than being hit or hurt physically. So the movie house is that secretive dark place where one can have a bit of the feelings anyway. The problem is that it gets to be like coitus interruptus—constant agitation and then frustration, because there is no emotional climax. I wonder what the contribution of those chronically suppressed tears is to symptoms such as post-nasal drip and stuffy noses.

One major contribution schools could make is to create an atmosphere around the showing of movies at school which would permit children to react emotionally and react strongly. So if the parental atmosphere at home were suppressive, at least the school situation could help alleviate some of that tension created at home. At the same time, it would reduce much of the acting-out of tension in antisocial forms by children.

It is really unfortunate that the first reflex of neurotic institutions, including family and school, is suppression. Somehow there is the delusion that when one has *behavior* under control, all is well. No matter that there is a seething cauldron inside the child. And, finally, when he goes to a movie with no one around, the child *suppresses himself*—the final neurotic denouement.

When suppression at home and at school fails to be efficacious, the child may be taken to a psychologist—a specialist in "behavior modification." He finishes the job the school and family could not achieve. The child is finished and he can no longer even feel in the movies.

22 *Post-Primal Life–Leslie Pam*

INTRODUCTION

What is post-Primal life like? It is different for everyone. No person's life is representative of any other person's life, and just because that person is "well" does not mean that he will lead a specific life-style. Primals do not produce a homogeneous group. Quite the opposite. The post-Primal person becomes highly individualistic; he is no longer "clubby" and involved in social organizations.

Leslie Pam is "cured." He talks about what a "cure" means. That cure is specific to him, and what is cure for him may not be for someone else. He did not stack himself against some norm or statistical table to see if he was well. He is well because he feels well and no longer suffers from tension and acting-out. I have selected his chapter to include in this book because he has been out of therapy for some time, which enables us to have a perspective on the lasting effects of Primal Therapy.

Perhaps this is a good time to say something about how long the "cure" takes. Radical changes take place in the first few weeks of Primal Therapy. Many patients, if not most, reach the "point of no return," the qualitative leap where they are more real than unreal, by the sixth month of treatment. Some patients leave at that time and continue Primaling at home for months or even years thereafter. Some continue on in treatment for many more months. This is particularly true of those with terrible childhoods where Pain was the order of each day—growing up in institutions or boarding schools is an example of this. Just because someone leaves therapy does not mean he is cured; and just because he stays in treatment does not mean he is preponderantly neurotic.

The key factor is whether the person can get to his feelings before he acts-out neurotically. Someone can have many Primals for many months and still not be cured if he has major unresolved Pains—the Pain of birth, for example. When a person with serious Pains blocks a feeling, instead of feeling it, he will be as neurotic as ever—because defenses are all-or-none. The same defense will spring up after one year of therapy if a Pain cannot be felt. That is why patients stay in treatment longer now than they did before. We are learning that the giant Pains often come up in the later months of treatment, once the lesser Pains have been felt. We know that patients need help with these serious hurts. They often cannot get to them without support and direction. This does not mean that they are not real during this time. It only means that their system is open enough for another major onslaught, and for that they need help. To be in Pain does not mean to be neurotic; to block Pain does, however.

Whatever failures this therapy has can be ascribed to a lack of appreciation of the fact that it is not a therapy for dilettantes. There comes a time in Primal Therapy when it becomes necessary to eschew all that is unreal around you—whether it is the job, a husband, a friend, or whatever. Some patients are unable or unwilling to do that. They know that relationships that are unreal will eventually devour them, but for various reasons they hang on. The salesman who is making a good living goes on selling things people don't need. The wife, out of financial insecurity, remains with a mentally sick husband. The point is, that the therapy cannot do it all. Living a new lifestyle is also part of the therapy. In short, the patient isn't a blob we perform magic on. He is an active participant in the process of change. There is no room for compromise because the person he is compromising is himself.

There are people who do not get cured in Primal Therapy. It is a very small percentage. There are many reasons for this, but perhaps the most important one is leaving too soon. Some individuals do not want all the Pain this therapy entails. They get impatient and decide to opt for the neurotic life. That is their choice. Other patients have been so locked up emotionally that it takes a lot longer than six or eight months to unlock them. They get discouraged and leave. Those who stay almost invariably get well.

Critics have often pondered about the post-Primal patient. They wonder how good a therapy is that doesn't prepare a person to live in this world. It is true that living in an unreal society becomes difficult for real people. But what are the alternatives? To be sick and enter into the sick games? To stay in sick relationships and "adjust" to everyone's unreality? Real people cannot do that. But there are advantages to being real. One does not get fooled by others, so that a person doesn't marry someone and discover six months later that the person is not a good human being. He doesn't have children for the wrong reasons and feel forevermore put-upon by them. He doesn't take on jobs or tasks he cannot do. He doesn't have friends who are only interested in exploiting him. Nor is he interested in exploiting anyone else. His life is simple, almost primitive, one might say. But he is most content. He is rarely sick; the people whom he relates to can give freely and warmly. He isn't agitated and restive. He isn't driven to do things that make him hate himself, like drinking, taking drugs, smoking and sexual perversions. Because he can feel, he can finally be loved.

LESLIE

It's been a little over two years since I first began Primal Therapy, and I consider myself to be cured. Since I'm now working as a Primal Therapist, people constantly question me about the effect of the therapy. "Does the Pain end?" "What's your life like now?" "What does therapy do to you?" These are the recurrent questions, and rather than answer them from a clinical viewpoint, I thought I'd talk about what my life is like now, where I am, and some of the things I've been doing. The one question that plagues most people probably is, "Does the Pain end?" A neurotic person, a prospective patient applying for therapy, reads the book and sees the word "cure"; I think people have a distorted idea about what that means. If a person is neurotic, obviously his hopes have to be neurotic. In short, hope is neurotic. In the beginning I was looking for that Godlike eternal bliss and its promise to us in the afterlife: some kind of place where there's no pain and no problems. After two years I've changed my ideas about what it's like to be finished with therapy; maybe in ten years I will have felt all the old Pain, but it's almost unimportant to me right now. That's something I try to tell people. When I tell a neurotic I had a Primal yesterday, he sometimes concludes that the therapy doesn't work. Actually, my having a Primal yesterday—or even two today—has nothing to do with whether or not the therapy works. If neurosis is the symbolically acting-out of one's real painful feelings, and if the cure for neurosis is feeling those pains, then as long as one doesn't act-out his needs and feels them instead, we then can say he's cured. That's quite different from the view most people have about therapy—at least quite a bit different than the one I envisioned when I first began therapy.

My answer to that question about "does the Pain end?" is: Do you ever suppose that someday you will give up eating, or sleeping, or breathing or anything else you do in your life? To me, Pains are just another thing that happens to me, just another event in my life. It might happen today and it might not happen for three weeks and then it might happen for three days in a row. But as long as I know that I can feel the Pain, then the Pain ceases to be any problem for me.

I'm aware that I still have Primal Pain—however imperceptible —and when it is triggered, I feel it. For example, I was asked to discuss the book *The Primal Scream* on a local TV program, and the day before my appearance, I had a tremendous amount of tension. I talked to one of the other therapists and I remembered a scene that I had completely blanked out of my memory; even after a year and a half of therapy I hadn't remembered it. When I was in the fourth grade, I had done something wrong and the teacher made me get up in front of the class and tell that I was bad, that I had lied. And after I felt that feeling, I realized something—it was a tremendous insight—that every time after that when I'd get up to speak in front of people, my body was getting ready for me to say that I'd been bad. It was like my confessional. Because of that initial scene I felt utterly, intolerably uncomfortable in front of groups, throughout my entire life. After I had the Primal, I went on the show and it was really easy. The tension was gone. I know I could do it again and with no problem at all.

After two years in therapy I find that there is very little time between when I first get tense and when I get to the real feelings. Now when I don't know something, I no longer feel uptight. There's a tremendous freedom in just being me without suffering from the tension produced by fear or constraint. This is a result of being in this therapy. In the beginning, I'd lie down and I'd cry for two or three hours about one particular Pain, which was intolerable to my body, to my entire system, to my being. As time has gone on, I can have the same amount of feeling in less time because of my increased tolerance to Pain. And the beauty of feeling is that I can trust myself to feel, and can allow myself to experience the intensity of any feeling. Today, feeling a particular Primal Pain takes a shorter time because it's like going into charted waters. Now I'm not afraid to feel; I'm not afraid to allow myself to be that little baby or that crying child.

Feeling my Primal Pain has replaced the acting-out, and it's not even a conscious effort. Part of the therapy process is, as I say, that the more one feels, the more one allows himself to feel, and the less he will find himself acting-out. Someone can't will away his acting-out—he has to feel the feeling that drives it. I've seen quite a few patients who have tried to act as though they are not sick, and yet they have all this inexplicable tension. They wind up acting-out something else; they make the therapist into the daddy or mommy they want. Until these patients feel their own Primal feelings, the acting-out will linger. There have been times even in my own therapy when I, too, thought I was really straight only to find out weeks or months later that I had not been. These things are so subtle at times that perhaps several weeks will have to elapse during which time new insights provide deeper understanding. And true understanding of the self shows me how I've acted out and even where I have to go in my next Primal; true understanding is a continuous, cyclical process.

What does all this have to do with my ability to live in society? I feel at ease around people because I don't want anything from them. I have already felt that I needed a mommy and a daddy, and now I can deal with people as they are—on their terms. Regardless of the fact that they might be neurotic, I can deal with people without needing them to be someone they can never be. And that is one of the greatest things that I have gotten out of this therapy—that I can be with people and really know people because I am not hung up with my own unfulfilled needs. So now I can talk to a girl and not struggle to make her into a mommy, and I can talk to a guy and he's not a Daddy. And not only that, but it makes me a better therapist. If a therapist needs a good mommy and daddy and he's seeing a patient, then he's going to make that patient into a mommy or a daddy, no matter how hard he may try not to. And it's only after someone has felt all of that pain, or a great part of it, that he will be free enough to see that patient just as a patient rather than as someone to fulfill a need of his own. You have to be a totally free human being to do this therapy.

I am supersensitive to changes in my body—I can feel it changing when I get a little tense. It's only when I don't get right to it that the tension builds. And so in that sense, I could lie down in a couple of minutes and get right to the feeling and get up and be completely straight and not need from anyone. That's what I've gained from Primal Therapy—the ability to feel a lot of Pain and get right to it.

I've found that my life has become extremely pleasant in one respect and sad in another. What's nice about my life now is that I won't compromise myself. There's no need to immerse myself in a wretched job or even in a lucrative one if it means working so many hours a week that I lose the chance to appreciate my life. There's no fear once I've felt the feelings of needing Mommy and Daddy. I can complain about the service in a restaurant if it's complainable about, or I can compliment them. It's the same with anybody. If I don't like someone, I don't have anything to do with them. If they really intrude on me, I'll tell them that I don't like them. And if I really like someone, I can tell them and I don't feel uptight about doing that either. I can get terribly angry at an injustice that might be done to me, but on the other hand, I can feel sympathetic and warm toward someone who is really hurting. My point here is that I am free to be me all the time. This does not mean that I walk around telling people off, only that I remain disengaged from the neurosis of others.

Philosophers have spent thousands of years developing theories about what's the meaning of life, why are we here, and so on. To me, the magnitude of this intellectual enterprise seems completely absurd. If I'm interested in history, I see history from a Primal standpoint. I extrapolate from my own feeling and I generalize it to what's happening in the world. And it makes perfect sense to me. Political movements, education systems, economic models—all are social extensions of the original Primal model.

Feeling Primal Pains explains many of the unanswerable questions that men have pondered ever since they could speak. And this puts me at ease with the world. I don't ponder infinity or the existence of God—I understand all of these things. I understand from my own feelings, of course, why people believe in God, what religion means to people, how it substitutes for a need that people have never had fulfilled.

Part of believing in what I feel means I can be a good therapist, because if I believe and know what I feel, then I can't be altered. I know my truth and my patients' truth. I can truly help people because I don't approach them with an eclectic viewpoint. I know where their pain is. I know what their pain is.

Is it possible that someone doesn't have Primal *need*? In all the patients that I have seen it has never happened. Everyone has the same basic need. That Mommy and Daddy didn't love them, and that without that love they would die. The need for love begins at birth.

I know what love is because I've felt the need for it in a baby Primal. I think it was one of the most tremendous feelings I've ever gotten to, in the sense that it answered so much for me. It brought together many fragmentary pieces of feelings that I had been having. I was just sitting in group and Art was doing the post-group session and I just felt that something going on inside and I didn't know what it was. So I went into the other room and I lay down. I found my head doing therapy on my body and I felt I had to turn that off. Instead, I went with my body. And little by little I stopped thinking. Finally, I just felt my body; my eyes were open, but I couldn't see very well and I couldn't understand anything that was being said around me. And I didn't even know I existed—I didn't know where I was or what was happening. All I could do was feel my body. And my body kept saying something that I couldn't connect to a memory. My body just hurt. Finally, after going with that for a while, I felt the need to be fed. And how did that need feel? It was purely a body reaction. I found my mouth puckering and I started sucking in an involuntary, automatic manner. And the feeling was that I was just a tiny baby. I didn't know how old I was. In fact, I had no conception of what age meant. There were no thoughts involved in this Primal at all. And I felt myself hungry. I didn't know what it was that would make me feel good. All I knew was that my body was hurting and then the Pain began to spread. This process began with the sucking reflex and a little pain in my stomach began to envelop my entire body. And as this particular Pain increased, there was no "love" to interfere with the Pain. And "love" at that moment would have been Mommy picking me up and feeding me. That's what I needed. That's what love is . . . having your need fulfilled, whatever that need happens to be at that moment as an infant. When I finished that feeling I knew that I had not gotten what I needed, and that not getting as that infant was the beginning of my neurosis. Even without reading about the neurophysiology of neurosis, even without knowing that, I felt that my Pain had begun at a cellular level, and it was as though there was a little spot in my gut that said, "I'm hungry." And my lips began to move in a sucking fashion. Because the need was not met, the real physical Pain became intolerable for that small area in my stomach. I know now that cells have a threshold for Pain. Groups of cells can tolerate more Pain. As each group of cells reaches its larger group threshold for maximum Pain, more and more cellular bodies become involved, until the body is enveloped in complete, wracking, physical Pain. Ultimately the organism will die. This is what could have happened to me as an infant. Dehydration is similar. First, a person is thirsty—the throat is parched. Soon the mouth becomes swollen, the stomach distended, and the body starts to ache. It's as though when the need isn't met the physical pain continues to increase and increase. In dehydration, the person enters a semi-coma and eventually dies. Neurosis is what prevented my ultimate death. In the Primal I felt my head shut down that physical Pain; I could feel the beginning of the neurotic process.

The head is what saves man's life. Among animals, there are certain wild ones in captivity who don't breed because there is some natural force that keeps them away from each other sexually. These animal parents, being neurotic, are unable to take care of any young, so they don't mate. When they do, the offspring born in captivity often die. I believe it's because those babies can feel that Mommy can't take care of them in the way that they need. Deprived of caring, they die. They have no brain mechanism to shut off the Pain when it gets too great, so instead they die. Neurotic humans, nevertheless, ignore that natural instinct not to have children, even though they are unable to take care of them properly. To survive while not getting what they need, their offspring have to utilize defense mechanisms.

The next day I got back into this baby Primal feeling while I was visiting a girlfriend, and I realized that something else had come out of that baby Primal. Quite suddenly I felt my body come alive as though there was a sixth sense, an awareness of other people. I could feel my body coming alive as a sensing mechanism, and it was more powerful than my sight, hearing, taste, or smell. I think those senses are highly undeveloped when we're first born. But one sense that isn't undeveloped is the body, and my body was like a radar system. As my girlfriend came close to me, I could gauge the distance between her and myself purely from my body. I could feel when she would move away and I could feel when she got closer. She got up and walked out of the room. And I just started wailing, uncontrollably, as a screaming little baby whose mommy had left him when he needed her. My friend came back in the room toward the bed and I could feel her getting closer. I couldn't see her but my body was feeling this feeling. And at that point another amazing thing happened: I actually felt the first time I became aware of what I had to do to relieve Pain. I know it sounds unbelievable but I experienced it. And my first thought was that crying feels good. It helped make the Pain tolerable. And I felt I was a baby and I knew I was a baby. I was back somewhere in my past and it was fantastic that I could cry to relieve the pain as I lay there, helpless.

I was still into this experience, when suddenly I saw my father's face and I saw his eyes. In past Primals I'd feel complete, utter terror when I saw his eyes. And I truly believed that he was really there at that moment and he was young and his hair was black. And I saw his eyes and they were the eyes of a crazy man. I could barely see, I had an image, but I could *feel* him with my body. My body was telling me something, and suddenly I began screaming in terror, the terror of knowing how unable he was to take proper care of me. The instant I saw that I felt my brain click as though that Pain were so intolerable that I had to shut it off immediately. And because I finally allowed myself to be that completely helpless infant and to feel that feeling, I could let myself experience the terror as I hadn't in the past. And the only place I could find refuge from my Pain was in my head.

The physical pain had increased beyond the point where I could have handled it, and I would have died from such an onslaught of physical pain. And so I shut it off with my head. My entire body was engulfed with this terror which I felt as a physical pain, and when my head shut off, my body went into shock— shock against that feeling.

That evening, after the Primal, I felt exuberant and freed of a tremendous burden. I never realized how this old feeling had prevented me from doing things. I felt greater than I'd ever felt in my life. As I walked down the street there was no fear, because I had felt the initial, early Primal fear. I no longer had any fear of walking up to strangers and entering into their conversations. I no longer feared whether they were going to like me or not. The Primal had explained so much to me—why I had been so afraid my whole life and what that fear had done to my life. Feeling the Pain had freed me from the fear. I'd been in other therapies and I had done other therapies but never had I experienced anything like that in my life.

Now I understand the beginnings of neurosis and how it happens to people. How it happens to anyone. I felt the beginnings of my neurosis. I felt the physical pain spreading throughout my body, and I could feel the shutoff that saved my life. At this point I see neurosis as a mechanism that is very worthwhile and useful. We stay alive at the expense of feeling. It's like living death, but it's a survival mechanism. And it's a very good one.

All I can say is that Primal Therapy saved my life. And not only that, it's made me completely aware of everything that goes on in the world around me. I'm at peace with the knowledge of how the world works and why we are where we are as people. That knowledge, in itself, is sad. It's one of the saddest things I know. I understand and know that what we talk about the most is what we have the least of. We talk about freedom because we don't have it; we talk about peace because we don't have it. We talk about equality and we talk about love because we don't have it. And because we don't, and because we try to get—because we try to fulfill those needs—because we can't—because the Pain is too great—we end up destroying in an attempt not to feel what's real. So we create institutions like schools, prisons and mental hospitals. The Pain is being a tiny, helpless, screaming infant at the mercy of two parents who are not capable of loving. Such parents are really, in effect, a child's executioners. And so we create a monstrous world where everyone strives to be important, useful, big, and helpful. And in doing all of these things, we make it miserable for ourselves, more miserable than it ever has to be. We insist that people work forty hours a week and wait for the two weeks at the end of the year when they can take a vacation. Mass media influence leads people into getting married, buying a home, having children, and going into debt—all to keep us under control so that we don't have to feel how little control we really had as that infant. And we create rules and elect people to enforce those rules: other people we appoint to control us so that we don't have to feel our needs. This is all sad because it doesn't have to be.

My life is easy. I'm the easiest person in the world to get along with. I make no demands on people, I make no judgments, I make no requests that are beyond what others can give. I can finally live alone. Sometimes this means I have to cry, but that's okay. As long as I know that all I have to do is keep feeling, then I'm cured. All is well.

Primal Therapy is more than a new psychological theory. For in its ability to cure neurosis, it is that which men have been looking for since the beginning of time—freedom. People seek freedom from oppression, from unconsciousness, from karma, from evil spirits, from a multitude of sicknesses, from fate, from reincarnation, from anything but themselves.

Primal Therapy does not preach a system of rules by which to live. It is instead a process through which men may feel their Pain. It is each man's personal revolution against the tyranny of his neurosis. As long as man is sick, the world will reflect his Pain. Primal Therapy is an end to that Pain.

23 *In a Real World—Conclusions*

Humanity is near the time when we shall either have a real world or no world. I believe that there is a chance for that real world; and that belief is not Utopian. Nature's dialectic provides that the conditions of unreality simultaneously produce the necessary conditions for reality. The more suppressive the society, the greater the force suppressed. That force must have its day, just as the force of real feelings must, or the organism (personal or social) will succumb.

The problem is: "Which force will ultimately prove victorious?" It may well be that those forces of unreality that are bent on destruction and pollution will create such havoc as to make restitution impossible. We can see this in neurosis, when the organism undergoes such assaults as to make a healthy body impossible. We see this in suicide, when the unreal system literally eradicates the real one. The social system is analogous to the personal one, though not coterminous with it. By that I mean systems have a viability of their own, and a social system is not a simple extrapolation of a personal one. But we can learn from the dynamics of the psychological system something about other systems.

What do we learn from neurosis that has social implications? First, that when a system is "sick," the symptoms of the sickness proliferate in whatever channels are available. Second, that the treatment of symptoms can never change the system. Third, that one cannot live healthily within a sick system because that system incorporates everything in its terms. Fourth, a sick system will prevail once set in motion and will continue to maintain itself no matter how unproductive or destructive it is. Fifth, there is no way to significantly alter the system without an understanding of its central dynamics and contradictions. Sixth, once understood, the system must be overthrown.

Why must the system be overthrown? Because a sick system will fight to maintain itself so long as any part of it exists. There is no way to accommodate or juxtapose a real and unreal system without one incorporating the other. The strongest system will predominate. In neurosis, we see this clearly in terms of the defense system; it is all or nothing. Even when there is a little tension left, the unreal defensive system operates as a totality. Under threat, the intellectual will fall back on his intellectual defenses no matter how far he has gone in therapy . . . until the real system prevails. In society we see this in the continuous failures of Utopian commune societies dating back more than one hundred years to the Fourier experiment. Those micro-societies tried to exist within exploitative macrocosms and expired accordingly.

No matter how good the intent of the society, no matter how altruistic its members (no matter how well-intentioned the neurotic is to quit drugs), the system dictates. In neurosis the dynamics of underlying tension overwhelm proper intentions just as the dynamics of exploitation suffuse the altruism of the factory owner.

How does a neurotic overthrow his system? and what social implications can be drawn from this? First, one needs a theory about the dynamics of the sickness of the system. If a theory states that understanding dreams is the key, then understanding dreams ought to lay the conditions for upheaval—which it does not. If a theory states that sickness is due to a defense against Pain, and that exposing Pain cures the sickness, and, indeed, the sickness is eliminated predictably and systematically, then we have the beginnings of a valid theory.

The second step is the actual treatment—the exposition of truth in every area possible. The "doctor" in the social situation is the one armed with the theory and techniques to help others understand the dynamics of change. The real elements of society will gather together to bring about change, only to be met inevitably by the unreal system bent on crushing them. We see this in neurosis when each time a repressed neurotic starts to laugh, his hand reflexively covers his mouth. The suppression is automatic.

The unreal society will move against its real elements *commensurate with the level of consciousness* of those individuals. The more "real" the members of society, the more they will be the target of the unreal. By level of consciousness, I am speaking about an understanding of the *central* contradictions in society. Someone can be a reformer, working within the system on particular symptoms (too many billboards, for example), and not become an enemy of the unreal. Again, in neurosis we note that when a feeling starts its rise to the level of consciousness, it is defended against most strongly. One may work on one's smoking too much and the personal system may readily accept for a time the dictates of a smoking clinic; but to feel the feelings underlying smoking is another matter. *Consciousness is a necessary condition for change.* That is why therapies that do not involve consciousness, such as body-manipulative approaches, do not make permanent changes. The sick neurotic system does not change precisely because reality never makes it to consciousness.

Consciousness is revolutionary, just as suppression of consciousness is antirevolutionary. But revolutionary consciousness does not simply involve an understanding of external realities—how the social system works; revolutionary consciousness is Primal consciousness—a mind integrated with and then liberated from internal realities—Pain. Without this Primal consciousness, a neurotic may externalize his inner conflicts and his rebellion will be symbolic; that is, he may make the world the "bad daddy" he must rail against. Even though the issue he is dealing with may well be justified, the reason for the rebellion would be sick. Thus, no matter what the conditions, the person would find a reason to revolt. So, even when in power he would be destructive and unstable. We sometimes see this in the women's liberationists we have treated. The issue they are coping with may well be justified. But in some of the cases we have seen, the women were lesbians who hated men (father) and discovered in therapy that they were projecting this hatred to the world and really were fighting to be men, not women. This in no way negates the validity of the social problem.

Because the unreal system automatically suppresses the real one, it is clear that moralizing, pleading, or the demonstration of facts will not significantly deter that suppression. It is not a matter of urging that unreal society to "get its priorities straight." Sick societies have their priorities straight—they are in accord with the sickness. Thus, the book exposing the abuses in the Arkansas prisons cannot change the Arkansas prison system so long as that system is tied to an unreal politico-economic system. What can be expected is what happened—the dismissal of the official who exposed the truth. Until the politico-economic system is completely reorganized to benefit rather than suppress the needs of the people, enlightened volumes on penal reform will be as useless as an insight given to a neurotic.

Can we work within the system? Psychoanalysis works within the neurotic system, and we see what a success it has been.

If we cannot plead or moralize with sick systems, how then do we change them? In neurosis, we find that evoking the truth makes the unreal system unnecessary. It is both an evolutionary and revolutionary process. Evoking the truth is a necessary but not sufficient condition for change. The defense system that ordinarily suppresses that truth must be stopped. The therapist is in a position of power to control the unreal defenses of the patient. In society, there have to be sufficient numbers of real people to generate enough power to control the sickness—such as wars. To block the symptom of war is to heighten the internal conflicts of a sick system and produce the conditions for change.

An example of this was recently illustrated in a small college which used *The Primal Scream* as a textbook. Having a glimpse of reality galvanized the students against sitting in boring classes, studying irrelevant psychological systems. They stopped going to class, and through that action brought about major changes in the curriculum. They did not change the educational system that generates irrelevant studies, but they did make a step.

One of the reasons that youth is the hope of the future is that they still have enough reality about them to want change. They are not yet old enough to have been totally crushed (called "adjustment") by the unreal system. It is analogous to young children who, though continually suppressed by neurotic parents, still have a vitality and reality about them that is not crushed for many years, despite the best efforts of neurotic parents.

Systems, real and unreal, tend to be self-perpetuating. Once an unreal system predominates, it produces subsystems (educational, penal, etcetera) in its own image. Each subsystem is characterized by a reflective repression of what is real. Thus, the educational system does not integrate the feelings of students into its programs. Feelings are considered something apart from academic pursuits, and the academic system is characterized by the split between mind and body. The unreal educational system must produce suppressed and therefore uncreative teachers, who will in turn suppress their students. No matter how brilliant the book on "What's Wrong with Education," little will change until the central, sick system is altered. In other words, the educational system is an outgrowth of the politico-economic one, and is determined by it.

In the interaction between social and personal, which system must change first? I think the psychological revolution is crucial. Well people will logically produce a well society. But it is not impossible for a radically changed social system to eventually produce well people even when that revolution was brought about by neurotics. However, the danger is that the new social system will be *superimposed* on sick people, who might corrode the essence of that system. Sick people rarely can solve social problems in a real way.

This does not mean that the new system will not ultimately prevail and produce well people, but I think it is crucial for people to get well, because in their getting well they will neither produce nor tolerate life under unreal conditions.

Why am I optimistic about this change? Because the truth has been found about how to produce the inner revolution; and because people are eager to overthrow their psychological afflictions. Numerous individuals who would never agree with me about society are drawn to Primal Therapy (and Primal theory) out of their own misery and because they sense a truth in it that they can feel. Nothing now can suppress the truth of personal change, because nothing can suppress truth, in the long run. What happens to people, irrespective of initial outlook, is that becoming well *automatically* changes their views. To feel violent, for example, is to believe in its necessity as a social force. To be relieved of all inner violence removes that belief without any brainwashing whatsoever. Real people could never shoot down a stranger in the name of some abstraction such as "loyalty." Thus, with the inner revolution there will be no war because we know now that man is *not* innately violent. He rages against death—against being forced to be unnatural. He rages when his needs are suppressed and when his life, therefore, is in danger. A society that fulfills needs will have no violence, no mental hospitals, prisons, or specialists in psychotherapy.

Is this Utopian? How can we get all the people well? We can't. But there is a class in society that is ready—a class suppressed because it is the enemy of the unreal—the youth. If we can get the youth straight, they will bring about a new society. What kind of society will they bring about? No one knows, and there can be no blueprint for that society, any more than I can see what kind of a life a well person will lead. Well people will make their own way—some will want to sit on the beach and sunbathe all the time, and the others might want to write songs or build bridges. The young people, sick though they are with drugs and crime, still have so many elements of health—in their music, in their outlook about money, in their attitudes about politics and power, in their questioning of authority, and in their relationships to one another. They are the hope. They want to feel—the widespread use of LSD and marijuana is testimony of that as-yet unconscious desire. They feel their suffering and want to feel better. They know there is a better way even if they don't know what it is. They have thought that drugs (thanks to Timothy Leary, et al) are the way, which they are not. Primal theory at least begins to offer them a real understanding of what inner change is about; they will do the rest.

When you don't feel, you can do almost anything or have almost anything done to you. You can abandon a child, trick with fifteen men a day, switch political allegiance from one extreme to another, allow your freedom to be taken away, kill someone, let others be killed, tolerate prison, and so on. When you don't feel, nothing has any real meaning, so whatever happens is accepted without introspection. Read any of the nonfiction prison stories by ex-inmates and, for the most part, one will read of one bizarre exploit after another, one abandoned relationship after another, without a drop of feeling.

When you don't feel, you can send your child away to boarding school even when you know it's deleterious. Or, you can keep children with a drunken father who beats them periodically. The point is, you can do anything when you don't feel. And the anything you do will always be in the service of your personal need to the detriment of anything outside yourself. If a husband demands that you send your children away because they annoy him, then away they'll go, so that the wife can continue to have a husband. An employer can continue to keep his employees on starvation wages when he cannot feel their struggle and misery. A government official can think more about costs than human welfare when he makes up a budget, and a prison official can keep a young person in a dark solitary dungeon, when there is no feeling.

We can be told to kill people we've never met, and we can voluntarily place ourselves in danger of death by the enemy when we don't feel. We can rationalize the most horrendous of events and watch children starve when we don't feel. There are no limits to the horror one can perpetrate without feelings. The answer for so many social problems lies in the ability to feel and therefore to empathize with suffering humanity. The criminal will return to crime no matter how liberal the prison program without feeling, just as the addict will shoot up again no matter how benevolent and therapeutic his incarceration. The mother will be cruel to her children when she doesn't feel, no matter how sophisticated her education, just as the boss will be cruel to his underlings.

Feeling will be the salvation of mankind, just as nonfeeling has been the destroyer of civilization. Feeling is what will return humanity to humans, and will make society humane again.

The most important thing that Primal Therapy has to offer is a chance to redo (and undo) history. The idea that we can go back decades to our early life and reverse things that happened then is truly a remarkable notion. We now have the power to eliminate the causes of personal sickness and to be liberated from our past. This means to be free to organize a healthy society, irrespective of what has gone before.

Just take one area of existence—crime and the judicial process—and imagine what would happen in a healthy, feeling society. First of all, very little crime, because people would neither be violent toward their fellow man nor would want to take from him. They would not be acting out their rebellion against their parents toward society. Feeling judges would be truly objective and not inflict personal Primal prejudices against defendants. Prisons, if they existed, would really be hospitals concerned with treatment of offenders. Offenders who had sufficient therapy would not spend the rest of their lives in jail; nor would they be a threat to society when paroled, as they can be now when they are released in exactly the same psychological condition as they entered. Feeling people cannot hurt others; and whether a prisoner—inmate—is feeling or not can be measured neurophysiologically and psychologically, so that there can be ways to determine scientifically how ready a person is to rejoin society. Prisons would be far less populated, with the resulting costs, both financial and in human misery, lessened significantly. As it stands now, just to survive in prison a person has to shut off feeling so he can stand living in a cage for years. How could we possibly expect him to feel and be compassionate toward others later on?

Our waiting list for treatment is very long. Many people begin having Primals while on the waiting list. *The Primal Scream* is being used as a textbook at a number of colleges. On one campus, a number of students have left school and formed a Primal community, where they give each other Primals. A religious group has written to me that they have converted their church to a Primal center. They report radical changes in the congregation. A lifetime of symptoms has been eliminated in some of them through Primals in church.

People who cannot come into therapy are finding their own way. I think if various elements of society got together and thought through possible alternatives to the way we are working now—slowly and by the "ones"—ways of bringing about Primal change on a broad level could be achieved. As I write, a local government agency is embarking on a program with the Primal Institute in which trained lay therapists who have had Primal Therapy will treat criminals. When we can document how a housewife or secretary can cure a chronic exhibitionist in a matter of months, we will have important evidence to indicate how the lay public can be used as agents of change.

I am optimistic about broad change because Primal Therapy is relatively quick. The social change I foresee need not be futuristic. Just reading *The Primal Scream* has produced Primals in great numbers of people. The letters and calls we get indicate that those self-induced Primals are producing radical changes.

What are some of the possibilities of a real world? Consider the effects of a Primally-oriented school system. Children with behavior problems would not be isolated, punished, or sent to the principal. They would be understood to be driven by historical forces and would be allowed their Primals in a system where feelings, no matter how intense, would be a matter of course. Children would learn that feelings are not something separate from education but of its essence. Feelings would be integrated in the overall educational scheme so that children would not be baffled by their tensions, their bedwetting, their belligerence and distractibility. They would learn *in class* the meaning of those things and how to rid themselves of the pressure. Very soon, it would be a school without discipline problems and without the interminable staff meetings about how to control children. The very fact that so much emphasis in education is placed on discipline and control is another indication of how unreal social institutions reflexively suppress feelings and reality; and how these educational systems can continue for years to teach things that are irrelevant to the lives and feelings of the students. A real education system that produces real people cannot have unreal, irrelevant courses because the students wouldn't tolerate it. A real educational system would have inspiring, "turned-on" teachers, not the turned-off disciplinarians who control that system today.

There are other implications of that real world, so relatively easy to achieve if we can get together. Take the field of illness. I have already pointed out how even the educational system would help prevent deepening psychological problems. At the same time, children freed of their pain would not be so physically ill; and there would be little of the allergies, asthmas, arthritis, headaches, stomach aches, etcetera, which plague all of us and make us run to doctors. What truly physical ailments exist would be given priority for study and research. As it is now in this unreal society, the priority is destruction. Thus, we have the socialization of death and the individuation of health. The government supports and subsidizes arms factories, and we as individuals are forced to raise pennies for health research.

When people are healthy, government expenditures will go for people's needs. There will be no overarching drug industry, drug commercials, drug-abuse programs, drug vigilantes, and professional drug witch hunts.

Healthy parents will not flee from their children and will not be perpetually crabby and critical and tired. They will enjoy those children and automatically do what is right with them without recourse to specialty books. The same is true for sex. Real, feeling people will not need courses and books in sexual problems. They will do what comes naturally.

Healthy people would not have latent fears that would make them want to arm themselves against fantasied enemies. No one could make them give up their loved ones to go kill strangers. They would be loyal to themselves.

In a real world people would not pollute and destroy a nature they feel so much a part of. It is those who are unnatural and unreal who can destroy nature with little remorse. There could be no false needs drummed into people to make their total aspiration one of consuming more and more. Thus, no new wardrobe every year; no need for the latent power in an automobile that helps produce so much carnage on the roads. The reader can fill in the blanks; a real world is much more relaxing.

One of the ways the unreal system perpetuates itself is to make itself sacrosanct; the true patriot upholds the system, believes in it, and treats anyone who wants to change it as a traitor. He sells himself out to the system, just as he sold himself out to his parents in order to be the "good, loyal son" who might be loved. He is the one who might exhort those who question the system, "If you don't like it, get out!" And he is the one who might well have heard that phrase from his parents early in his life and decided to "like it." When that person can feel the hopelessness of ever having his needs fulfilled, no matter how loyal and obedient he is, the conditions will arrive for change.

The problem with those who have been snuffed out by repression is that they often come to believe in it as necessary. Otherwise, they would have to feel the senselessness of their early years. They come to think that children must be kept in line, for otherwise they would run wild. And, of course, by keeping their children in line, they often do run wild when out of parental reach. To be totally repressed and to believe in it leads to a *general* philosophy of repression, so that a repressed person not only keeps his children in check but thinks that the government must keep its youth in line. Helping this person *feel* his repression (rather than *acting* repressed) is what would enable him to change his philosophy.

Here again we are faced with the dialectic. Repressed people produce repressive societies, and repressive societies produce repressed people. So which comes first? What is the cause of which? Where must we direct our energies? If we think nondialectically, we might say we have to begin with society, or others might urge that we begin with the individual. But life is not like that. We begin in both spheres. We don't get straight and *then* change society, just as we don't change society and then get straight. It is a constant interaction because man and his society are reciprocals. It is unfortunate that some Marxist states have left psychological man out of the social equation. It should be obvious to them that in our capitalist society where rich people have the best of the system with every material convenience there is overwhelming misery among them.

The point I am making is that repressive social systems generate ideologies which must be internalized and maintained by much of the populace if the system is to continue.* The populace becomes at once the prisoners of the system and its maker. The trick is to suppress people so that they lose touch with their needs and operate on the basis of ideology alone. That ideology will then support the system in every facet: education, penal and, most importantly, psychological. That is one reason why Conditioning Therapy enjoys such broad governmental support. It is an

* This is no different from the process by which neurotic repression produces unreal ideas which are perpetually supported by the blocked Pain.

ideology based on repression—not only repression of feelings, but repression of the symptoms which are reminders of the existence of feelings.

Ideology becomes a force which will not easily be countered by other, perhaps more real, ideologies, because an unreal ideology grows out of a repressed personal system and is used to block Pain. It then is no longer a matter of infusing correct notions into the heads of the exploited. The unreal person has a Primal stake in his ideology; he needs it to keep from feeling the facts of his misery and exploitation. A crucial factor in his ideology is hope. Every unreal ideology must contain unreal hope or it is not viable. The neurotic must think that in the end he will get something. It is only when social conditions obliterate hope that there is a chance to change that ideology. This is certainly true in Primal Therapy, where a key condition for change is to help people feel the hopelessness of their neurotic struggle.

Are those in power who control the unreal system cruel and evil? Do they really want smog and war? To answer that in the affirmative would be to psychologize a *social* phenomenon. Policies of the arms and oil industry remain constant no matter who the representatives are, just as the policies of the American Legion remain constant despite who is in leadership. It is not a matter of changing people's minds, just as it is not a matter of changing the mind of a drug addict so that he considers drugs an evil. It is a matter of changing an underlying system.

To summarize: Neurosis is of a piece. It not only determines one's inner life but shapes one's social philosophy. Changing that inner state provides the basis for change in social outlook; and that is the hope—the transformation of the members of society *is* inevitably the transformation of that society. That world is within our reach because in an unreal society, the simple truth is revolutionary.